Science PUZZLERS

Nancy De Waard and Jack De Waard

Illustrated by Doug Klauba

Good Year Books

An Imprint of Addison-Wesley Educational Publishers, Inc.

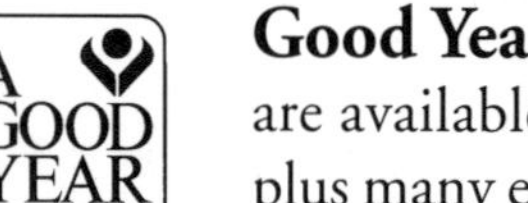

Good Year Books
are available for most basic curriculum subjects plus many enrichment areas. For more Good Year Books, contact your local bookseller or educational dealer. For a complete catalog with information about other Good Year Books, please write:

Good Year Books
1900 East Lake Avenue
Glenview, IL 60025

Book design by Foster Design.

Printed in the United States of America.

ISBN 0-673-36378-3
2 3 4 5 6 7 8 9 - PRO - 05 04 03 02 01 00 99 98

Preface

As parents and teachers ourselves, we have a strong interest in encouraging learning. Some of the strongest motivators for learning are wonder, fun, and competition. We have also found that one of the biggest barriers to adults learning science is the intimidating vocabulary involved. (One researcher has found that introductory biology involved learning more new terms than in a first-year foreign language class.) However, the "vocabulary barrier" is more in the minds of teachers and parents; children don't know that science words are hard until some adult tells them. Thus, if kids are left to have fun, explore, and compete, they can grow up enjoying learning science terminology, gaining a solid foundation before they realize they weren't supposed to like it.

Background

The word lists upon which the puzzles in this book are based were drawn from the most widely used fourth-, fifth-, and sixth-grade science textbooks. Thus, they comprise much of the specialized vocabulary that most upper elementary students will be expected to master.

Organization

The book is organized into four units that mirror the major areas of science that most elementary science programs cover—Life Science, Earth/Space Science, Physical Science, and the Human Body. These units are further broken down into topics such as Plants, Motion, Solar System, and Digestive System. While most modern elementary programs integrate multiple disciplines into each of their chapters, our goal was to provide a generic volume that would be useful to all.

Each topic has a single word list consisting of about twenty words that are used to construct five different types of puzzles—matching, word search, fill-in, crossword, and word jumble puzzles. This sequence introduces the children first to the words and then to the definitions (clues) in a progressively more challenging format. If they do all of the puzzles in a topic, they will have mastered the age-appropriate vocabulary usually introduced at the upper elementary level.

Ideas for Using This Book

Parents

We suspect that a good number of these books will be selected by parents and grandparents for either budding science whizzes or kids that are struggling with a topic. The science whizzes will do the puzzles because they are fun and challenging. You can use the puzzles to help a "struggler" by "preteaching" the vocabulary through the puzzles and giving a child a boost in self-confidence. Then they will be able to focus on other aspects of science as they progress through their program.

We strongly suggest that you actively participate in a child's progress, working with him or her as they do the puzzles or review the results together. Remember that the clue format used with puzzles limits the extent of the definitions that can be given and that there are major differences between a broad dictionary definition of a word and a precise scientific definition. (To prove this point to yourself, look up the words *insect* and *energy* in a dictionary.)

To encourage interaction, control the solutions to the puzzles printed at the back of this book. Either tear out one or more puzzles for the children to solve or remove the answers for use when the two of you review the child's solutions.

Teachers

You probably know how you want to use these puzzles. However, a quick read through this section may give you some additional ideas. We have found the puzzles useful in three areas: pre-teaching the vocabulary, reviewing the vocabulary, and using puzzles as extra credit and enrichment activities. Here are some additional ideas for each type of puzzle.

Matching: Solving this puzzle demonstrates the student's knowledge of the relationship between a word and its definition, but it does not help the child demonstrate knowledge of either the word or its definition. Thus, the matching puzzles are most useful as seatwork or homework, familiarizing children with a word list. To introduce the entire word list, combine a matching puzzle with one of the following puzzles.

Word Search: These puzzles fascinate kids but don't develop any particular skill. However, they do give us the chance to introduce the entire word list and provide students an initial brush with some unfamiliar words.

Fill-In: These puzzles combine an introduction to the word list along with some logical thinking. For example, if the initial given letter is a P and is followed by 13 empty boxes, the unknown word is 14 letters long and begins with a P. Consulting the word list yields *photosynthesis,* which fits perfectly.

One very enjoyable way to use these puzzles is to have a student reproduce the puzzle on the chalkboard and then divide the class into two teams. Using your own criteria, such as a coin toss, decide which team goes first. Hand out copies of the word list to the teams and have them confer on the first word. Caution them to respond only through their captain. Accept only the first answer you hear. If correct, fill in the word on the chalkboard and award one point for each letter. If it is incorrect, award double points to the other team for a correct answer. Next let the other team choose which intersecting word they want to identify. Continue until the puzzle is complete.

Crossword: These are the most familiar and straightforward of the puzzles. Use them as seatwork or homework, or copy the puzzle grid on the chalkboard or hand out copies. Make up clue slips containing a clue and its position (1 Down; The ability to do work.). Mix the slips up in a bowl and have the students draw one slip apiece. Then, in any order you determine, have them come up and pantomime the position and clue, like a game of charades, while the rest of the class tries to guess the word. If the class gets frustrated on one or two words, set a time limit, give them the word, and go on.

Word Jumble: These are tough. Use them for extra credit and for those students that are always done early and want something else to do. They do involve some logic and require a certain kind of mind to enjoy.

Puzzles are a fun and challenging way for kids to learn science terms. When a child solves a puzzle, there is more going on than rote learning. For example, solving the fill-In puzzles involves quite a bit of logical thinking, a higher-level skill. This is also true of the word jumble puzzles. However, we don't want to mislead you— the purpose of this book is age-appropriate vocabulary development and fun! Anything else is a bonus.

Science PUZZLERS

Contents

Life SCIENCE

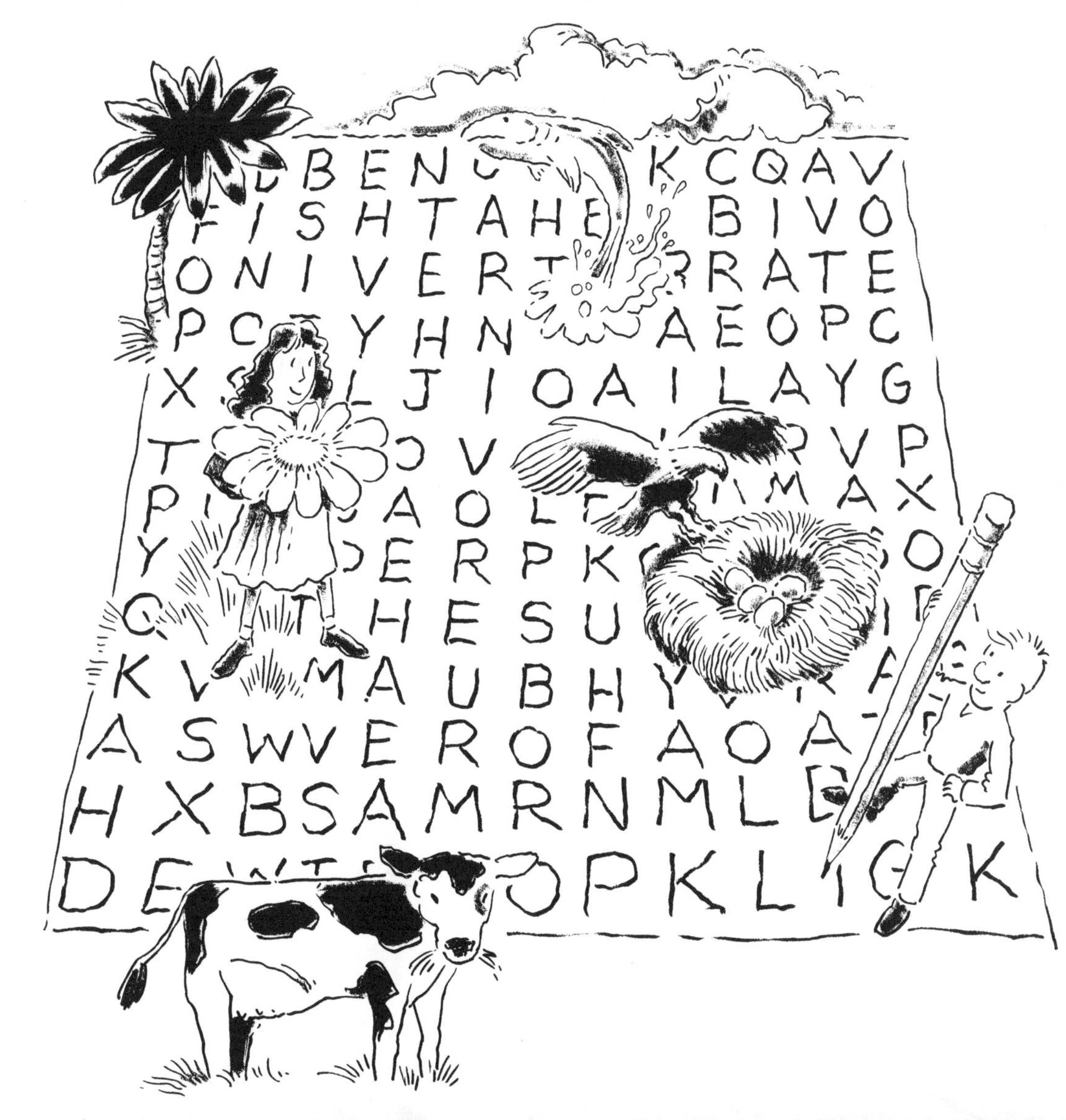

Life SCIENCE

Animals

This puzzle has two lists—words and definitions. Match the words with their definitions by drawing a line between them.

fish	An organism that lives by eating plants.
earthworm	Vertebrates that have fins, scales, and gills.
nocturnal	A kind of vertebrate that starts out with gills and later develops lungs.
amphibian	A mammal whose young develop in a pouch on the mother.
chordates	A segmented worm commonly found underground in gardens and lawns.
carnivore	Term for animals that are active at night.
marsupial	An organism that survives by eating meat.
herbivore	Vertebrates and their relatives that have a notochord.

Life SCIENCE

Animals

This puzzle contains hidden words. They can go up and down, across, at an angle, forward, or back. All the hidden words are in the list below. When you find one, circle it and look for another.

G	D	B	E	N	C	L	T	O	K	C	Q	A	V	W
F	I	S	H	T	A	H	E	R	B	I	V	O	R	E
O	N	I	V	E	R	T	E	B	R	A	T	E	T	V
D	O	T	Y	H	N	J	R	I	A	E	O	O	P	C
X	S	Y	L	J	I	O	A	I	L	A	Y	G	C	H
T	A	J	M	D	V	H	C	I	L	R	V	G	P	O
P	U	M	W	A	O	P	T	T	A	O	M	A	X	R
Y	R	T	P	E	R	P	L	K	U	R	B	S	O	D
S	S	E	N	H	E	S	U	A	O	R	L	I	R	A
Q	C	K	D	R	I	E	U	W	C	A	N	O	T	T
K	V	A	M	A	U	B	H	P	M	E	W	A	E	E
Q	T	S	L	N	T	T	I	M	I	Z	N	F	L	S
A	S	W	V	E	R	O	A	A	O	A	U	T	L	F
H	X	B	S	A	S	M	R	N	N	M	L	R	A	T
D	E	W	E	P	C	H	O	O	P	K	L	I	G	K

Vertebrate
Amphibian
Nocturnal
Dinosaurs
Marsupial
Chordates
Placenta
Mammals
Scales
Hair
Carnivore
Earthworm
Trilobite
Herbivore
Predator
Reptile
Fish

Animals

Using the words in the list, you can build your own crossword puzzle. Start with the letter printed at the top and count the number of letters in its word. Now you know what letter that word begins with and how many letters it has. Look at the list and find the word. Write it in and build from there.

Hair	Chordates	Mammals	Dinosaurs
Scales	Amphibian	Marsupial	Vertebrate
Reptile	Trilobite	Carnivore	
Herbivore	Fish	Earthworm	

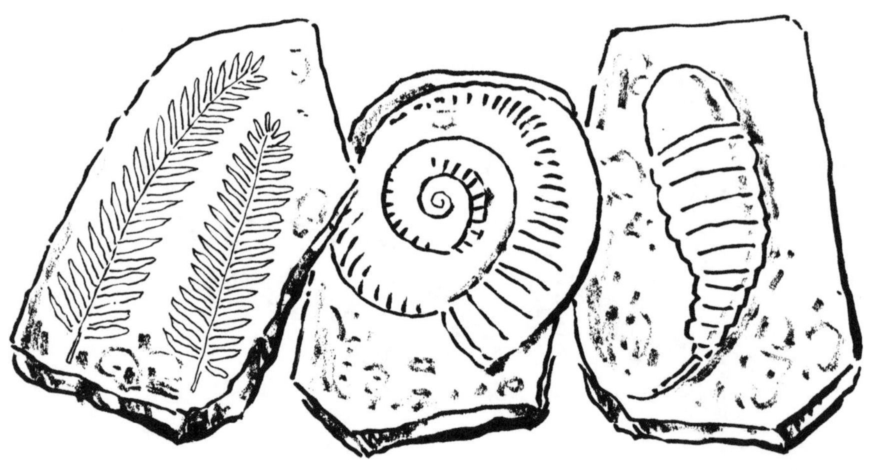

Animals

Across

1 An organ in most mammals that provides nourishment to the young before birth.

3 Term for animals that are active at night.

6 An extinct arthropod with an oval body segmented in three parts.

8 The outer body covering of most mammals.

12 Member of a large group of animals that have backbones.

14 A class of animals that have hair and feed their young milk.

Down

2 A group of animals that start out with gills and later develop lungs.

4 Vertebrates and their relatives that have a notochord.

5 Organisms that survive by eating meat.

7 A segmented worm commonly found underground in gardens and lawns.

9 A mammal whose young develop in a pouch on the mother.

10 An organism that lives by eating plants.

11 An animal that hunts others for food.

13 Vertebrates that have fins, scales, and gills.

Animals

Unscramble the letters into words and write them in the boxes to the left. Now unscramble the letters in the boxes with circles to find the last word.

HISF

MMMLAAS

TMEQAWRRHO

TURNNLCAO

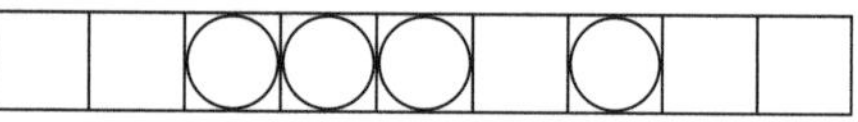

ROIEBRHEV

An extinct arthropod with an oval body segmented in three parts.

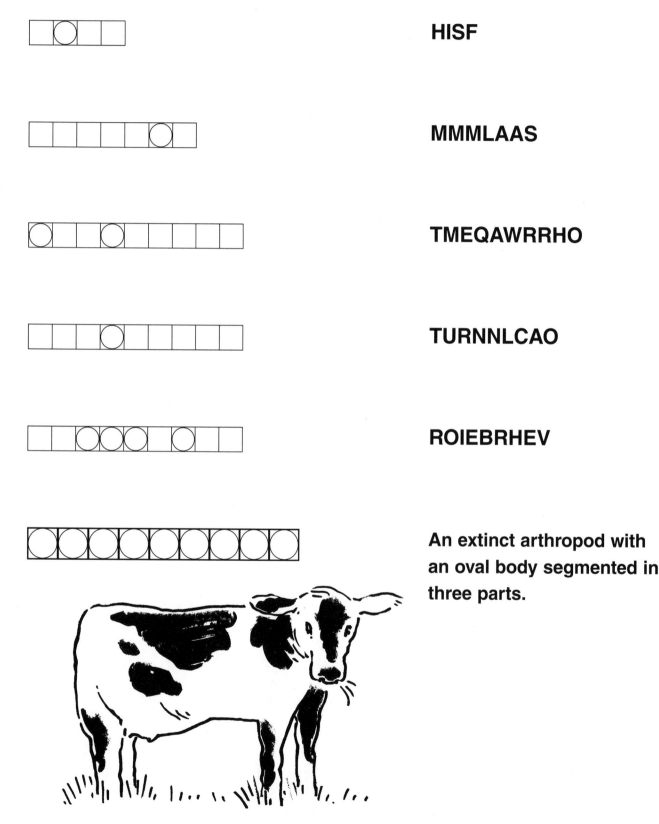

Birds

This puzzle has two lists—words and definitions. Match the words with their definitions by drawing a line between them.

eagle	A medium-sized red songbird.
robin	Falcon brought in to cities to control pigeon populations.
tern	A small seed-eating songbird; Darwin used the ones on the Galapagos Islands to show evolution.
lift	An arctic seabird that migrates more than 8,000 miles.
cardinal	Nocturnal bird of prey with eyes that look forward.
peregrine	The bird that is the symbol of the United States.
owl	The red-breasted bird that signifies the return of spring.
finch	The force that keeps birds and aircraft in the air.

Life SCIENCE

Birds

This puzzle contains hidden words. They can go up and down, across, at an angle, forward, or back. All the hidden words are in the list below the puzzle. When you find one, circle it and look for another.

```
I O P E R E G R I N E N S W M
J V E G M O C T A L E A I J S
M Q Y G B A J Z T P F N G X Q
V D N K D V E F I H T K E L M
I H M I G R A T I O N O J G E
P O T D X D A T S L C W R L F
B T R H I T S G Q L A L L R R
F E A T H E R S X O R T M W A
T U J R N A O H M W D D N J V
E A H U M M I N G B I R D B D
R Z L R F I W H A O N P O D Q
N D V O I L G D B N A D N L B
A A C B N R I A U E L B L K Z
M F S I C S Q F N S A R Y M L
Z S D N H M O H T N Y K I U C
```

Hummingbird
Peregrine
Ptarmigan
Cardinal
Talons
Eagle
Drag
Nene
Lift
Egg

Hollow Bones
Migration
Feathers
Raptor
Robin
Finch
Tern
Beak
Nest
Owl

Birds

Using the words in the list, you can build your own crossword puzzle. Start with the letter printed at the top and count the number of letters in its word. Now you know what letter that word begins with and how many letters it has. Look at the list and find the word. Write it in and build from there.

Owl
Drag
Lift
Nene
Eagle
Robin
Raptor
Cardinal
Ptarmigan
Hummingbird
Egg
Tern
Nest
Beak
Finch
Talons
Feathers
Migration
Peregrine
Hollow Bones

R

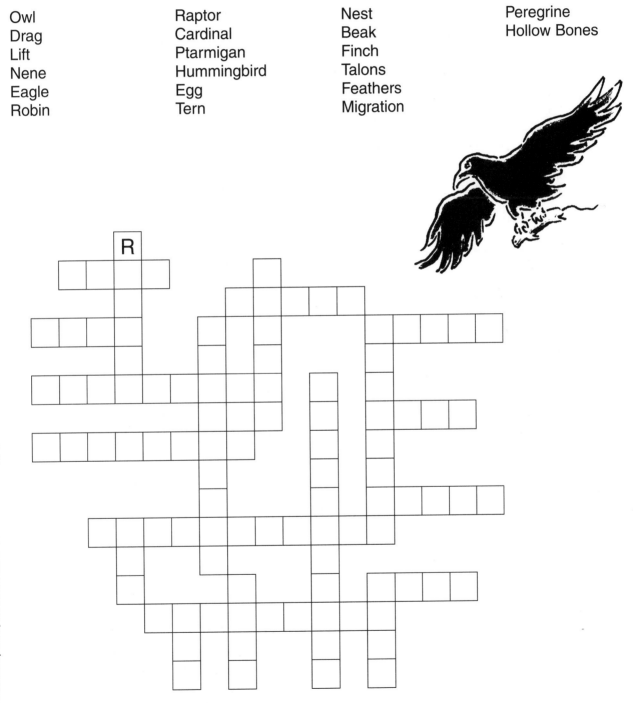

Birds

Across

4 The force that keeps birds and aircraft flying.
6 Falcon brought into cities to control pigeon populations.
9 An Arctic seabird that migrates more than 8,000 miles.
10 A medium-sized red songbird.
12 The bird that is the symbol of the United States.
14 What makes bird skeletons different and helps lighten them (two words).
17 An Arctic bird that changes color with the seasons.
18 A small seed-eating songbird; Darwin used the ones from the Galapagos Islands to show evolution.
19 Nocturnal bird of prey with eyes that look forward.

Down

1 Where baby birds develop.
2 Moving from where there is little food or water to where there is more.
3 The home that many birds build.
5 Bird covering that conserves heat and permits flight.
7 A tiny, brightly colored bird that can fly backwards.
8 The force that slows down birds and aircraft.
11 A native Hawaiian goose that is endangered.
13 The red-breasted bird that signifies the return of spring.
15 The claws on a bird of prey.
16 A bird of prey.

Birds

Unscramble the letters into words and write them in the boxes to the left. Now unscramble the letters in the boxes with circles to find the last word.

TLIF

KAEB

MMUHNDGBRII

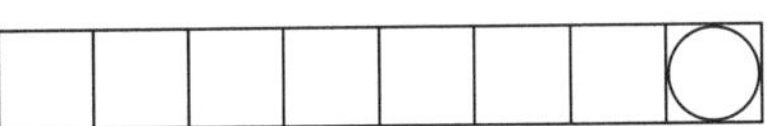

EFSETRHA

WOL

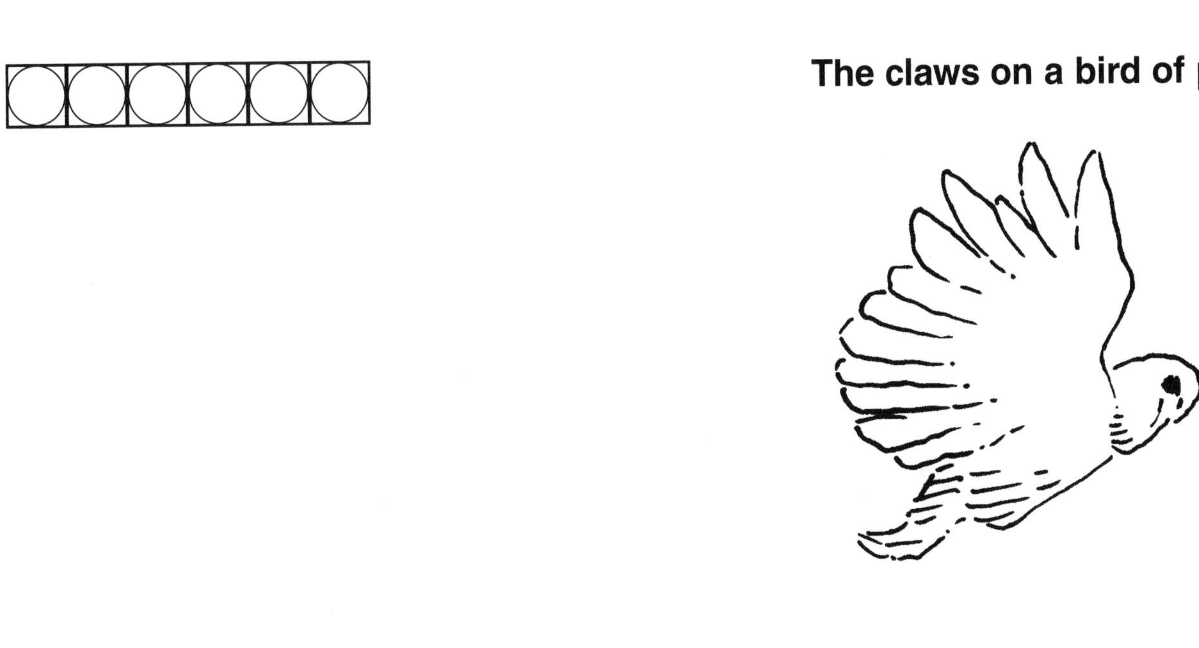

The claws on a bird of prey.

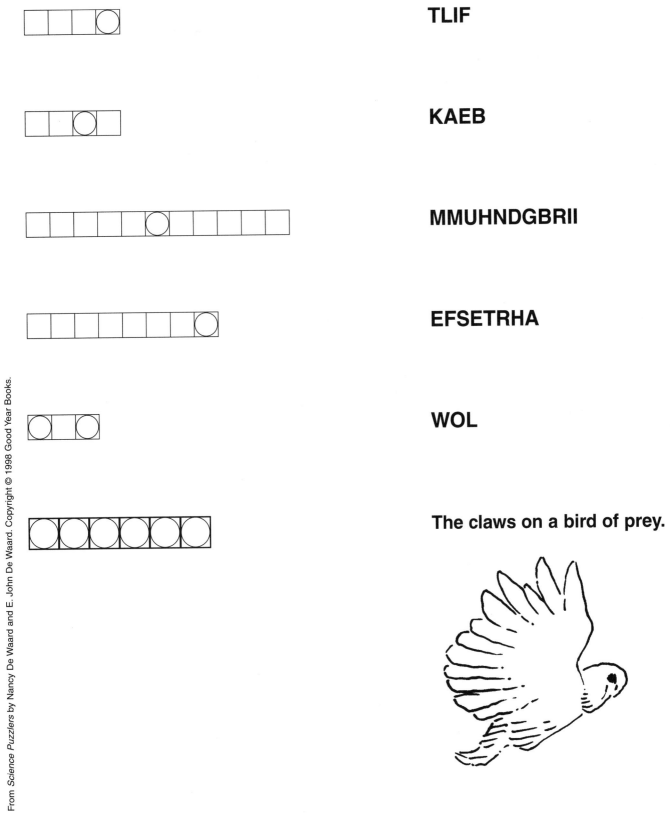

Plants

This puzzle has two lists—words and definitions. Match the words with their definitions by drawing a line between them.

oxygen	A reaction in green leaves that provides energy for almost all life.
pollination	The male reproductive cells in plants.
photosynthesis	The reproductive structure of most plants.
diffusion	Populations of plants grown for food.
osmosis	The process of a substance spreading out, usually through a fluid.
flower	The process of molecules passing through a membrane.
pollen	The gas given off by plants that is essential to animals.
crops	The process of transferring pollen from an anther to a stigma.

Plants

This puzzle contains hidden words. They can go up and down, across, at an angle, forward, or back. All the hidden words are in the list below the puzzle. When you find one, circle it and look for another.

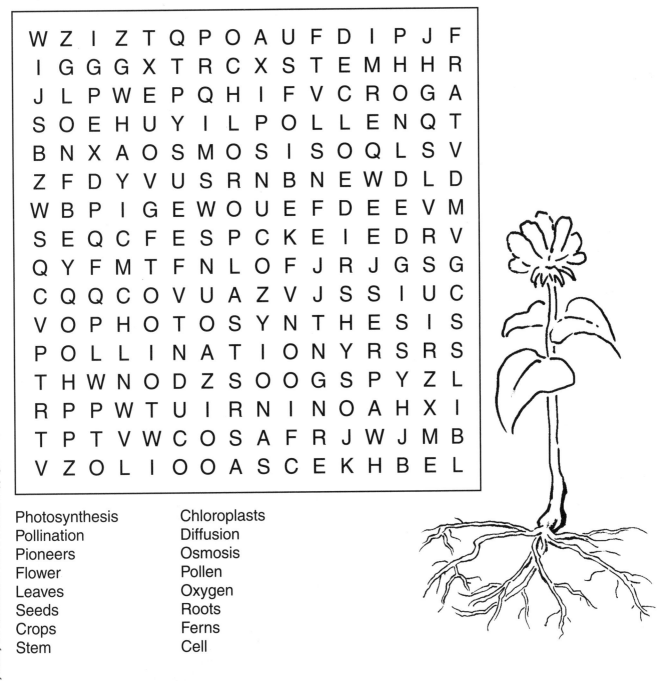

W Z I Z T Q P O A U F D I P J F
I G G G X T R C X S T E M H H R
J L P W E P Q H I F V C R O G A
S O E H U Y I L P O L L E N Q T
B N X A O S M O S I S O Q L S V
Z F D Y V U S R N B N E W D L D
W B P I G E W O U E F D E E V M
S E Q C F E S P C K E I E D R V
Q Y F M T F N L O F J R J G S G
C Q Q C O V U A Z V J S S I U C
V O P H O T O S Y N T H E S I S
P O L L I N A T I O N Y R S R S
T H W N O D Z S O O G S P Y Z L
R P P W T U I R N I N O A H X I
T P T V W C O S A F R J W J M B
V Z O L I O O A S C E K H B E L

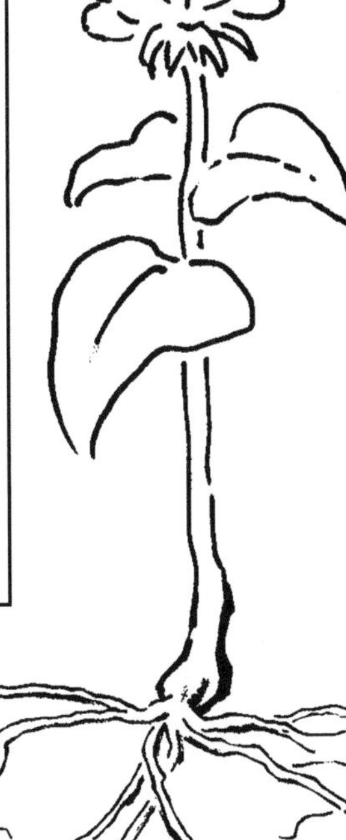

Photosynthesis
Pollination
Pioneers
Flower
Leaves
Seeds
Crops
Stem
Chloroplasts
Diffusion
Osmosis
Pollen
Oxygen
Roots
Ferns
Cell

Plants

Using the words in the list, you can build your own crossword puzzle. Start with the letter printed at the top and count the number of letters in its word. Now you know what letter that word begins with and how many letters it has. Look at the list and find the word. Write it in and build from there.

Stem	Leaves	Cell	Digitalis
Ferns	Pioneers	Seeds	Pollination
Roots	Diffusion	Crops	Oxygen
Pollen	Chloroplasts	Osmosis	

Plants

Across

7 A seedless group of plants that reproduce by spores.
8 Plants that repopulate an area, such as after a forest fire.
9 A reaction in green leaves; provides energy for almost all life.
11 The process of transferring pollen from an anther to a stigma.
12 A chemical from the foxglove plant used to treat heart disease.
13 The process of molecules passing through a membrane.
14 The structures that feed most plants; where photosynthesis occurs.

Down

1 The process of a substance spreading out, usually through a fluid.
2 The gas given off by plants that is essential to animals.
3 The reproductive structure of most plants.
4 Plant parts that anchor the plant and get water and minerals.
5 Populations of plants grown for food.
6 Bodies in the cells of leaves that contain chlorophyll.
10 What you plant to grow new plants.

Plants

Unscramble the letters into words and write them in the boxes to the left. Now unscramble the letters in the boxes with circles to find the last word.

ELCL

LOPINOILTNA

MTSE

OCPRS

SREFN

Plants that repopulate an area, such as after a forest fire.

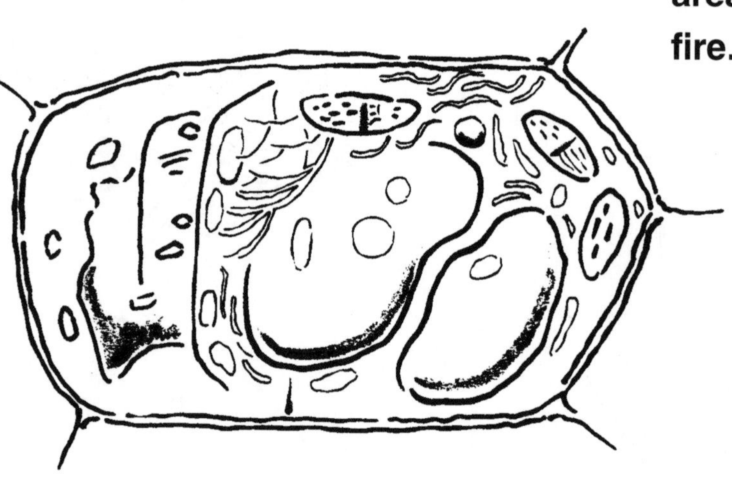

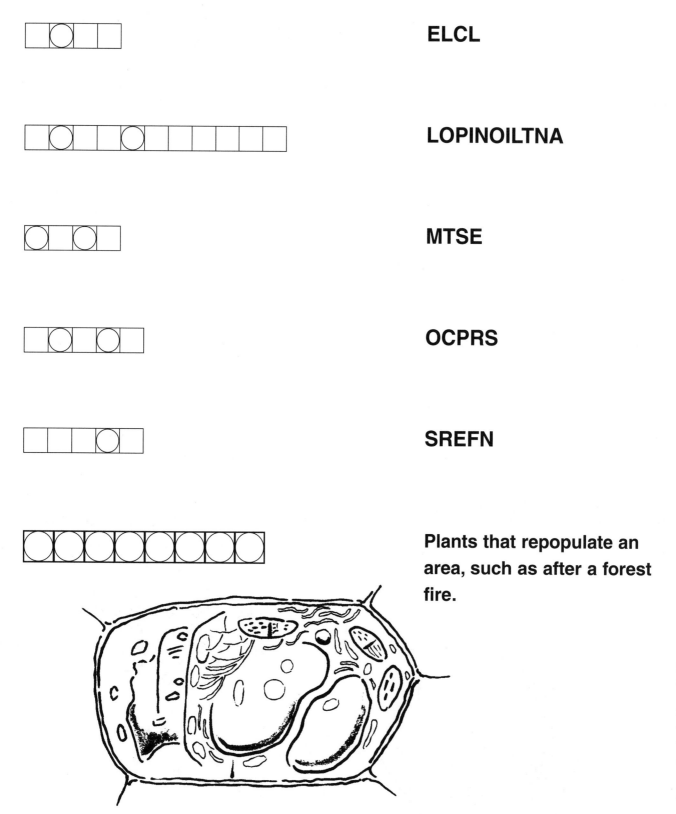

Mammals

This puzzle has two lists—words and definitions. Match the words with their definitions by drawing a line between them.

beaver

elephant

whale

vertebrate

carnivore

dolphin

kangaroo

bears

An animal with a backbone.

Forest-dwelling omnivorous mammals that hibernate through winter.

Large Australian marsupial, with large rear legs, and a long, tapered tail.

An organism that eats meat.

A stream-dwelling mammal that builds dams.

A marine mammal; some are the largest animals that have ever lived.

A medium-sized marine mammal that navigates by sonar.

A large mammal from Africa and Asia that has a prehensile trunk.

Mammals

This puzzle contains hidden words. They can go up and down, across, at an angle, forward, or back. All the hidden words are in the list below the puzzle. When you find one, circle it and look for another.

Q	I	K	N	A	K	I	Q	P	C	T	Y	N	U	M	F
G	L	B	A	T	S	N	Q	Q	F	G	I	S	N	A	W
M	I	L	K	N	H	K	M	P	R	O	R	G	T	R	H
D	J	R	Q	K	G	G	P	M	J	A	X	K	L	S	A
U	R	P	A	X	F	A	W	R	E	T	Y	T	O	U	L
T	G	K	L	F	H	E	R	B	I	V	O	R	E	P	E
D	A	R	A	A	F	B	C	O	Y	M	E	O	A	I	L
Y	R	R	W	K	C	E	A	Y	O	C	A	Y	K	A	H
M	A	M	M	A	L	E	R	T	O	Z	T	T	M	L	W
Q	D	O	L	P	H	I	N	N	S	Q	X	A	E	V	G
H	S	Y	T	E	C	A	I	T	I	M	T	R	N	O	R
G	I	L	N	S	H	H	V	D	A	M	C	G	K	U	B
N	G	U	C	P	R	P	O	R	C	U	P	I	N	E	D
Y	U	B	E	A	V	E	R	D	S	F	G	A	H	L	X
D	Q	L	H	A	D	L	E	L	B	C	U	Y	A	V	N
F	E	O	R	J	V	E	R	T	E	B	R	A	T	E	S

Vertebrate
Carnivore
Herbivore
Elephant
Placenta
Dolphin
Beaver
Whale
Bats
Milk

Rhinoceros
Marsupial
Porcupine
Kangaroo
Primate
Giraffe
Mammal
Bears
Goat
Fox

Mammals

Using the words in the list, you can build your own crossword puzzle. Start with the letter printed at the top and count the number of letters in its word. Now you know what letter that word begins with and how many letters it has. Look at the list and find the word. Write it in and build from there.

Fox
Whale
Beaver
Primate
Kangaroo

Placenta
Carnivore
Herbivore
Vertebrate
Goat

Bears
Giraffe
Dolphin
Elephant
Porcupine

Marsupial
Rhinoceros

Mammals

Across

6 An order of mammals that includes apes, monkeys, and humans.
8 Animals that bear internal young, give milk, and are covered by hair.
9 A marine mammal; some are the largest animals that have ever lived.
10 The food given to young mammals from birth to weaning.
13 A hollow-horned and bearded herbivore; source of milk, wool, and meat.
14 Animals with backbones.
15 A large, forest-dwelling rodent that is covered with quills.
16 The organ in most mammals that feeds the young before birth.

Down

1 A stream-dwelling mammal that builds dams.
2 Forest-dwelling omnivorous mammals that hibernate through winter.
3 An African mammal; the tallest land animal.
4 An animal that eats plants.
5 An organism that eats meat.
7 A large African herbivore that has one or two horns on its nose.
11 Large Australian marsupial, large rear legs, and a long, tapered tail.
12 A mammal that rears its young in a pouch.

Mammals

Unscramble the letters into words and write them in the boxes to the left. Now unscramble the letters in the boxes with circles to find the last word.

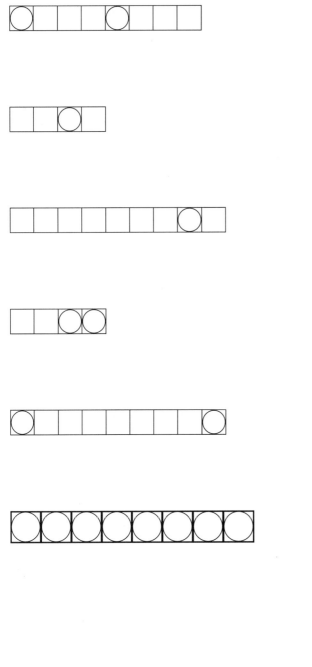

ANPEATLC

LMIK

UPREOICPN

GAOT

EIVEOBRRH

A large mammal from Africa and Asia that has a prehensile trunk.

Insects

This puzzle has two lists—words and definitions. Match the words with their definitions by drawing a line between them.

nymph	Hard outer covering of an insect.
invertebrate	The larva of a butterfly or moth.
mandibles	Stinging insects that have a narrow waist and build houses of paper.
wasps	A jointed sense organ on the head of an insect.
antenna	A wingless insect that lives in highly organized colonies
exoskeleton	An animal that does not have a backbone.
caterpillar	An early stage of an insect that has incomplete metamorphosis.
ant	The first pair of mouthparts on an insect.

Insects

This puzzle contains hidden words. They can go up and down, across, at an angle, forward, or back. All the hidden words are in the list below the puzzle. When you find one, circle it and look for another.

V	I	W	Y	V	I	T	E	R	M	I	T	E	S	J	S
W	V	T	P	B	X	A	N	T	A	Z	N	K	R	Z	U
L	D	D	U	C	E	P	R	V	C	O	C	O	O	N	D
B	A	R	P	V	A	E	D	T	T	B	E	E	S	B	T
N	C	C	A	N	J	T	T	L	H	T	H	G	I	Y	N
A	W	I	N	G	S	F	E	L	A	O	P	P	X	T	Q
D	R	U	C	N	O	K	I	R	E	J	P	O	U	W	M
S	G	A	M	A	S	N	B	R	P	S	T	O	R	Y	D
C	A	P	C	O	D	E	F	M	E	I	U	I	D	J	Z
M	Y	B	X	H	T	A	N	L	U	F	L	V	Z	S	F
F	S	E	S	R	N	S	B	Q	Y	Q	L	L	P	U	X
B	A	X	E	N	P	I	S	Y	M	R	O	Y	A	X	R
P	U	V	E	S	D	O	D	F	D	V	Y	N	O	R	L
F	N	T	A	N	M	O	N	A	R	C	H	X	H	L	C
I	N	W	A	L	K	I	N	G	S	T	I	C	K	W	U
A	Z	M	C	N	Y	M	P	H	K	I	B	L	T	U	U

Walking Stick
Caterpillar
Mandibles
Mosquito
Antenna
Firefly
Cicada
Nymph
Wasps
Ant

Invertebrate
Dragonfly
Arachnida
Termites
Monarch
Beetle
Cocoon
Wings
Bees

Insects

Using the words in the list, you can build your own crossword puzzle. Start with the letter printed at the top and count the number of letters in its word. Now you know what letter that word begins with and how many letters it has. Look at the list and find the word. Write it in and build from there.

Nymph	Invertebrate	Mandibles
Cicada	Bees	Arachnida
Firefly	Cocoon	Caterpillar
Mosquito	Monarch	Walking Stick
Arthropods	Antenna	

Insects

Across

4 A class of carnivorous arthropods that have eight legs; spiders.
6 The larva of a butterfly or moth.
9 An animal that does not have a backbone.
10 Butterfly that migrates long distances to and from Mexico.
12 Stinging insects that have a narrow waist and build houses of paper.

Down

1 An early stage of an insect that has incomplete metamorphosis.
2 This noisy insect has a life cycle of up to 17 years.
3 A predatory insect that looks like a twig (two words).
5 A silky covering spun by a larva that protects the pupa.
7 Insects that can digest wood; some species build giant mounds.
8 A jointed sense organ on the head of an insect.
11 A wingless insect that lives in highly organized colonies.

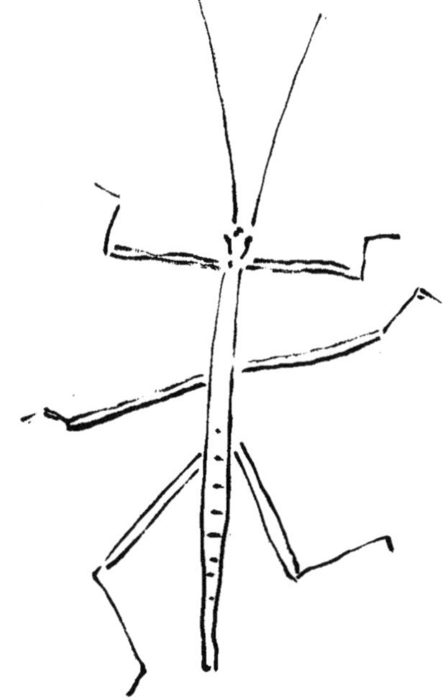

Insects

Unscramble the letters into words and write them in the boxes to the left. Now unscramble the letters in the boxes with circles to find the last word.

☐☐◯☐☐☐☐ **EFFYRIL**

☐☐☐☐☐◯ **IAADCC**

◯☐◯☐☐☐☐☐☐ **BNLSAEMID**

☐☐◯☐☐☐☐☐☐☐☐ **LKTXEOSENOE**

☐☐☐◯◯☐☐☐☐ **HAANCIRDA**

◯◯◯◯◯◯◯ **Butterfly that migrates long distances to and from Mexico.**

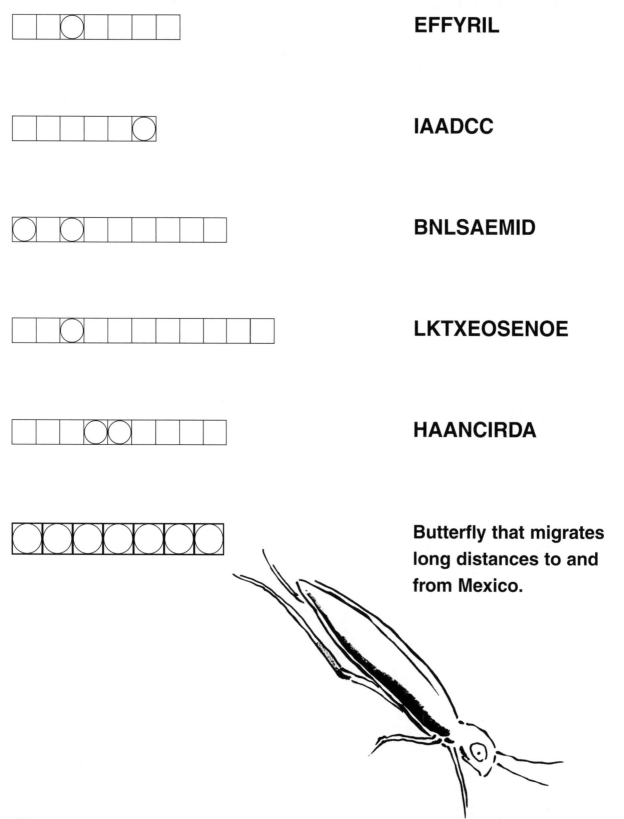

Adaptation

This puzzle has two lists—words and definitions. Match the words with their definitions by drawing a line between them.

coloration	Plant structures that gather and store energy, where photosynthesis happens.
fins	Color that helps with recognition and camouflage.
gills	The process of species changing over time by natural selection.
environment	An adaptation of plant species that helps them spread over large areas.
seeds	A British scientist; one of the first to describe adaptation.
evolution	An adaptation in fish that makes them good swimmers.
leaves	An adaptation in fish that allows them to take oxygen from water.
Darwin	All of the things and conditions that surround an organism.

Adaptation

This puzzle contains hidden words. They can go up and down, across, at an angle, forward, or back. All the hidden words are in the list below the puzzle. When you find one, circle it and look for another.

C	A	X	O	P	E	N	V	S	D	Z	F	U	R	S	Z
C	H	F	E	A	T	H	E	R	S	A	T	Y	R	R	C
K	A	P	G	R	L	U	N	G	S	Z	R	P	T	S	K
E	B	R	U	A	A	T	A	G	I	A	E	W	M	U	L
B	I	I	N	S	C	Q	I	Z	V	N	P	S	I	S	E
D	T	W	X	I	S	O	F	T	O	E	I	Q	I	N	A
Q	A	A	G	T	V	F	L	I	U	L	N	S	J	L	V
Q	T	X	O	I	Q	O	T	O	A	D	O	K	P	B	E
S	E	O	M	S	L	A	R	U	R	I	E	T	B	M	S
O	R	N	H	M	N	L	T	E	B	A	K	A	I	V	T
D	G	V	L	R	E	U	S	M	S	D	T	G	K	D	D
T	L	I	E	K	M	I	Y	E	K	G	Y	I	O	I	M
O	E	B	G	U	J	S	E	E	D	S	O	X	O	N	B
F	I	N	S	B	Y	E	V	O	L	U	T	I	O	N	R
H	U	J	C	L	I	M	A	T	E	Z	X	Y	U	E	B
W	Q	E	N	V	I	R	O	N	M	E	N	T	V	T	T

Environment
Carnivores
Coloration
Mutualism
Altitude
Habitat
Leaves
Seeds
Lungs
Fins
Hibernation
Parasitism
Evolution
Symbiosis
Feathers
Climate
Darwin
Roots
Gills
Fur

Adaptation

Using the words in the list, you can build your own crossword puzzle. Start with the letter printed at the top and count the number of letters in its word. Now you know what letter that word begins with and how many letters it has. Look at the list and find the word. Write it in and build from there.

Fur	Altitude	Fins	Feathers
Gills	Symbiosis	Roots	Evolution
Lungs	Parasitism	Seeds	Coloration
Darwin	Carnivores	Leaves	Hibernation
Habitat	Environment	Climate	

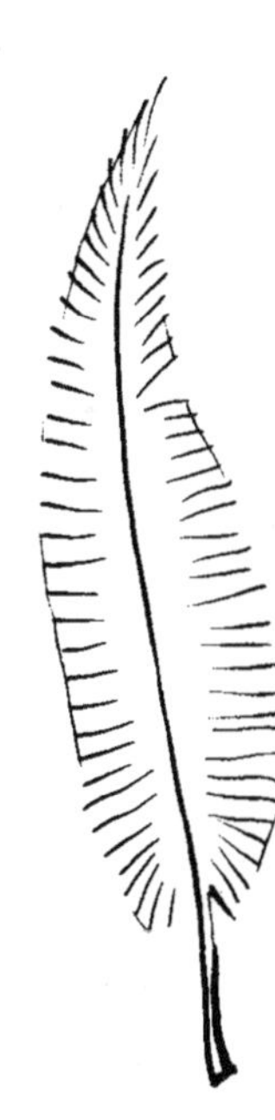

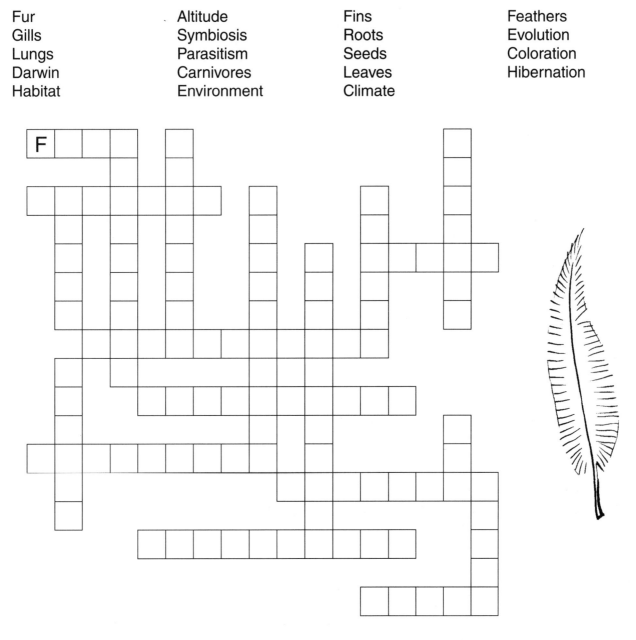

Life SCIENCE

Adaptation

Across

1 Special protective covering of birds.
4 Relationship in which organisms are essential to each other.
5 A relationship between organisms where one benefits and one is hurt.
6 Color that helps with recognition and camouflage.
8 All of the things and conditions that surround an organism.
10 Organisms that eat only meat.
11 Surroundings to which an organism is adapted and usually found.
13 Organisms that live high on a mountainside are adapted to _________ .
14 An adaptation in fish that makes them good swimmers.
15 An adaptation of plant species that spreads them over large areas.

Down

2 An adaptation of bears to cold and lack of food.
3 An adaptation of most plants that anchors them to one place.
7 Organs that take oxygen from the air.
9 Structures that help plants gather and store energy; where photosynthesis happens.
10 Long-term weather patterns that influence adaptation.
12 An external adaptation of mammals that conserves body heat.

Adaptation

Unscramble the letters into words and write them in the boxes to the left. Now unscramble the letters in the boxes with circles to find the last word.

□□○□□○□○	ULAMITUMS
□□□□□□□□○□	OEISRARVNC
○□□□□□□□	ATEDITLU
□□□□○□	WNAIDR
○□□□□□□□□□	COAOTOLNRI
○○○○○○○	**Long-term weather patterns that influence adaptation.**

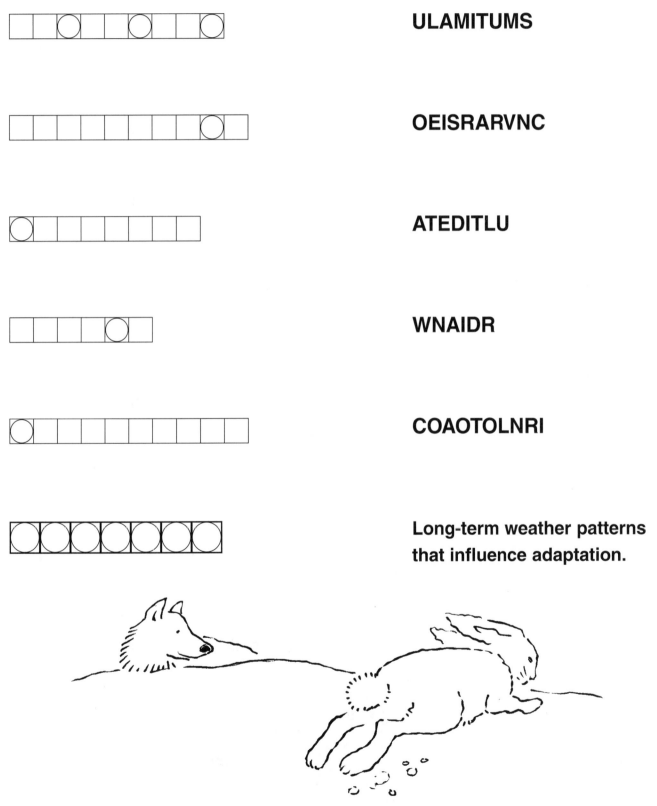

Ecology

This puzzle has two lists—words and definitions. Match the words with their definitions by drawing a line between them.

biosphere	Organisms alive after a natural disaster, such as a flood or eruption.
human	A substance, usually a manufactured chemical, used to kill pests.
pesticide	Food, minerals, and vitamins that sustain an organism.
ecosystem	A primate that has a large brain, walks upright, and has little hair.
photosynthesis	All of the interacting living and nonliving parts within an environment.
survivors	A process by which plants store energy from sunlight in sugars.
community	Ecosystem that includes every place that life exists on earth.
nutrients	Groups of living things that interact within an area.

Life SCIENCE

Ecology

This puzzle contains hidden words. They can go up and down, across, at an angle, forward, or back. All the hidden words are in the list below the puzzle. When you find one, circle it and look for another.

```
S Q W M C I C I A U E E L P H T
N H E E C O M P E T I T I O N C
P E C N C A L L G V X Y N L C O
S R O P U O R O S C T I V L E N
G B S E S T M N N H M J I U Y S
E I Y S N U R M I I U S F T D U
N V S T Z V R I U V Z M Q I E M
D O T I E G I V E N O E A O C E
A R E C B T V R I N I R R N O R
N E M I M N L B O V T T E S M N
G C M D L V B G I N O S Y S P C
E J W E J A Z Y V Y M R W E O R
R P H O T O S Y N T H E S I S F
E V X I X L S K R R Z L N S E B
D Z S G R A I N F O R E S T R R
Y H D I V E R S I T Y J E C S Q
```

Photosynthesis
Environment
Rain Forest
Endangered
Pesticide
Survivors
Nutrients
Diversity
Consumer
Competition
Carnivores
Decomposer
Colonizers
Community
Ecosystem
Herbivore
Pollution
Human

Ecology

Using the words in the list, you can build your own crossword puzzle. Start with the letter printed at the top and count the number of letters in its word. Now you know what letter that word begins with and how many letters it has. Look at the list and find the word. Write it in and build from there.

Human
Producer
Community
Survivors
Decomposer

Carnivores
Rain Forest
Environment
Human

Plants
Consumer
Nutrients
Ecosystem

Endangered
Colonizers
Competition
Photosynthesis

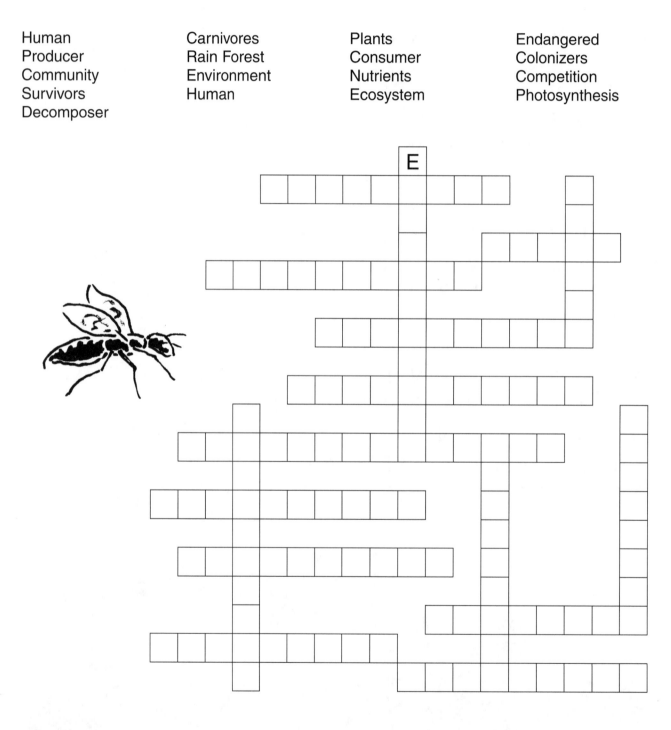

E

Ecology

Across

7 An organism that helps break down dead organisms.

10 The struggle among organisms for food, water, and/or space.

12 In serious threat of becoming extinct.

13 Ecosystem that includes every place that life exists on earth.

15 Organisms alive after a natural disaster, such as a flood or eruption.

16 The dumping of harmful substances into the environment.

Down

1 Organisms that repopulate an area, such as after a volcanic eruption.

2 Organisms that survive by eating meat.

3 A process by which plants store energy from sunlight in sugars.

4 An animal that survives by eating plants.

5 Food, minerals, and vitamins that sustain an organism.

6 All of the interacting living and nonliving parts of the environment.

8 All of the things and conditions present in a place.

9 A tropical forest in an area with high precipitation.

11 An ecosystem that has many different kinds of organisms shows ______ .

14 A primate that has a large brain, walks upright, and has little hair.

Ecology

Unscramble the letters into words and write them in the boxes to the left. Now unscramble the letters in the boxes with circles to find the last word.

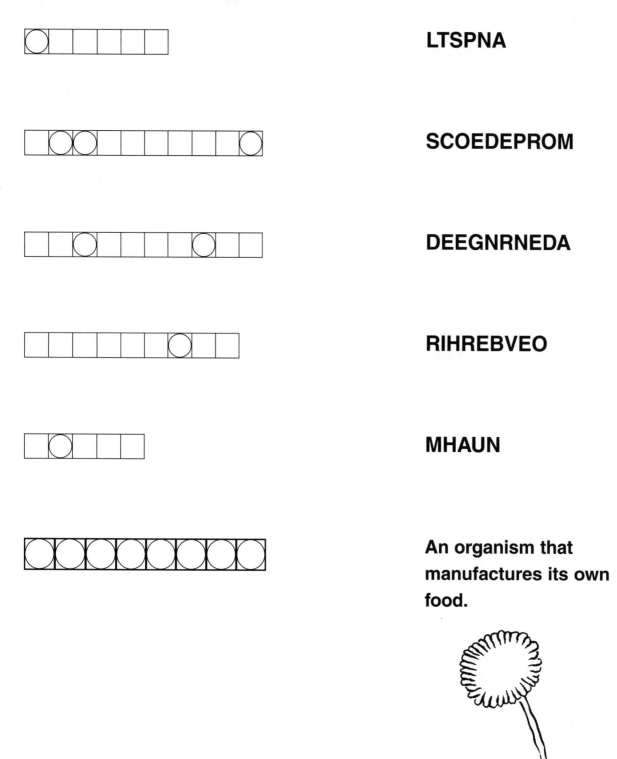

LTSPNA

SCOEDEPROM

DEEGNRNEDA

RIHREBVEO

MHAUN

An organism that manufactures its own food.

Biomes and Habitats

This puzzle has two lists—words and definitions. Match the words with their definitions by drawing a line between them.

taiga	Trees that bear needles and cones.
tundra	A biome that receives little usable moisture each year.
reef	A rocky projection from the earth typically having alpine ecosystems.
mountain	The living and dead bodies of coral at or near the ocean's surface.
colonizer	All of the water on the surface of the earth.
conifers	An arctic desert with few trees and little usable water.
hydrosphere	Huge evergreen forests that cover subarctic Canada and Europe.
desert	An organism that moves into a new area such as after an eruption.

Life SCIENCE

Biomes and Habitats

This puzzle contains hidden words. They can go up and down, across, at an angle, forward, or back. All the hidden words are in the list below the puzzle. When you find one, circle it and look for another.

Z	J	Z	T	T	U	N	D	R	A	G	M	C	B	L	J
T	V	A	A	L	S	A	L	T	W	A	T	E	R	L	X
E	S	E	I	M	U	B	E	R	E	E	F	J	L	S	U
O	C	A	G	G	A	I	I	N	P	O	L	A	R	R	I
W	C	O	A	C	R	R	I	O	P	I	M	M	S	T	C
D	P	E	N	I	O	A	S	Z	S	E	Z	D	A	A	Z
E	O	C	A	I	T	L	S	H	T	P	N	K	J	L	Y
C	K	R	G	N	F	H	O	S	O	A	H	T	U	P	P
I	P	Z	U	D	S	E	Y	N	L	U	Q	E	P	I	O
D	G	O	S	B	A	S	R	T	I	A	E	O	R	N	I
U	M	A	M	Q	O	A	E	S	B	Z	N	G	N	E	C
O	W	Z	L	C	Y	W	H	V	K	C	E	D	Q	T	J
U	L	M	E	H	Y	D	R	O	S	P	E	R	E	K	T
S	X	L	H	A	B	I	T	A	T	I	L	T	H	R	G
F	R	E	S	H	W	A	T	E	R	A	Z	U	C	T	B
C	D	Q	C	L	F	O	R	E	S	T	V	X	B	S	H

Ecosystem
Grassland
Salt Water
Mountain
Conifers
Prairie
Oceans
Tundra
Marsh
Reef
Fresh Water
Colonizer
Deciduous
Wetlands
Habitat
Alpine
Forest
Polar
Taiga
Biosphere

Biomes and Habitats

Using the words in the list, you can build your own crossword puzzle. Start with the letter printed at the top and count the number of letters in its word. Now you know what letter that word begins with and how many letters it has. Look at the list and find the word. Write it in and build from there.

Taiga	Salt Water	Oceans	Biosphere
Alpine	Colonizer	Desert	Fresh Water
Tundra	Grassland	Prairie	
Habitat	Hydrosphere	Deciduous	
Wetlands	Polar	Ecosystem	

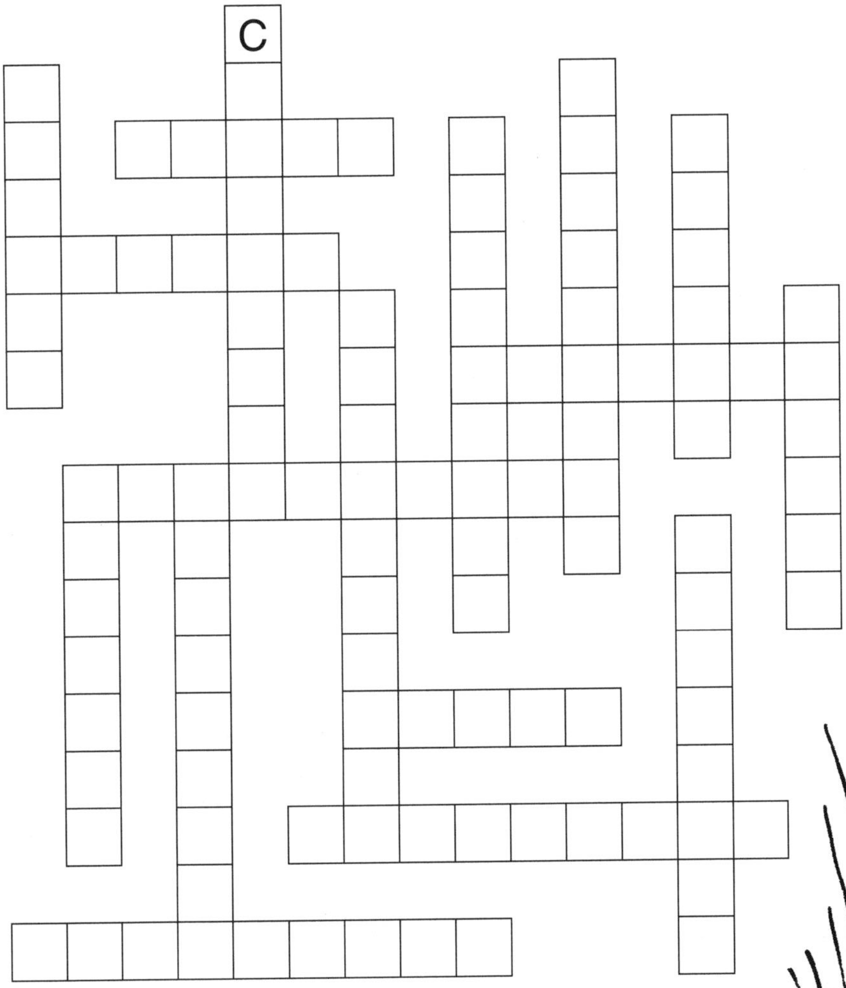

C

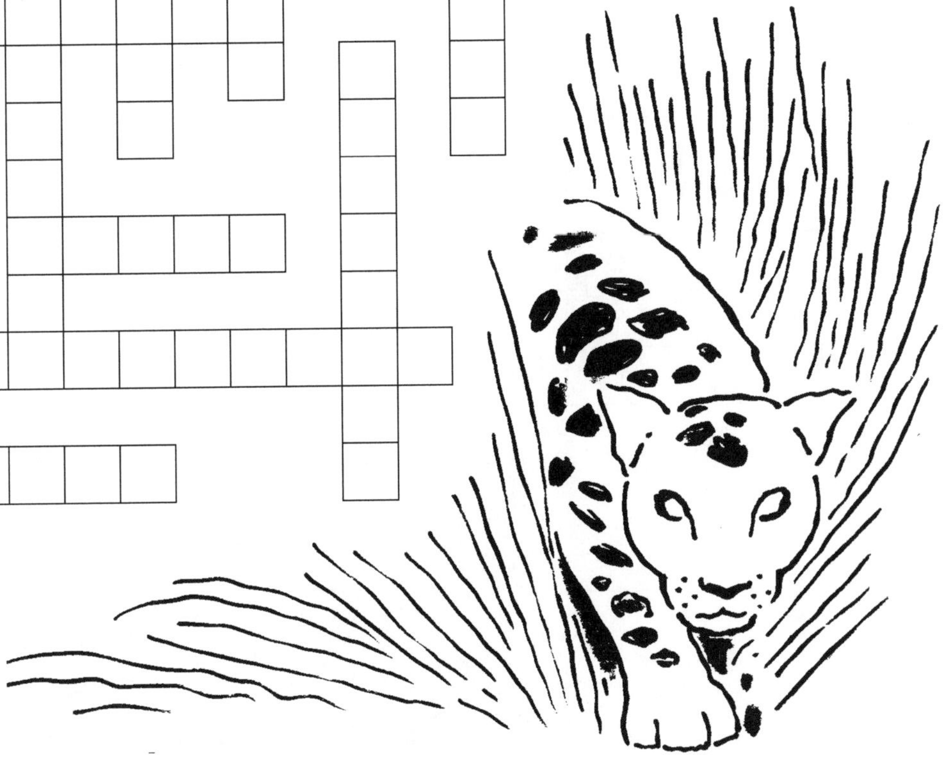

Biomes and Habitats

Across

3 A grassland biome that covers the upper Midwest of the U.S.
9 A tree that sheds its leaves each year.
10 Areas with wet and spongy soil such as a swamp, marsh, or bog.
12 Water that has little salt dissolved in it (two words).
13 Ecosystem that includes every place that life exists on earth.
15 Trees that bear needles and cones.
17 A high-altitude biome.
18 A rocky projection from the Earth, typically having alpine ecosystems.

Down

1 Water with a significant amount of salt dissolved in it (two words).
2 An arctic desert with few trees and little usable water.
4 A biome that receives little usable moisture each year.
5 A large area covered by trees.
6 The whole system, living and nonliving, that affects an organism.
7 An organism that moves into a new area such as after an eruption.
8 All of the water on the surface of the earth.
11 An area with few or no trees, such as a prairie.
14 Large bodies of salt water covering about three-fourths of the earth.
16 The living and dead bodies of coral at or near the ocean's surface.

Biomes and Habitats

Unscramble the letters into words and write them in the boxes to the left. Now unscramble the letters in the boxes with circles to find the last word.

OIEFSCRN

RSDPEREHYOH

MYTEOSECS

NEALPI

EDDUSICOU

A biome that receives little usable moisture each year.

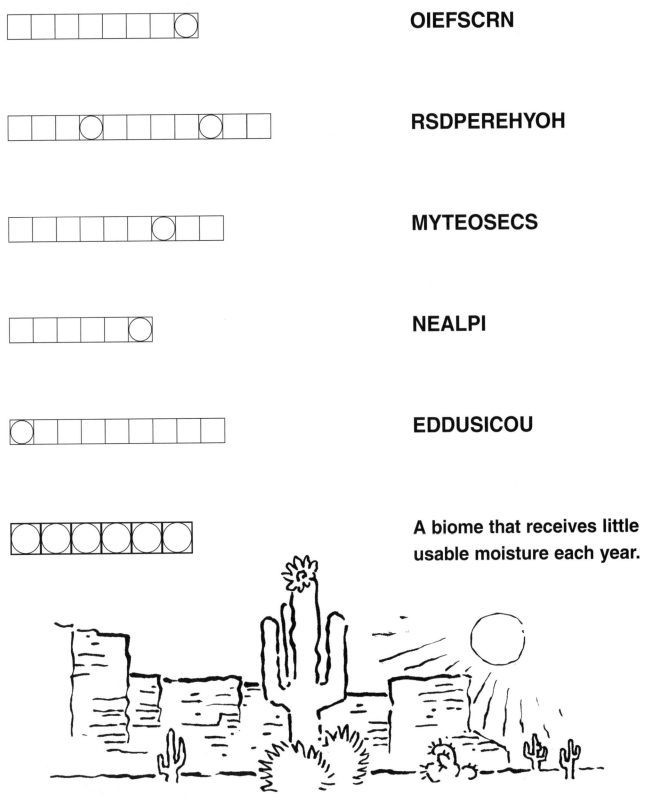

Food Chains

This puzzle has two lists—words and definitions. Match the words with their definitions by drawing a line between them.

decomposers	An animal that eats only plants.
predator	Organisms that break down dead organisms into simpler chemicals.
nutrients	An organism that eats both plants and animals.
sugars	Food, minerals, and vitamins that sustain an organism.
herbivore	An organism that hunts others for food.
omnivore	The process by which oxygen cells combine oxygen with sugar and release energy.
respiration	The source of almost all energy on earth.
sunlight	Chemical compounds produced by photosynthesis.

Food Chains

This puzzle contains hidden words. They can go up and down, across, at an angle, forward, or back. All the hidden words are in the list below the puzzle. When you find one, circle it and look for another.

```
H G R I C O N S U M E R S T M C
T C D P R O D U C E R S L V C X
E I H C Y E G S T A F L Y P F C
N X S L Z P S L D R R Z G D S C
G T G X O I L P D L I B V Q U R
E H E N E R G Y I J L E O L G A
D E C O M P O S E R S L N N A K
I R N R O P B P W J A R H T R O
G B G P I X R Y H T L T A Y S Y
E I Y T K E Y E W Y L T I Z C X
S V P W X M L G D N L B F O G B
T O M U U L W D E A R L C X N Q
I R P H O T O S Y N T H E S I S
O E A I P L A N T S O O M V T O
N I S U N L I G H T O X R V X T
J U E O M N I V O R E U D K W E
```

Photosynthesis
Decomposers
Producers
Herbivore
Consumers
Sunlight
Oxygen
Carbon
Energy
Respiration
Chlorophyll
Nutrients
Digestion
Predator
Omnivore
Sugars
Plants

Food Chains

Using the words in the list, you can build your own crossword puzzle. Start with the letter printed at the top and count the number of letters in its word. Now you know what letter that word begins with and how many letters it has. Look at the list and find the word. Write it in and build from there.

Heat	Nutrients	Energy	Producers
Plants	Herbivore	Oxygen	Digestion
Food Web	Chlorophyll	Predator	Decomposers
Sunlight	Respiration	Consumers	Photosynthesis

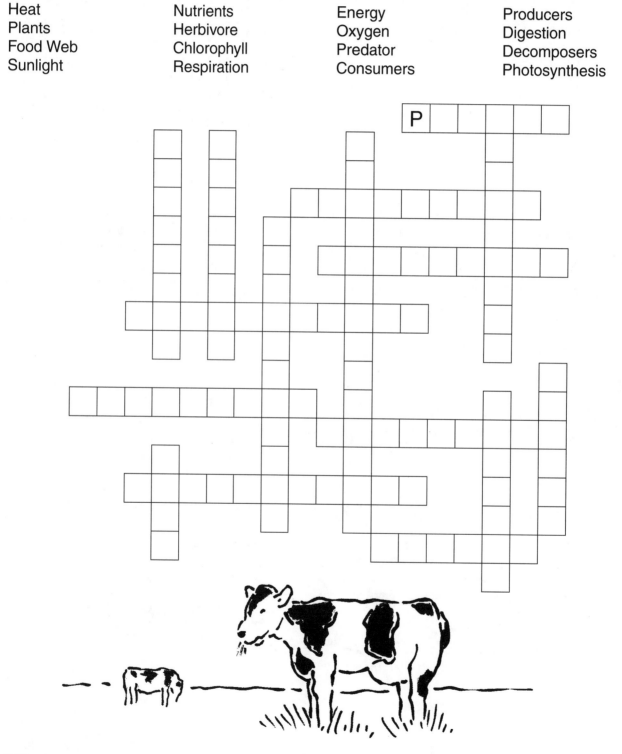

Food Chains

Across

7 The process by which cells combine oxygen with sugars, releasing energy.
9 The ability to do work.
12 Chemical compounds produced by photosynthesis.
13 Organisms that make their own food.
14 The source of almost all energy on earth.
15 An organism that hunts others for food.

Down

1 A natural reaction that stores energy from sunlight in sugars.
2 The process of breaking down food into molecules the cells can use.
3 The catalyst that makes photosynthesis go.
4 Food, minerals, and vitamins that sustain an organism.
5 Organisms that break down dead organisms into simpler chemicals.
6 An atmospheric gas that, when combined with food, releases energy.
8 An animal that eats only plants.
10 All life on earth is based on chains of atoms of this element.
11 The major producer in most ecosystems.

Food Chains

Unscramble the letters into words and write them in the boxes to the left. Now unscramble the letters in the boxes with circles to find the last word.

ETIPRRAIOSN

ASRGSU

EODEPRMOCSS

LNTASP

OREVONMI

The process of breaking down food into molecules the cells can use.

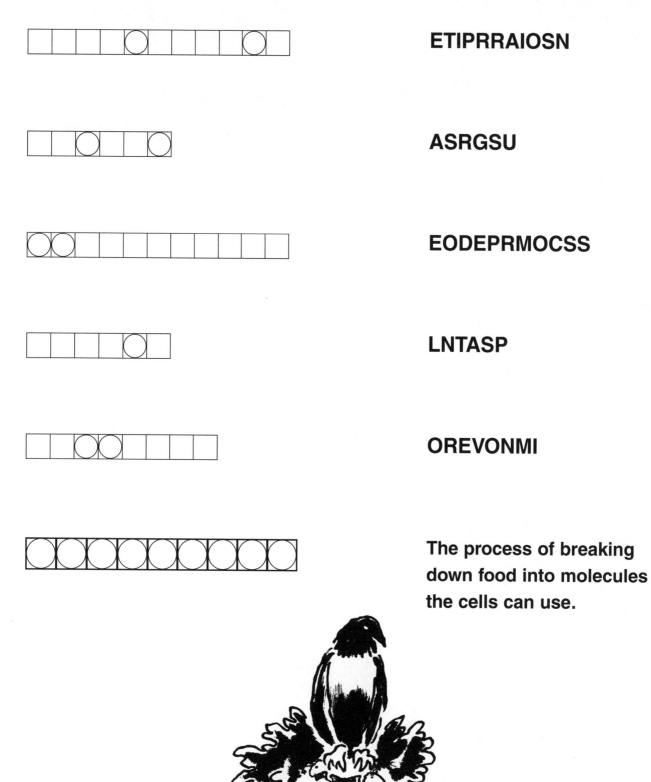

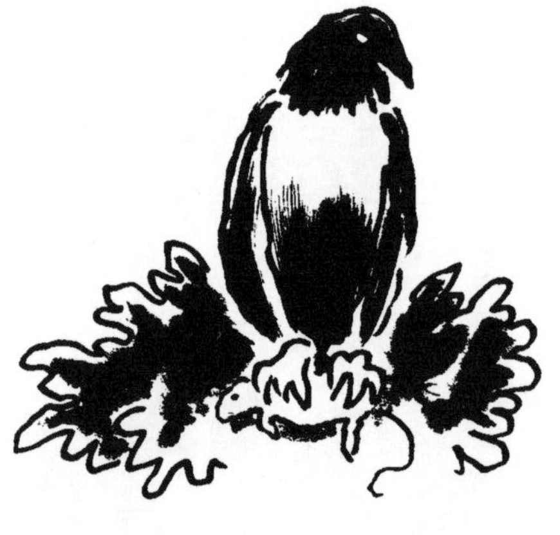

Heredity

This puzzle has two lists—words and definitions. Match the words with their definitions by drawing a line between them.

recessive	Genetic engineering is possible because of gene _____.
DNA	A gene that does not express itself when paired with a dominant gene.
genes	Traits that come from a parent's genes are called _____.
Mendel	Small organisms used in the laboratory to study genetics (two words).
fruit flies	A change in the DNA that determines an organism's traits.
inherited	Areas on a chromosome that control individual traits.
splicing	An Austrian monk who first described the rules of inheritance.
mutation	Initials of the chemical deoxyribonucleic acid.

Heredity

This puzzle contains hidden words. They can go up and down, across, at an angle, forward, or back. All the hidden words are in the list below the puzzle. When you find one, circle it and look for another.

D	S	P	V	Q	K	L	P	C	K	S	W	W	V	E	G
F	O	I	W	O	E	Z	L	H	J	F	P	Q	E	H	S
M	R	M	B	Y	R	K	R	R	M	B	D	T	E	U	I
M	G	U	I	L	A	R	N	O	T	W	Z	L	E	V	O
F	H	S	I	N	I	Z	R	M	M	R	D	K	T	R	C
R	P	C	D	T	A	N	R	O	E	E	A	A	H	Q	N
P	S	O	L	H	F	N	G	S	J	C	N	I	S	B	P
S	P	H	H	O	W	L	T	O	C	E	P	D	T	B	J
H	L	M	J	Y	N	U	I	M	F	S	V	P	E	A	Y
U	I	B	I	O	D	I	V	E	R	S	I	T	Y	L	F
G	C	D	V	R	Q	T	N	U	S	I	P	Z	H	A	E
S	I	G	E	N	E	S	O	G	Q	V	T	F	Z	I	D
L	N	A	I	N	H	E	R	I	T	E	D	G	D	N	G
Z	G	E	N	R	R	T	N	R	N	H	V	U	Y	L	I
S	H	U	B	R	E	E	D	I	N	G	Q	R	L	P	B
U	P	M	U	T	A	T	I	O	N	Z	N	S	L	R	X

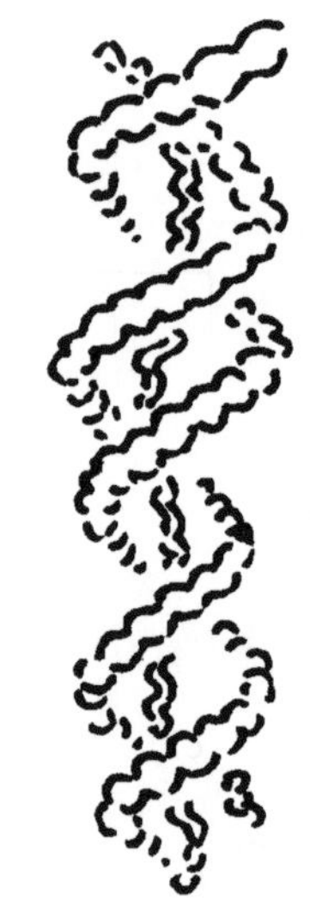

Biodiversity
Chromosome
Inherited
Breeding
Mutation

Sibling
Mendel
Genes
Pea

Fruit Flies
Recessive
Dominant
Splicing

Cloning
Punnet
Trait
DNA

Life SCIENCE

Heredity

Using the words in the list, you can build your own crossword puzzle. Start with the letter printed at the top and count the number of letters in its word. Now you know what letter that word begins with and how many letters it has. Look at the list and find the word. Write it in and build from there.

Pea	Dominant	Trait	Recessive
Genes	Inherited	Mendel	Fruit Flies
Punnet	Chromosome	Predict	
Cloning	Biodiversity	Breeding	
Sibling	DNA	Mutation	

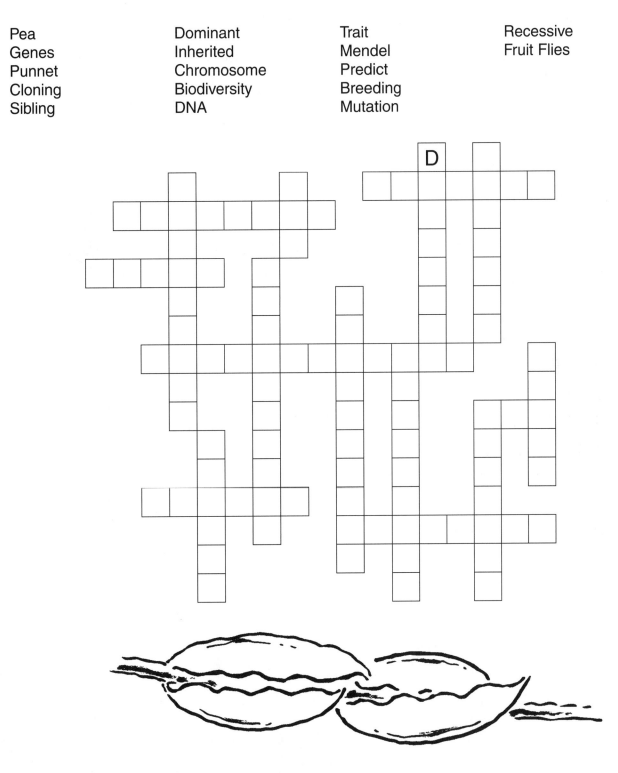

Heredity

Across

5 A gene that does not express itself when paired with a dominant gene.
7 Initials of the chemical deoxyribonucleic acid.
9 The kind of plant Mendel used to study inheritance.
10 Traits that come from a parent's genes are called _____.
11 Small organisms used in the lab to study genetics (two words).
13 A long molecule in the nucleus that contains the genes.
14 A gene which expresses itself in a hybrid.
15 A brother or sister born of the same mother and father.
16 _____ squares allow us to predict what offspring will look like.

Down

1 An Austrian monk who first described the rules of inheritance.
2 An inherited characteristic.
3 Areas on a chromosome that control individual traits.
4 The range of different organisms in an area.
6 Genetic engineering is possible because of gene _____.
8 Mathematics can help _____ the characteristics of offspring.
12 Controlled and supervised reproduction.
13 The process of reproducing an exact duplicate of an organism.

Heredity

Unscramble the letters into words and write them in the boxes to the left. Now unscramble the letters in the boxes with circles to find the last word.

NAD

EGESN

ENPTNU

DVTIIOIEBRYS

NEDLEM

Controlled and supervised reproduction.

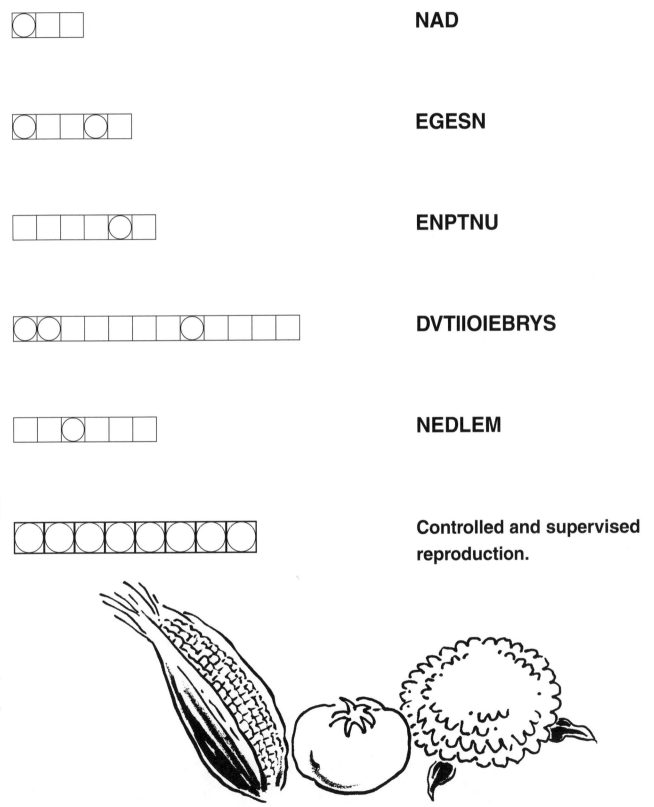

Evolution

This puzzle has two lists—words and definitions. Match the words with their definitions by drawing a line between them.

habitat	Those characteristics that make an individual or species different.
selection	The area where a particular organism is found.
beaks	A species that is no longer in existence is _____.
biodiversity	The process of a better-adapted organism surviving.
extinct	Darwin used the shape of these parts of certain birds to show adaptation.
traits	An inherited trait that increases an organism's chances of survival.
adaptation	Birds that Darwin used to show adaptation.
finches	—— The range of different organisms in an area.

Evolution

This puzzle contains hidden words. They can go up and down, across, at an angle, forward, or back. All the hidden words are in the list below the puzzle. When you find one, circle it and look for another.

A	C	S	G	M	A	F	I	N	C	H	E	S	L	N
D	E	C	B	S	M	U	T	A	T	I	O	N	O	L
X	M	I	Z	K	A	Z	R	M	M	G	F	I	N	T
Q	V	V	B	L	D	T	Z	S	A	P	T	I	K	Y
E	J	Y	V	S	A	M	R	P	H	C	W	E	S	W
R	Y	H	K	T	P	O	A	L	E	R	O	V	U	H
T	E	A	I	V	T	L	L	L	A	B	F	O	F	D
F	E	B	F	S	A	E	E	D	E	T	M	L	E	F
B	A	S	E	G	T	S	Y	V	C	A	Z	U	M	N
H	X	C	Z	I	I	A	E	N	S	U	S	T	R	C
A	N	H	B	I	O	D	I	V	E	R	S	I	T	Y
A	W	Z	R	T	N	T	R	A	I	T	S	O	Z	L
A	W	N	S	M	X	O	G	Z	I	Q	U	N	O	V
T	O	S	P	E	C	I	E	S	J	T	O	I	P	K
Q	P	K	E	J	H	Z	M	C	P	J	O	Q	U	Y

Biodiversity
Evolution
Ancestors
Mutation
Extinct
Habitat
Darwin
Fish
Adaptation
Galapagos
Selection
Finches
Species
Traits
Beaks

Evolution

Using the words in the list, you can build your own crossword puzzle. Start with the letter printed at the top and count the number of letters in its word. Now you know what letter that word begins with and how many letters it has. Look at the list and find the word. Write it in and build from there.

Beaks	Survival	Habitat	Ancestors
Traits	Evolution	Species	Adaptation
Extinct	Selection	Mutation	
Fossils	Biodiversity	Galapagos	

B

Evolution

Across

2 The process of living and having offspring that can breed.
6 Darwin used the shape of these parts of birds to show adaptation.
8 The British scientist who first described natural selection.
9 The process of a better-adapted organism surviving.
11 The range of different organisms in an area.
13 Those characteristics that make an individual or species different.
14 Birds that Darwin used to show adaptation.
15 The area where a particular organism is found.

Down

1 The islands where Darwin first observed evidence of evolution.
3 Some of the most primitive of these are sharks.
4 An inherited trait that increases an organism's chances of survival.
5 Directly related organisms that lived in earlier times.
7 The process of organisms changing over long periods of time.
10 A change in the DNA that determines an organism's features.
12 A species that is no longer in existence is _____.

Evolution

Unscramble the letters into words and write them in the boxes to the left. Now unscramble the letters in the boxes with circles to find the last word.

OLTOIENUV

IPSECES

DPOAAIATNT

RVSUAILV

FECSINH

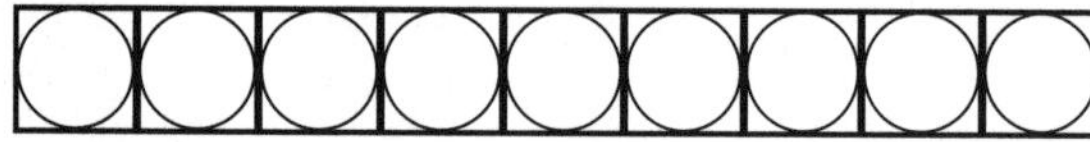

The process of a better-adapted organism surviving.

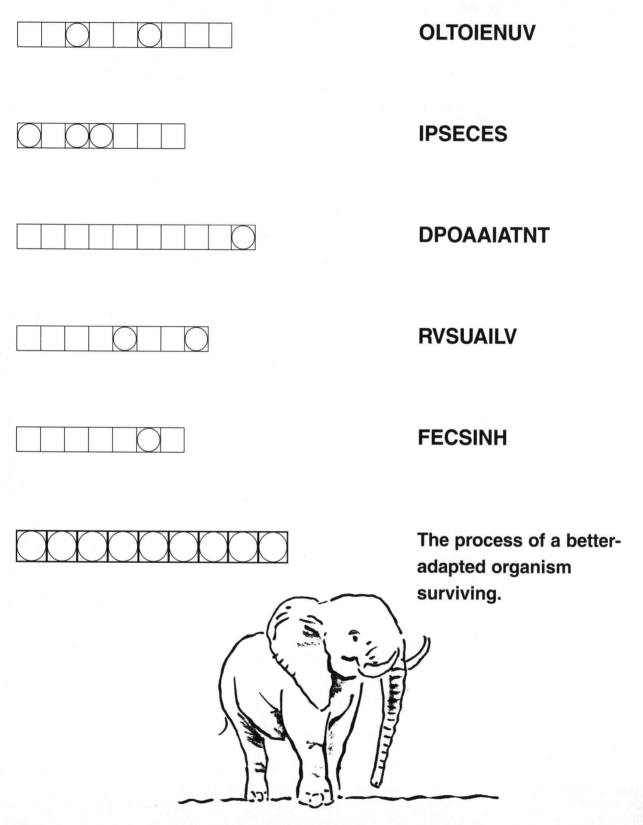

Earth SCIENCE

Dinosaurs

This puzzle has two lists—words and definitions. Match the words with their definition by drawing a line between them.

teeth	A type of animal that has a backbone.
extinct	A dinosaur that could fly.
nests	Describes a species whose members are totally dead and gone.
mesozoic	Changes in a species over a long period of time.
triceratops	Flesh-eating dinosaurs had pointed ones for grasping and ripping.
pterodactyl	A large dinosaur that had three horns.
vertebrate	A period in earth's history from 245 to 65 million years ago.
evolution	Where dinosaurs laid their eggs and raised their young.

Dinosaurs

This puzzle contains hidden words. They can go up and down, across, at an angle, forward, or back. All the hidden words are in the list below the puzzle. When you find one, circle it and look for another

```
Y H C E T B E V O L U T I O N I
W E E T X E I W T L C F S T P G
P T I R M H E R B I V O R E F U
G Y S I D E G T D V M S Z D M A
Z R V C O S S H H S E S R E C N
P A L E O N T O L O G I S T L O
R N E R R S T R Z B G L G Y R D
E N C A N T R K P O B H T Y Q O
D O N T E Q E E P W I C U N A N
A S K O S X P B R M A C Z P H Z
T A R P T N T E R D M Z C S C B
O U P S S R I I O A Y P J D O Y
R R C P Z H L R N F T D Z Y L I
Y U L Z Q I E I Z C M E I U P K
O S F O O T P R I N T S I S S J
G E K E P H Y T O S A U R Y W Z
```

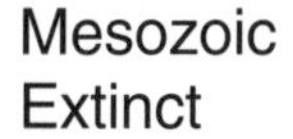

Paleontologist
Triceratops
Vertebrate
Evolution
Iguanodon
Predator
Reptile
Fossil
Nests
Herds
Tyrannosaurus
Pterodactyl
Footprints
Herbivore
Phytosaur

Mesozoic
Extinct
Teeth
Birds
Egg

Dinosaurs

Using the words in the list, you can build your own crossword puzzle. Start with the letter printed at the top and count the number of letters in its word. Now you know what letter that word begins with and how many letters it has. Look at the list and find the word. Write it in and build from there.

Egg	Phytosaur	Herds	Herbivore
Teeth	Vertebrate	Nests	Footprints
Fossil	Stegosaurus	Reptile	Pterodactyl
Extinct	Triceratops	Mesozoic	Tyrannosaurus
Predator	Paleontologist	Evolution	

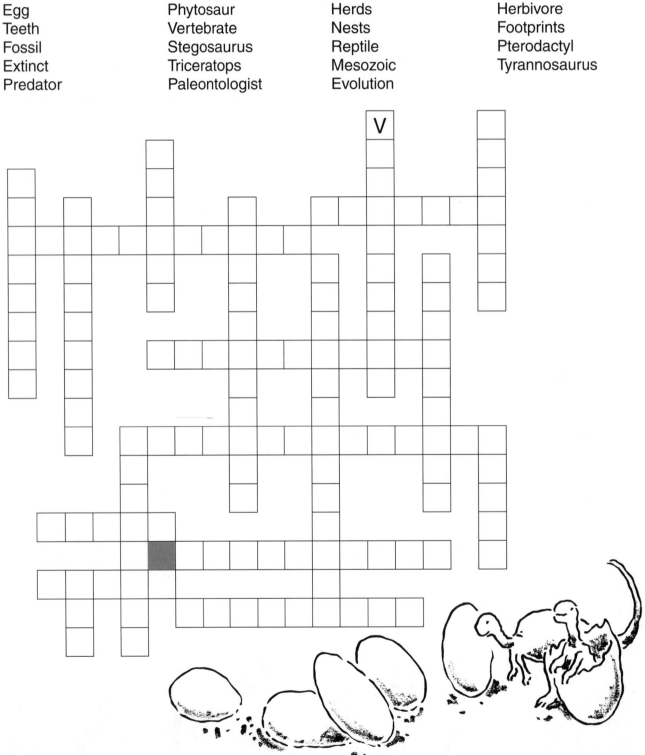

V

Earth SCIENCE

Dinosaurs

Across

1 An animal that lives by hunting and eating other animals.
2 Changes in a species over a long period of time.
3 A carnivorous dinosaur that looked much like a modern crocodile.
5 A large dinosaur that had a series of pointed plates down its back.
7 Describes a species whose members are totally dead and gone.
8 A large dinosaur that had three horns.
10 A scientist who studies fossils.
13 Fossils of these indicate how dinosaurs walked.
14 A type of animal that has a backbone.
15 Some dinosaurs traveled in groups called ______.
16 A plant-eating dinosaur that was the first dinosaur fossil found.

Down

1 A dinosaur that could fly.
4 Where dinosaurs laid their eggs and raised their young.
6 A giant flesh-eating dinosaur.
9 A plant-eating animal.
11 These feathered vertebrates and dinosaurs likely had a common ancestor.
12 Flesh-eating dinosaurs had pointed ones for grasping and ripping.

Dinosaurs

Unscramble the letters into words and write them in the boxes to the left. Now unscramble the letters in the boxes with circles to find the last word.

☐☐☐☐◯☐☐☐☐☐ **ORNFTSTPOI**

☐☐◯◯☐ **HRSED**

☐☐◯☐☐ **HETET**

☐◯☐◯☐☐◯☐☐☐☐ **OCALDRYPTET**

☐☐☐◯☐☐☐☐ **OSCMEZOI**

◯◯◯◯◯◯◯◯ **An animal that lives by hunting and eating other animals.**

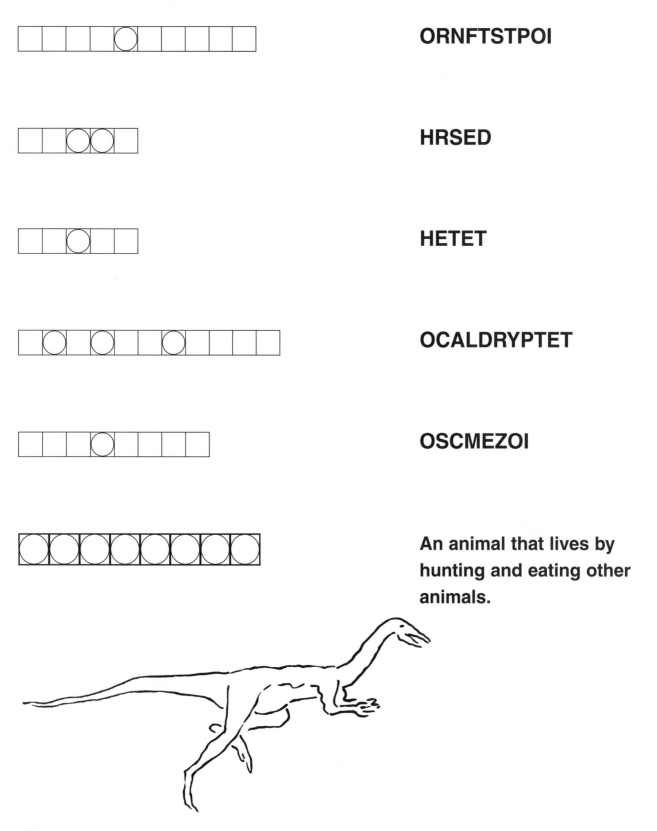

Earthquakes

This puzzle has two lists—words and definitions. Match the words with their definition by drawing a line between them.

mantle	A crack in the earth's crust along which rocks can move.
magnitude	A push or a pull.
fault	The middle layer of the earth.
aftershock	The solid part of the earth.
force	Earth movements that occur after an earthquake.
lithosphere	The relative strength of an earthquake.
epicenter	Areas under the earth where earthquake waves bounce off.
reflectors	The point in the earth where an earthquake started.

Earth SCIENCE

Earthquakes

This puzzle contains hidden words. They can go up and down, across, at an angle, forward, or back. All the hidden words are in the list below. When you find one, circle it and look for another.

Aftershock	Friction	Richter
Blocks	Lithosphere	Rift
Boundary	Magnitude	Seismograph
Collide	Mantle	Shaking
Crust	Movement	Sliding
Energy	Pacific	Tiltmeter
Epicenter	Plate	Tsunami
Fault	Pressure	
Force	Reflectors	

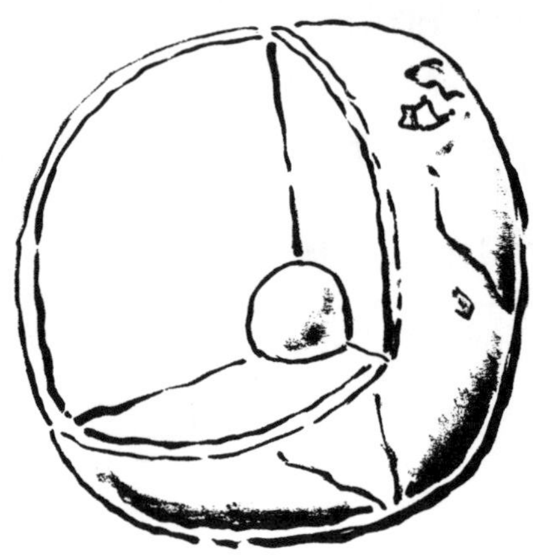

Y M E N E E R R A N N E I N N T Y T

B I P R L C F I D B O U N D A R Y E

L F I S O I R A F C T L C O E G D A

O R C L O R T U U T E F E R R I E F

C I E I U O E H S L P S U E L C D T

K C N D S E D F O T T S N L R E U E

S T T I H C D M L S S E O O T A D R

E I E N A K C I M E P C F R E R I S

E O R G K P M B R O C H I E K I O H

E N T C I A O P E B V T E N Y C A O

P M A G N I T U D E F E O R W H U C

T A D U G R D E N T S S M R E T H K

O N S A U C P A C I F I C E S E N E

N T E T I L T M E T E R D P N R R O

A L L A E E T L L D A I O N L T T T

N E T K E I U D I A C E S E L A C N

E A A O I A C Q O E C D E T M H T T

S E I S M O G R A P H I C L N R S E

Earthquakes

Using the words in the list, you can build your own crossword puzzle. Start with the letter printed at the top and count the number of letters in its word. Now you know what letter that word begins with and how many letters it has. Look at the list and find the word. Write it in and build from there.

Plate	Boundary	Fault	Pressure
Mantle	Epicenter	Blocks	Tiltmeter
Richter	Magnitude	Sliding	Reflectors
Pacific	Aftershock	Tsunami	Lithosphere
Shaking	Seismograph	Friction	

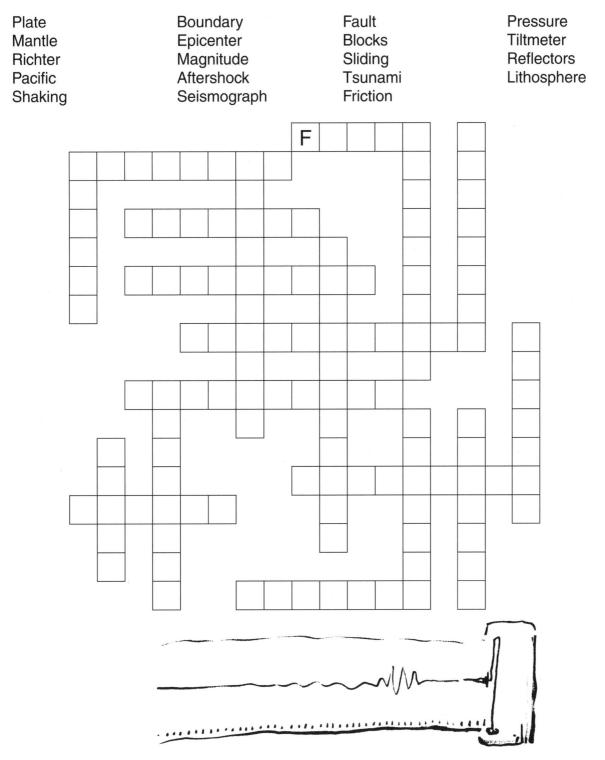

F

Earth SCIENCE

Earthquakes

Across

2 The middle layer of the earth.
6 The force that keeps rocks from moving along a fault.
7 Movement along the earth's surface caused by an earthquake.
11 Areas under the earth where earthquake waves bounce off.
12 An instrument that measures earthquakes.
15 The force that keeps the interior of the earth liquid.
16 Part of the California coast is part of this plate.
17 The point in the earth where an earthquake starts.

Down

1 The back and forth movement caused by an earthquake.
2 The relative strength of an earthquake.
3 An instrument that measures changes in the tilt of the earth.
4 The area where the edges of two tectonic plates meet.
5 A large and dangerous wave caused by an undersea earthquake.
8 Earth movement that occurs after an earthquake.
9 The solid part of the earth.
10 The scientist who invented the scale used to measure earthquakes.
13 A crack in the earth's crust along which rocks can move.
14 A crack in the earth opened when two plates pull apart.

Earthquakes

Unscramble the letters into words and write them in the boxes to the left. Now unscramble the letters in the boxes with circles to find the last word.

TITTRLMEE

ROIPSSEAGMH

IEEEPRNTC

BSOKLC

AMNUTSI

The scientist who invented the scale used to measure earthquakes.

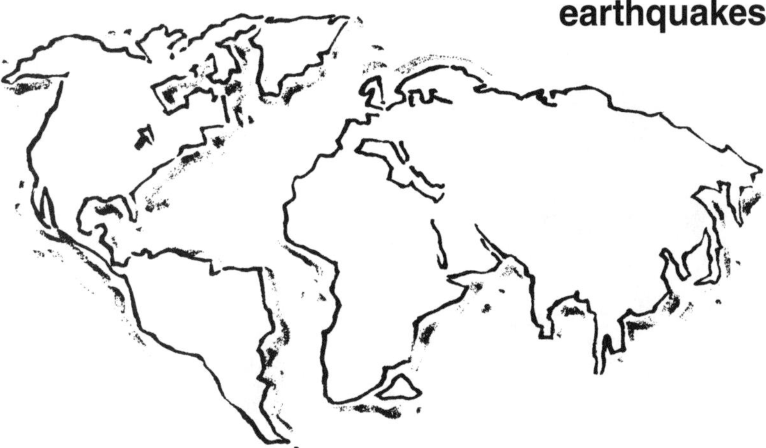

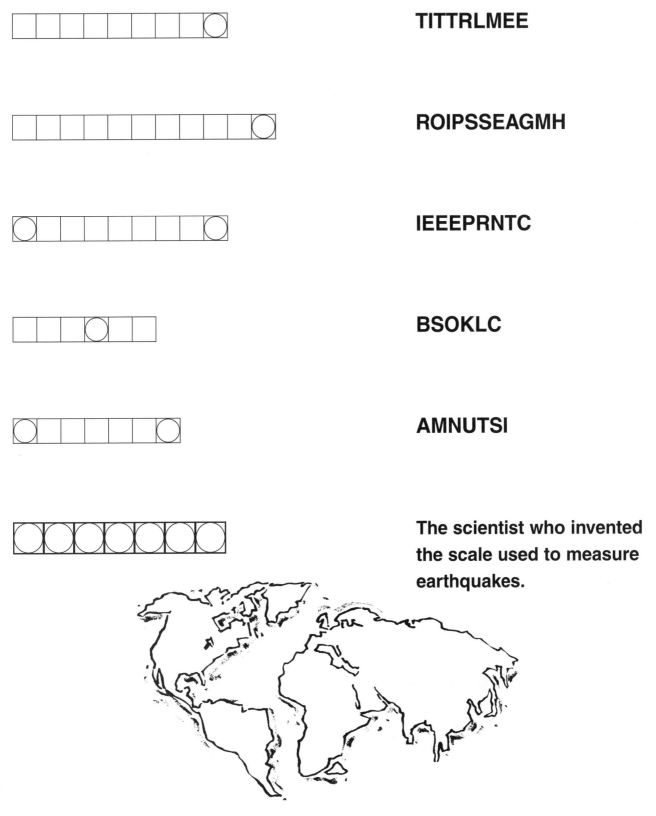

Earth SCIENCE

The Moon

This puzzle has two lists—words and definitions. Match the words with their definition by drawing a line between them.

astronaut	The name of a series of missions that took humans to the moon.
weight	The first man on the moon.
atmosphere	A small body that orbits the sun.
Armstrong	On the moon this would be a fraction of what it is on earth.
gravity	Your weight on the moon would be less, but this would be the same.
Apollo	A person who goes into space.
asteroid	The force that keeps the moon in orbit around the earth.
mass	The layer of gases around the earth.

The Moon

This puzzle contains hidden words. They can go up and down, across, at an angle, forward, or back. All the hidden words are in the list below the puzzle. When you find one, circle it and look for another.

I L O Y Y T I E D E E J C A N L C Y
N D I O W C S O Y C R S A B S A R T
O E E F T A N A N T E S D S E O E A
P H Y S E T S A S S W O A R A S S E
N F O A T M T D A T C A E T S H C C
K N R R Y S M H T R E H N T D O E R
M E M D I S P G E L P R F I I F N B
W C G D L A B T I S A R O I N C T O
A L R F D Y R I O B A P B I E G A O
X I A T R A O M T R B T O N D P I H
I P V U U H T U S O L O E L A F R H
N S I Q C A A A R T N E U L L C T N
G E T C N N O T T D R M P S L O P F
E T Y T O H H I M H D O A A D I E T
I U Z R N G B E M T H E N S T C T M
D W T D I R B T D W O U I G S T S E
P S R E O E T I D E S E W D T O C D
A S W F A A T T R A C T I O N H U E

Air
Apollo
Armstrong
Asteroid
Atmosphere
Attraction
Crescent
Distance
Eclipse
Gibbous
Gravity

Life
Mass
Orbit
Phases
Quarter
Tides
Waning
Waxing
Weight
Astronaut
Satellite

The Moon

Using the words in the list, you can build your own crossword puzzle. Start with the letter printed at the top and count the number of letters in its word. Now you know what letter that word begins with and how many letters it has. Look at the list and find the word. Write it in and build from there.

Air	Quarter	Mass	Gibbous
Tides	Eclipse	Orbit	Crescent
Waning	Asteroid	Phases	Satellite
Apollo	Astronaut	Weight	Armstrong
Waxing	Attraction	Gravity	Atmosphere

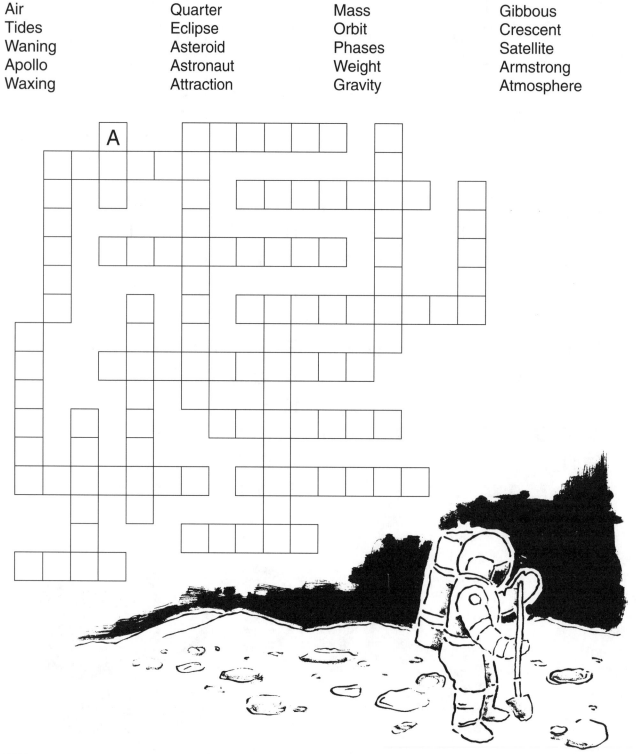

A

The Moon

Across

2 A celestial body that orbits another body.
3 A person who goes into space.
7 The name of a series of missions that got humans to the moon.
8 The first man on the moon.
13 The stage just before a full moon.
14 The moon is held in orbit by gravitational ____.
15 Changes in the appearance of the moon.
16 Lack of water and oxygen have prevented this on the moon.
17 The force that keeps the moon in orbit around the earth.
19 A mixture of gases, vital to humans, that is not present on the moon.
20 When one celestial body blocks the light from another.

Down

1 Your weight on the moon would be less but this would be the same.
4 The layer of gases around the earth.
5 The final half of the moon's cycle.
6 The first and last moon phases after a new moon.
9 The path traveled by the moon around the earth.
10 The first half of the moon's cycle.
11 On the moon this would be a fraction of what it is on earth.
12 When only one-half of the lighted side of the moon can be seen.
14 A small body that orbits the sun.
18 The effect of the moon on the earth's oceans.

Earth SCIENCE

The Moon

Unscramble the letters into words and write them in the boxes to the left. Now unscramble the letters in the boxes with circles to find the last word.

EQURRAT

MAPHETSREO

NSCEERTC

BSBOGIU

TINARACOTT

A person who goes into space.

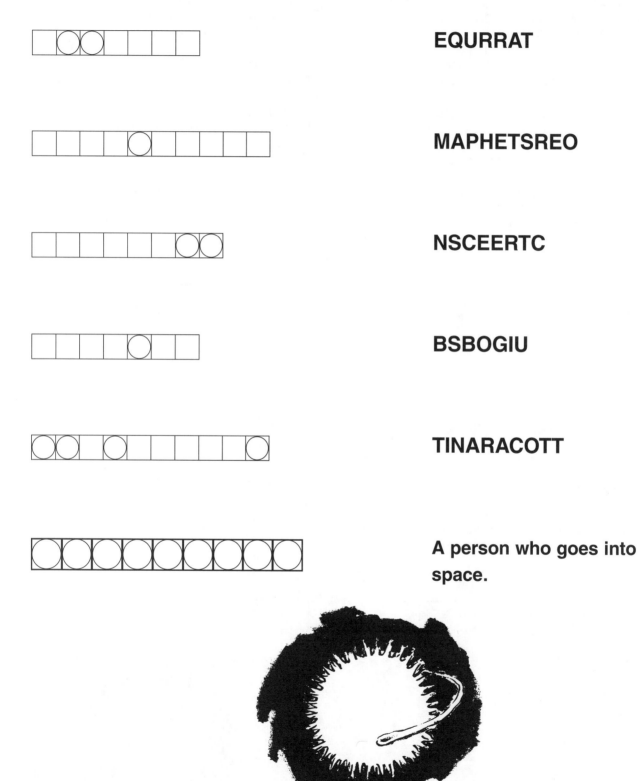

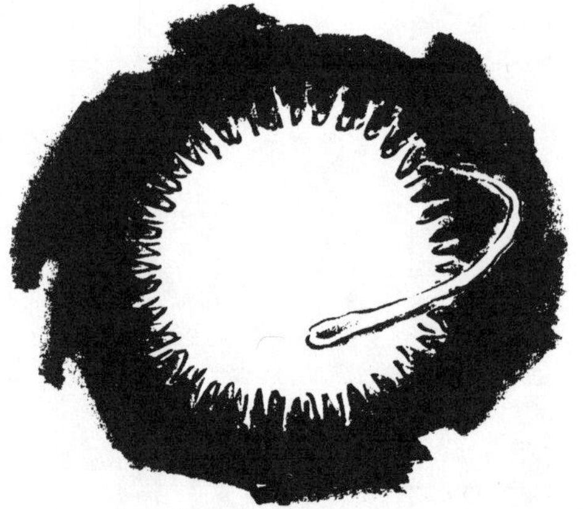

Natural Resources

This puzzle has two lists—words and definitions. Match the words with their definition by drawing a line between them.

iron	A mineral, consisting of carbon, that is mined and used as a fuel.
oceans	The principal natural resource taken from forests.
silver	The natural resource from which gasoline and oil are made.
lumber	The source of most of the water on earth.
hydroelectric	A shiny metal used to make photographic film and coins.
desalination	The metal contained in the ore hematite.
coal	A process that converts the energy in moving water to electricity.
petroleum	The process of removing salt from water.

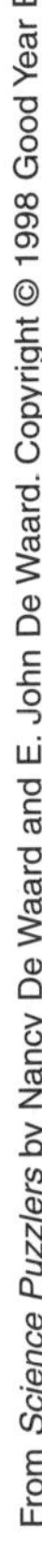

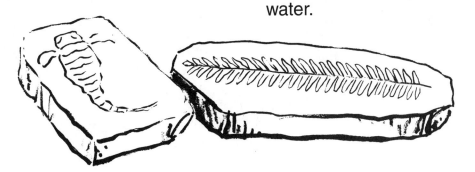

Earth SCIENCE

Natural Resources

This puzzle contains hidden words. They can go up and down, across, at an angle, forward, or back. All the hidden words are in the list below the puzzle. When you find one, circle it and look for another.

```
A C U R D S A D S E U R O S S S Y L
C L B H S O T E M S T E N E C G A M
T I M L T F R E H F N A T D R Y A I
N M B H A L C A N D E L O E G O E N
V A P H Y D T S F C A E N O S N H I
F T E E H D P A O A E E L A O N Y N
O E D E T O R C L E R O E I F R O G
R A R C R R E O R A N M T S E L D M
E S E C T X O E E H O A I N E V L I
S E N H B I V L C L N L I N R D U N
T S E A N R E E E I E F R M G C M E
C E W C Q O T I L U E C E N E O B R
K X A W P N N A B R M T T T T A E A
O D B A D L S B S P I L I R E L R L
I T L T C E O D A X R C W I I E A S
L R E E D P N E U N L E H R I C O O
A O E R H T D A S A D U E H E D R U
M E T A L S B E C S I L V E R S G Q
```

Bauxite
Calcite
Climate
Coal
Crops
Desalination
Energy
Farming
Forest
Hydroelectric
Iron
Lumber
Metals
Minerals
Mining
Oceans
Oil
Petroleum
Refinery
Renewable
Silver
Technology
Water

Natural Resources

Using the words in the list, you can build your own crossword puzzle. Start with the letter printed at the top and count the number of letters in its word. Now you know what letter that word begins with and how many letters it has. Look at the list and find the word. Write it in and build from there.

Coal	Refinery	Oceans	Petroleum
Crops	Renewable	Metals	Desalination
Forest	Technology	Energy	
Silver	Hydroelectric	Farming	
Climate	Iron	Minerals	

I

Earth SCIENCE — Natural Resources

Across

2 The natural resource from which gasoline and oil are made.
4 Natural resources that are grown or gathered for us.
7 A manufacturing plant where gasoline and oil are made.
9 A mineral, consisting of carbon, that is mined and used as a fuel.
10 A natural resource essential to life.
12 A group of natural resources that are usually solid, shiny, and can conduct heat and electricity.
14 Naturally occurring, nonliving material that makes up the earth.
15 The metal contained in the ore hematite.
16 A process that converts the energy in moving water to electricity.

Down

1 Any resource that can be replaced within a short time.
2 A large group of trees, often the source of lumber.
5 The application of scientific or technical knowledge for practical purposes.
6 The principal natural resource taken from forests.
8 The process of removing salt from water.
9 A mineral, common in sedimentary rocks, that contains calcium carbonate.
11 Many natural resources are burned to release this.
13 The process of raising organisms useful to humans.

Natural Resources

Unscramble the letters into words and write them in the boxes to the left. Now unscramble the letters in the boxes with circles to find the last word.

AOIDALTSENIN

EBLRMU

ITCMELA

PRCSO

OYNCEOHLGT

Naturally occurring, nonliving material that makes up the earth.

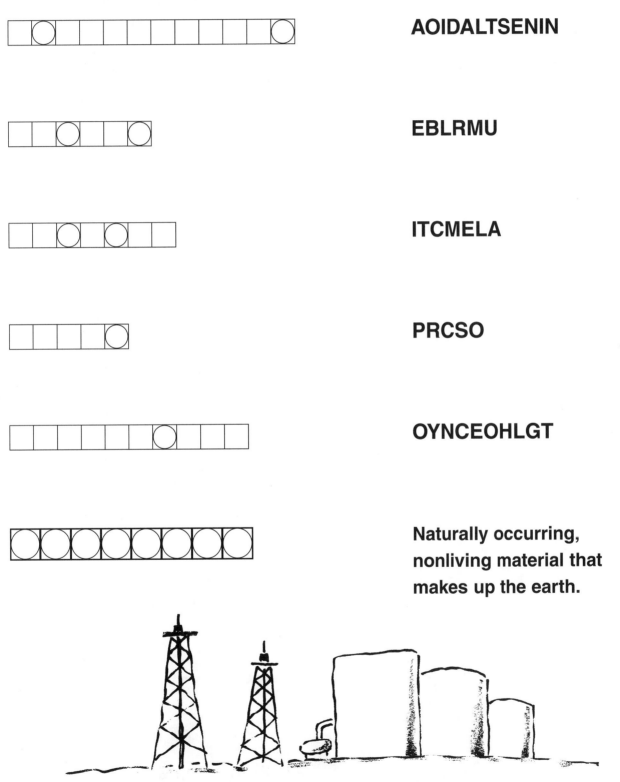

Oceanography

This puzzle has two lists—words and definitions. Match the words with their definition by drawing a line between them.

sediments	Another name for low tide.
waves	Openings in the earth's crust under the sea where gases and magma emerge.
vents	Movements of the sea floor along many rifts.
plankton	An undersea mountain.
spreading	Tiny living things that drift with the current in the sea.
neap	Solid particles that have fallen to the bottom of a body of water.
seamount	Animals that move through the water on their own.
nekton	The movement of water across the surface, usually caused by wind.

Earth SCIENCE

Oceanography

This puzzle contains hidden words. They can go up and down, across, at an angle, forward, or back. All the hidden words are in the list below the puzzle. When you find one, circle it and look for another.

A L O D A B E N T H O S S S N E A P
I S T S E D I M E N T S S T I D E R
A S P R D E I B A R N A C L E S T H
Y L H R E P L I D E S O N A R L E L
P H G O I N L S L I I I H C E A P O
S T A A R N C I P E A E D R P R C R
E A R I E E G H W R S T U E O C E R
A Y C L P S L C O E E S O N E H M E
M C C E P A I I V T S A T M P E C I
O D U S N L F A N E O P D A N E D O
U O R T E I W I R E P O R I E E T L
N S R U K N S P S E N G R G N T Z F
T B E A T I S W L H O A D A R G S O
E H N R O T E N S N M I N E R A L S
E D T Y N Y N O A S R D O M S R S V
U P S E B S U E E S A O E V E N T S
C O R A L N C T Q S H A R K U E A R
R E E F I O P P L A N K T O N I E F

Algae
Barnacles
Benthos
Coral
Currents
Diatom
Estuary
Fish
Marine
Minerals
Neap
Nekton
Oceanographer
Plankton
Pressure
Reef
Ridge
Salinity
Seamount
Sediments
Shark
Shoreline
Sonar
Spreading
Spring
Tide
Trench
Vents
Waves

Earth SCIENCE

Oceanography

Using the words in the list, you can build your own crossword puzzle. Start with the letter printed at the top and count the number of letters in its word. Now you know what letter that word begins with and how many letters it has. Look at the list and find the word. Write it in and build from there.

Neap	Nekton	Tide	Minerals
Fish	Pressure	Waves	Barnacles
Vents	Plankton	Shark	Spreading
Sonar	Sediments	Trench	Oceanographer
Algae	Shoreline	Diatom	
Marine	Reef	Benthos	

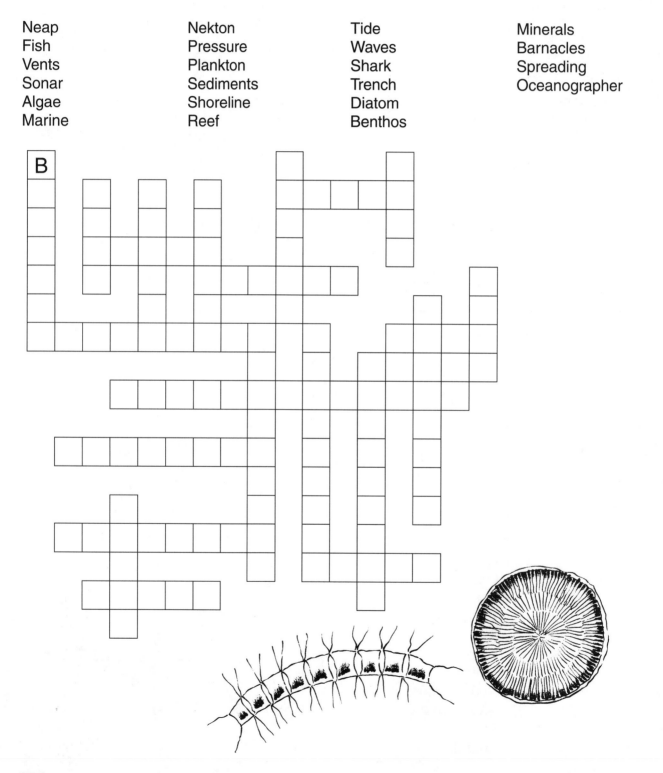

B

Earth SCIENCE

Oceanography

Across

2 Natural resources, many of which can be mined from the sea.
5 Marine animals that have a shell and attach to objects such as rocks and ships.
7 Movement of the sea floor along many rifts.
9 The point at which a body of water meets land.
13 The plants and animals of the sea bottom.
14 A narrow ridge of rock, sand, or coral near or at the water's surface.
17 A scientist who studies oceans.
20 An undersea mountain.
21 The movement of water across the surface, usually caused by wind.
22 A tiny plant with a shell of silicon.
23 Animals that move through the water on their own.

Down

1 Animals that have gills, fins, and scales.
3 Solid particles that have fallen to the bottom of a body of water.
4 A force that increases with depth.
6 The movement of water in response to the moon's gravitational pull.
8 Movement of water in a particular direction.
10 A deep valley in the bottom of the ocean.
11 A small marine animal that lives in colonies and is responsible for many of the reefs in the Pacific.
12 An ancient fish that has a skeleton made of cartilage.
15 Openings in the earth's crust under the sea where gases and magma emerge.
16 Another name for low tide.
18 The mouth of a river where it enters the ocean.
19 Tiny living things that drift with the current in the sea.

Oceanography

Unscramble the letters into words and write them in the boxes to the left. Now unscramble the letters in the boxes with circles to find the last word.

NUOSTAME

SRUEYTA

PTNKLNAO

RSPNADIEG

BEONTHS

A force that increases with depth.

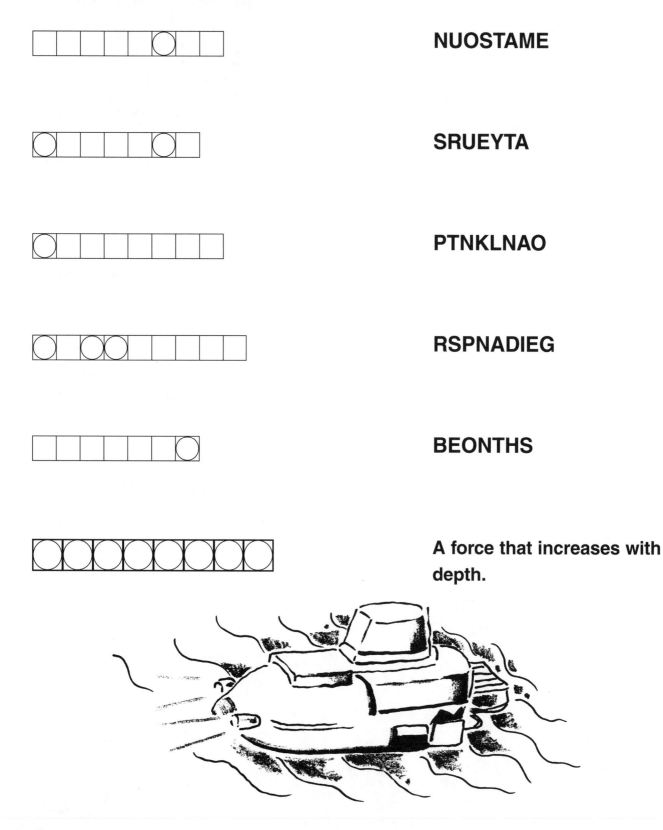

Rocks and Minerals

This puzzle has two lists—words and definitions. Match the words with their definition by drawing a line between them.

granite	A heavy element used in coins and jewelry.
gold	A green mineral that contains copper.
crystal	A kind of rock containing aluminum silicates and other minerals.
feldspar	A solid that has a regular internal structure.
soapstone	A sedimentary rock formed from the shells of sea creatures.
limestone	A very hard igneous rock containing mostly quartz and feldspar.
malachite	A soft metamorphic rock that feels soapy.
graphite	A form of carbon that has platelike crystals and is very slippery.

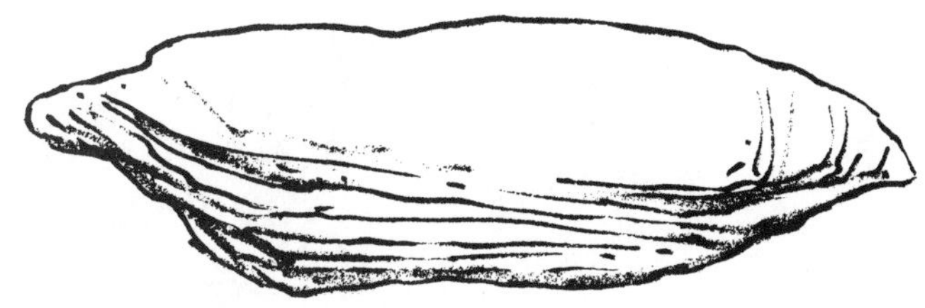

Earth SCIENCE

Rocks and Minerals

This puzzle contains hidden words. They can go up and down, across, at an angle, forward, or back. All the hidden words are in the list below the puzzle. When you find one, circle it and look for another.

F C O A L P T S E S C L U S T E R I
M E V E D Y U T S N E T C D N M R S
I E T E I O I E W N A I E O R I N I
N S H D E N N E O E H B T E I N S L
E E U N A D T T F P A S P A A I O I
R D G R R I S Y R G D T H A E N A C
A I G A L E G O M N Y I H O H G P O
L M H A M M M O A A A P R E I D S N
S E H I C A A S L E G A S E R N T P
T N L H T A I L D D P N T U A I O O
T T U E U E L N A S S I E I M E N E
T A M S A C E C D C H H D T H U E G
C R E C E L S L I P H I A I I D E T
L Y I O B S E S A T S I N L E T R D
A M K N M F A R A B E E T E E E E G
I H R E E K G A O L S E E E N B D U
L O G A T C R Y S T A L S A X U O M
H A T A S E C E S P O T A S S I U M

Magnetite
Hardness
Calcite
Mining
Feldspar
Gems
Mica
Silicon
Gold
Sandstone
Graphite
Metamorphic
Gypsum
Halite
Igneous
Shale
Limestone
Malachite
Crystal
Mineral
Obsidian
Potassium
Sedimentary
Hornblende
Granite
Soapstone
Luster
Weathering
Coal

Rocks and Minerals

Using the words in the list, you can build your own crossword puzzle. Start with the letter printed at the top and count the number of letters in its word. Now you know what letter that word begins with and how many letters it has. Look at the list and find the word. Write it in and build from there.

Coal	Feldspar	Shale	Limestone
Gems	Magnetite	Luster	Sandstone
Mining	Malachite	Crystal	Hornblende
Halite	Soapstone	Igneous	Sedimentary
Calcite	Weathering	Mineral	
Silicon	Metamorphic	Graphite	
Obsidian	Gold	Hardness	

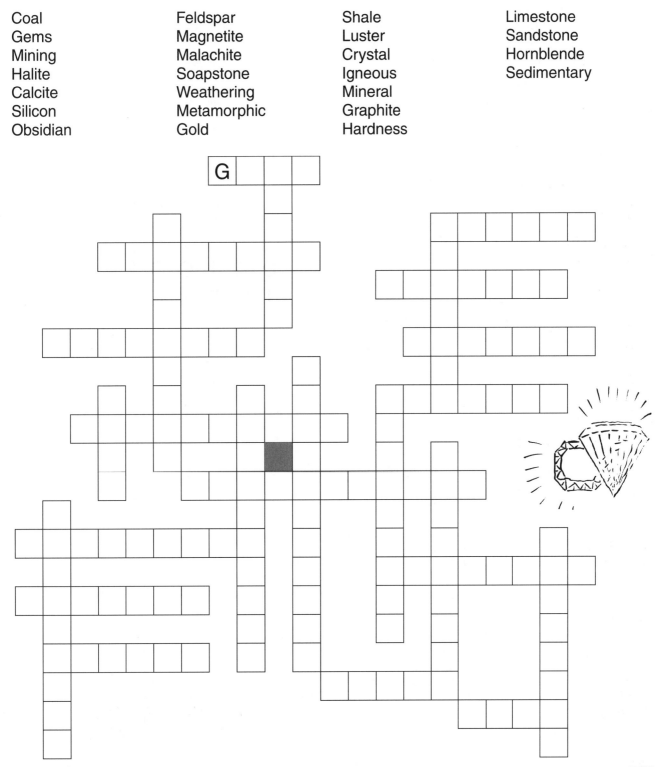

G

Rocks and Minerals

Across

1 A structural form of many solids that has a regular, internal arrangement.
4 A heavy element used in coins and jewelry.
5 The process of taking minerals from the earth
6 A fuel, mined from the earth, that is almost pure carbon.
8 A shiny mineral that occurs in sheets.
10 Rock formed from particles that have fallen to the bottom of a lake or ocean.
11 A kind of rock containing aluminum silicates and other minerals.
12 An ore that is almost pure salt.
13 A form of carbon that has platelike crystals and is very slippery.
15 An iron-containing mineral that has a magnetic field.
16 The process by which exposure to weather breaks down rocks and minerals.
17 A very hard igneous rock containing quartz and feldspar.
18 A sedimentary rock formed from clay or mud under pressure.
19 Rare rocks and minerals that are used in jewelry.

Down

2 An element that is in almost all rocks and is the second most abundant element on earth.
3 A transparent or translucent form of calcium carbonate.
5 A natural, nonliving substance that comes from the earth.
7 A glasslike igneous rock, often black in color.
9 A sedimentary rock formed from the shells of sea creatures.
14 The resistance of a mineral to scratching.

Rocks and Minerals

Unscramble the letters into words and write them in the boxes to the left. Now unscramble the letters in the boxes with circles to find the last word.

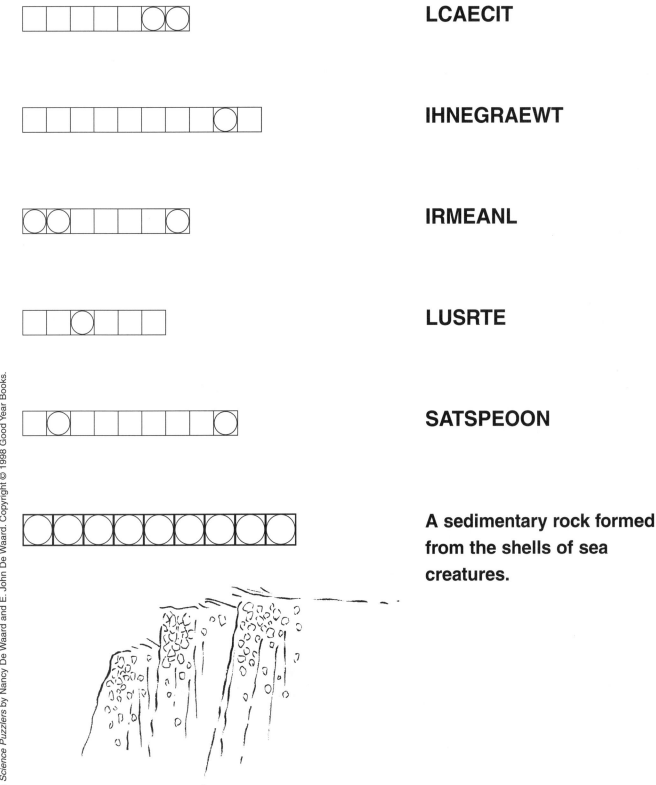

LCAECIT

IHNEGRAEWT

IRMEANL

LUSRTE

SATSPEOON

A sedimentary rock formed from the shells of sea creatures.

Solar System

This puzzle has two lists—words and definitions. Match the words with their definition by drawing a line between them.

radiation	Movement around a central axis.
rotation	The process of one body in space blocking light from another.
comet	The planet closest to the sun.
gravity	A frozen chunk of ice and dust from outside the solar system.
eclipse	The "red planet," fourth from the sun.
Mercury	A rocky body that orbits the sun between the planets.
asteroid	The process by which energy travels from the sun to the earth.
Mars	The force of attraction between two bodies.

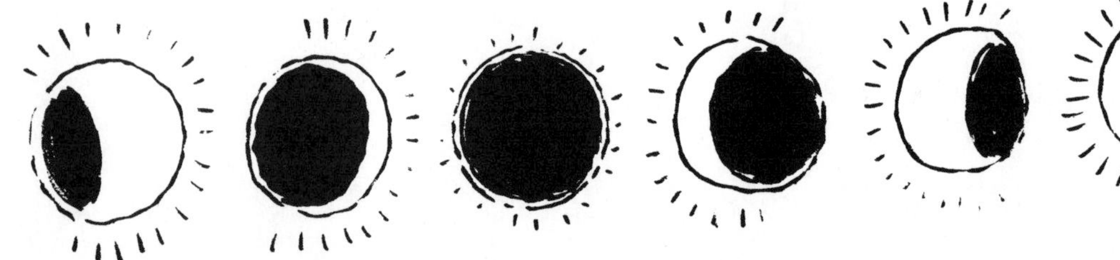

Solar System

This puzzle contains hidden words. They can go up and down, across, at an angle, forward, or back. All the hidden words are in the list below the puzzle. When you find one, circle it and look for another.

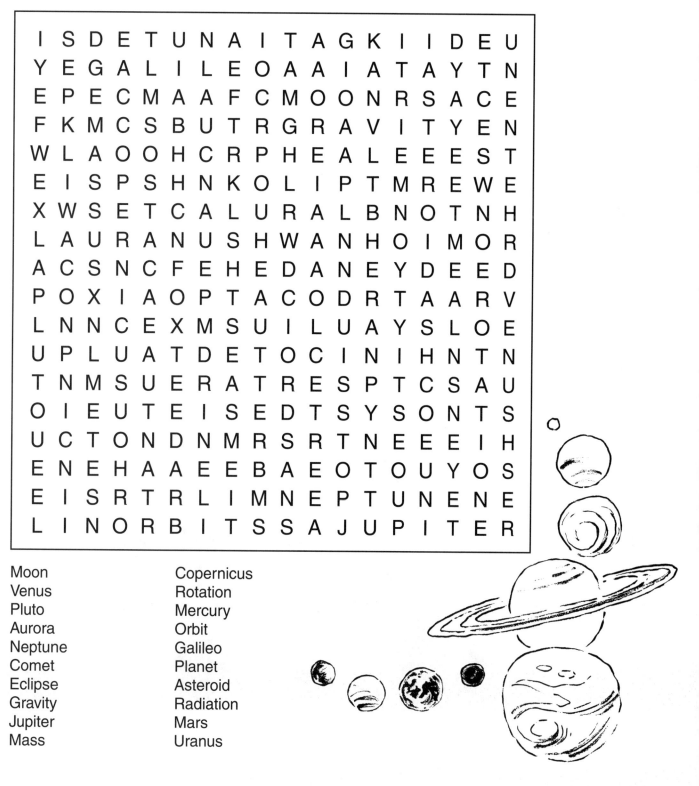

I S D E T U N A I T A G K I I D E U
Y E G A L I L E O A A I A T A Y T N
E P E C M A A F C M O O N R S A C E
F K M C S B U T R G R A V I T Y E N
W L A O O H C R P H E A L E E E S T
E I S P S H N K O L I P T M R E W E
X W S E T C A L U R A L B N O T N H
L A U R A N U S H W A N H O I M O R
A C S N C F E H E D A N E Y D E E D
P O X I A O P T A C O D R T A A R V
L N N C E X M S U I L U A Y S L O E
U P L U A T D E T O C I N I H N T N
T N M S U E R A T R E S P T C S A U
O I E U T E I S E D T S Y S O N T S
U C T O N D N M R S R T N E E E I H
E N E H A A E E B A E O T O U Y O S
E I S R T R L I M N E P T U N E N E
L I N O R B I T S S A J U P I T E R

Moon
Venus
Pluto
Aurora
Neptune
Comet
Eclipse
Gravity
Jupiter
Mass
Copernicus
Rotation
Mercury
Orbit
Galileo
Planet
Asteroid
Radiation
Mars
Uranus

Solar System

Using the words in the list, you can build your own crossword puzzle. Start with the letter printed at the top and count the number of letters in its word. Now you know what letter that word begins with and how many letters it has. Look at the list and find the word. Write it in and build from there.

Mass	Neptune	Mars	Mercury
Venus	Gravity	Comet	Eclipse
Pluto	Asteroid	Orbit	Rotation
Uranus	Radiation	Planet	Copernicus

Solar System

Across

5 The amount of matter, or "stuff," in a body.
8 The largest planet, fifth from the sun.
9 Movement around the central axis.
10 The process by which energy travels from the sun to the earth.
13 The "red planet," fourth from the sun.
14 The process of one body in space blocking light from another.
16 The seventh planet from the sun, made mostly of gas.
18 The eighth planet, a giant ball of gas, orbiting the sun in 165 years.

Down

1 A large body in orbit around a star.
2 An early Italian astronomer who explored the sky with a telescope.
3 A rocky body that orbits the sun between the planets.
4 The force of attraction between two bodies.
6 A Polish scientist, first to propose a sun-centered solar system.
7 The smallest and, usually, the planet farthest out from the sun.
11 Light in the northern sky, caused by solar particles interacting with the atmosphere.
12 The planet closest to the sun.
15 A frozen chunk of ice and dust from outside the solar system.
17 Second planet from the sun, sometimes called "the evening star."

1 2 3 4 5 6 7 8 9 10 11 12 13 14 15 16 17 18

Solar System

Unscramble the letters into words and write them in the boxes to the left. Now unscramble the letters in the boxes with circles to find the last word.

□□□○□□□ **NPEENUT**

□□□□○ **TULOP**

□□□○□○ **LAEPNT**

□○□□○□□ **AITGYVR**

□□□□○□□○□ **ADNITRIOA**

○○○○○○○○ **Movement around a central axis.**

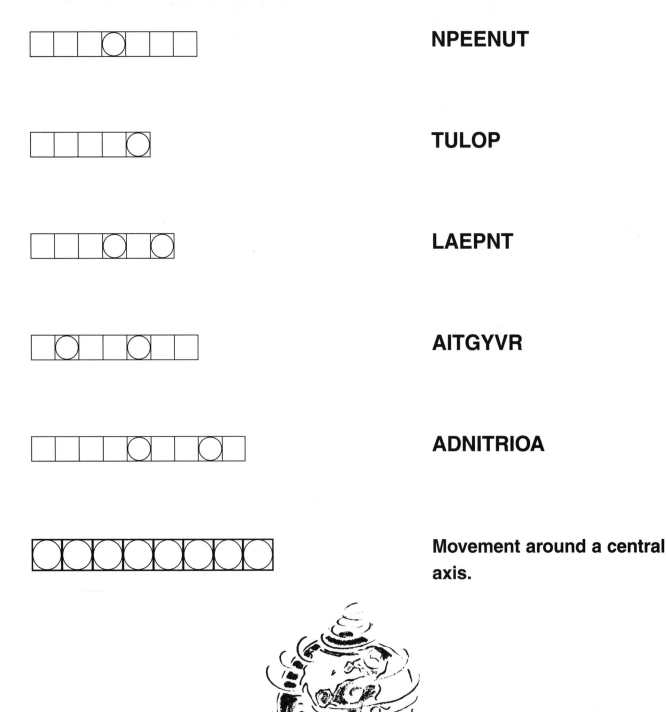

Space

This puzzle has two lists—words and definitions. Match the words with their definition by drawing a line between them.

Hubble	Vehicle that took the first astronauts to the moon.
satellite	The space telescope is named for this American astronomer.
moon	An area of space with gravity so strong that it traps light (two words).
light-year	A natural body in space that orbits a planet.
black hole	The distance that light can travel in one year.
sun	A space pioneer who first developed liquid-fueled rockets.
Apollo	Our nearest star.
Goddard	A body that revolves around another body in space.

Earth SCIENCE

Space

This puzzle contains hidden words. They can go up and down, across, at an angle, forward, or back. All the hidden words are in the list below the puzzle. When you find one, circle it and look for another.

H	E	N	P	U	I	U	M	E	T	E	O	R	V	C	Y
F	Y	N	F	L	G	H	A	A	P	H	G	C	N	N	M
S	A	T	E	L	L	I	T	E	R	I	L	J	N	B	B
D	Z	T	T	T	K	I	N	U	X	I	E	L	Z	E	I
G	S	P	A	C	E	C	R	A	F	T	N	A	Q	C	G
A	O	I	P	P	C	L	O	E	K	F	N	E	O	L	B
Q	S	D	H	J	W	C	E	S	S	B	U	L	R	I	A
U	O	T	D	L	U	B	C	S	M	Y	L	K	M	P	N
P	L	A	R	A	W	E	L	L	C	O	H	K	W	S	G
L	A	B	F	O	R	X	S	M	P	O	N	H	B	E	J
A	R	B	L	W	N	D	D	A	O	Z	P	A	N	F	W
N	G	G	A	B	L	A	C	K	H	O	L	E	U	Z	V
E	F	H	R	R	V	L	U	N	U	Z	N	O	P	T	W
T	U	F	E	K	N	P	J	T	I	U	H	D	Z	S	E
S	I	L	T	B	P	K	F	A	S	M	P	J	P	R	B
I	J	X	J	R	Q	R	L	X	L	X	W	R	R	O	W

Spacecraft
Cosmonaut
Satellite
Big Bang
Goddard
Apollo
Planet
Solar
Moon
Telescope
Black Hole
Astronaut
Mariner
Eclipse
Meteor
Glenn
Flare
Sun

Space

Using the words in the list, you can build your own crossword puzzle. Start with the letter printed at the top and count the number of letters in its word. Now you know what letter that word begins with and how many letters it has. Look at the list and find the word. Write it in and build from there.

Sun	Black Hole	Apollo	Cosmonaut
Flare	Astronaut	Planet	Satellite
Hubble	Telescope	Big Bang	
Meteor	Spacecraft	Eclipse	
Mariner	Solar	Light-year	

S

Space

Across

3 Pertaining to the sun.
5 A theory that the universe began in a giant explosion (two words).
6 The Russian name given to a person who travels into space.
8 The space telescope was named for this American astronomer.
10 A body that revolves around another body in space.
12 An area of space with gravity so strong that it traps light (two words).
14 A device that allows humans to travel in space.
16 A relatively large body that orbits a star.
17 A space pioneer who first developed liquid-fueled rockets.
18 The spacecraft that first visited the planet Mercury.

Down

1 The first American to orbit the earth.
2 The natural body in space that orbits a planet.
4 The distance that light can travel in one year.
7 An American name for a person who travels into space.
9 The process of one body in space blocking the light from another.
11 A device that allows distant objects to be seen more clearly.
13 Vehicle that took the first astronauts to the moon.
14 Our nearest star.
15 A sudden eruption from the surface of a star such as the sun.

Earth SCIENCE

Space

Unscramble the letters into words and write them in the boxes to the left. Now unscramble the letters in the boxes with circles to find the last word.

ODARDDG

GABGNBI

NEGLN

NOOM

ARNSATUTO

The spacecraft that first visited the planet Mercury.

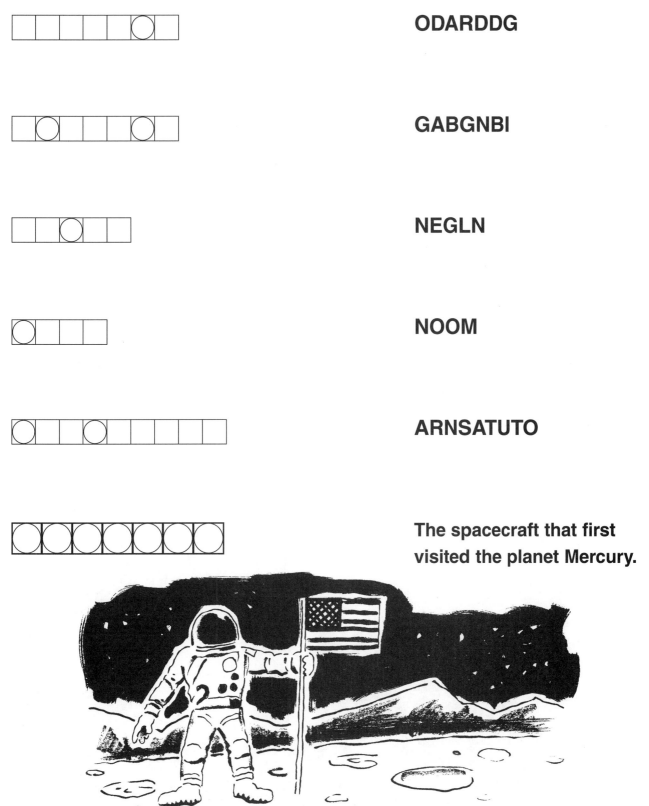

The Stars

This puzzle has two lists—words and definitions. Match the words with their definition by drawing a line between them.

Betelgeuse	Clouds of gas and dust between the stars.
Cassiopeia	The first maneuverable spacecraft; conducted the first rendezvous.
giant	A scientist who studies the universe.
telescope	One of the 20 brightest stars; it is 300 times as large as the sun.
Gemini	A constellation of five bright stars that form a *W.*
constellation	The first stage in the death of a star; red in color.
nebula	A device that allows humans to view the details of a far-off object.
astronomer	A group of stars that have been given a name by humans.

Earth SCIENCE

The Stars

This puzzle contains hidden words. They can go up and down, across, at an angle, forward, or back. All the hidden words are in the list below the puzzle. When you find one, circle it and look for another.

I S U P E R N O V A L M Z J A J

B N H M L D A K A P L A W R H N

Y N F E G L W D S F A G J B W S

A W G R U R E A T I T N A U O N

N I X B A M L S R A D I O D B N

R F E S O R T J O F E T O D P M

S N A R K S E I N P Y U D E C E

Q U D J C K O D O U Q D K T O G

Q N N A Y O L I M S E E F B R D

A T C C O N S T E L L A T I O N

K C V T G S V M R F U S I O N F

Q G G I A N T H O F U L V W A E

Y H C C F K D T L S C N V W S A

L G K S I D X N G E M I N I Y M

N Y B E T E L G E U S E G V D Z

Z M I M T S U E B Y T U Y D O G

Constellation
Betelgeuse
Andromeda
Magnitude
Nebula
Corona
Gemini
Giant
Radio
Sun
Astronomer

Cassiopeia
Supernova
Infrared
Cosmos
Fusion
Quasar
Dwarf
Rigel

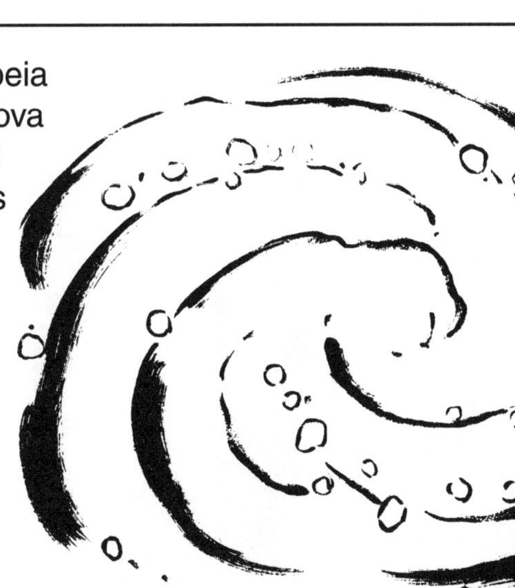

The Stars

Using the words in the list, you can build your own crossword puzzle. Start with the letter printed at the top and count the number of letters in its word. Now you know what letter that word begins with and how many letters it has. Look at the list and find the word. Write it in and build from there.

Sun	Telescope	Radio	Magnitude
Rigel	Supernova	Cosmos	Astronomer
Fusion	Betelgeuse	Corona	Constellation
Gemini	Cassiopeia	Infrared	
Nebula	Giant	Andromeda	

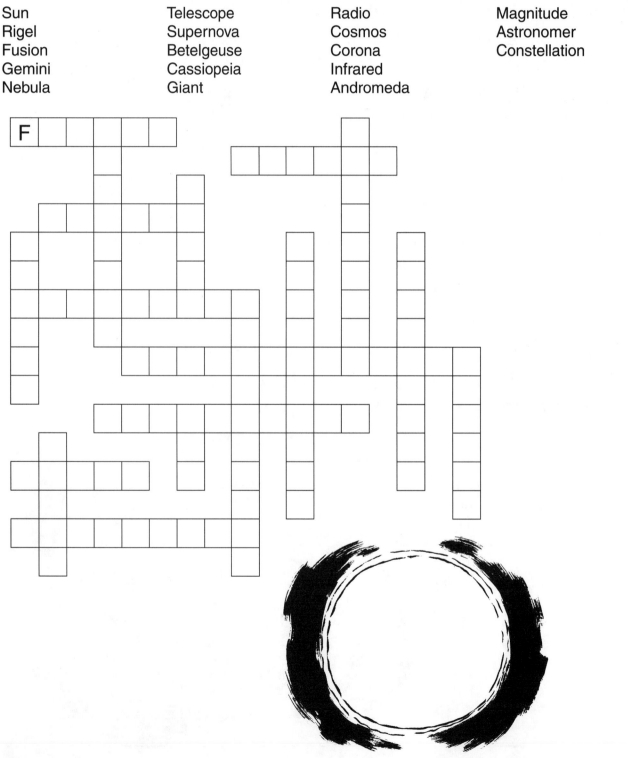

The Stars

Across

3 Clouds of gas and dust between the stars.
4 Object far away in the universe that emits strong radio signals.
5 A very bright star that is made of an enormous cloud of gas.
7 A constellation of five bright stars that form a *W*.
9 The first stage in the death of a star; red in color.
10 One of the 20 brightest stars; it is 300 times as large as the sun.
11 Wavelengths longer than visible light that can be converted to sound.
12 A device that allows humans to view the details of a far-off object.
14 A nuclear reaction that combines atoms of elements and releases energy.
15 How bright a star is.
16 The last stage in a star's life.
17 Light energy with wavelengths longer than visible red.
18 A large galaxy shaped like a pinwheel.

Down

1 A name given to the whole universe.
2 The first maneuverable spacecraft; conducted the first rendezvous.
6 A group of stars that have been given a name by humans.
8 A scientist who studies the universe.
13 The star closest to earth.

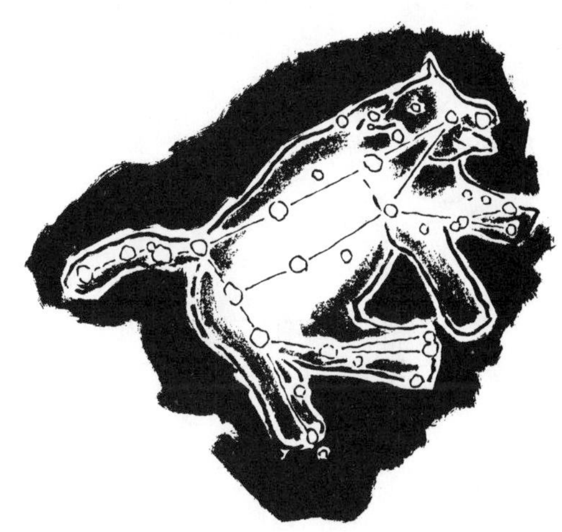

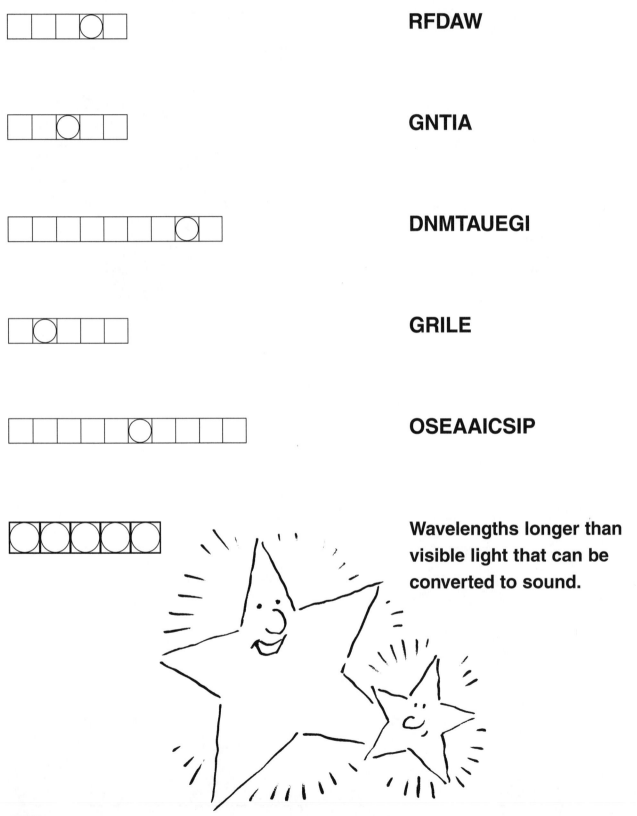

The Stars

Unscramble the letters into words and write them in the boxes to the left. Now unscramble the letters in the boxes with circles to find the last word.

RFDAW

GNTIA

DNMTAUEGI

GRILE

OSEAAICSIP

Wavelengths longer than visible light that can be converted to sound.

Earth SCIENCE

Volcanoes

This puzzle has two lists—words and definitions. Match the words with their definition by drawing a line between them.

pressure	The bowl at the top of a volcano, sometimes filled with water.
magma	The deformation of a volcano when pressure pushes the surface out.
caldera	An opening where volcanic gases escape.
eruption	The outermost layer of the earth.
crust	The force that causes volcanoes to erupt.
shield	The process of molten rock and gases flowing out of a volcano.
vent	Liquid rock inside the earth.
bulge	A volcano that has a low, broad shape.

Earth SCIENCE

Volcanoes

This puzzle contains hidden words. They can go up and down, across, at an angle, forward, or back. All the hidden words are in the list below the puzzle. When you find one, circle it and look for another.

Z Q M H S E I S M O G R A P H
X I A L Z E D K V T X P O C F
G P G U G O Y I T H A I N R M
L C M T V Z G I M A Y N K A I
X U A S H I E L D W B A C T S
Y E U L V A B R M A N T L E S
H M J I D E J R E I R U X R F
V G R C C E S E A I R B R O Y
U B N O R E R U P T I O N C A
L L Z N B U L A V I I W O W L
G A S E S N S A E I B O P P M
N S V S O X I T N Q U G N L G
U T E A M Z W X T D L S T S P
X R Z L S S C T S B G E J R Y
P K N U A S W M U I E V X M V

Seismograph
Eruption
Vesuvius
Caldera
Mantle
Hawaii
Magma
Gases
Blast
Lava
Heat
Vibrations
Pressure
Pinatubo
Iceland
Crater
Shield
Bulge
Crust
Cone
Vent
Ash

Volcanoes

Using the words in the list, you can build your own crossword puzzle. Start with the letter printed at the top and count the number of letters in its word. Now you know what letter that word begins with and how many letters it has. Look at the list and find the word. Write it in and build from there.

Ash	Crater	Vent	Pressure
Cone	Caldera	Magma	Vesuvius
Blast	Pinatubo	Gases	Vibrations
Crust	Eruption	Shield	
Bulge	Seismograph	Mantle	
Hawaii	Heat	Iceland	

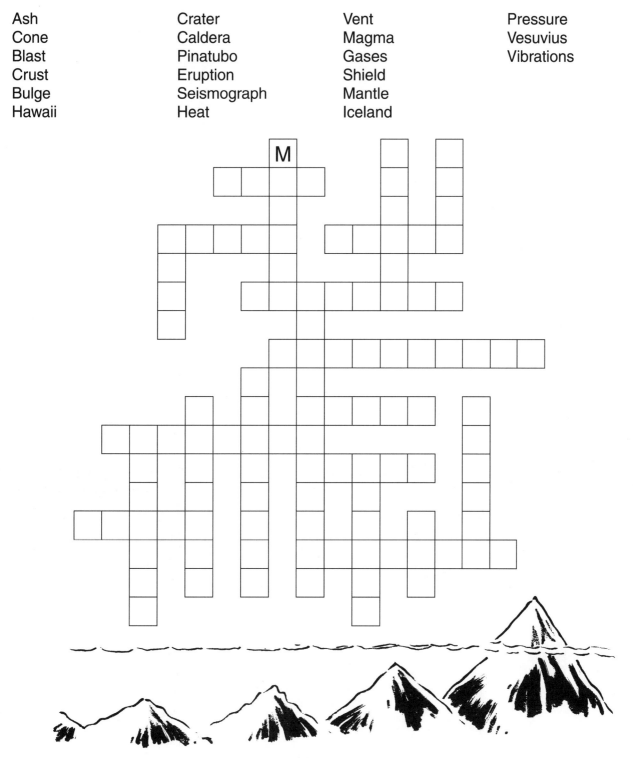

Volcanoes

Across

5 A rock that flows from volcanoes.
6 The process of the top of a volcano blowing off explosively.
7 A volcano that has a low, broad shape.
8 The middle layer of the earth.
10 The type of energy that causes rocks to melt.
14 The shape of a volcano formed by magma building up in steep slopes.
15 The kind of movement produced by earthquakes and volcanic eruptions.
17 A country where people use volcanic heat to warm their buildings.
18 Fine particles that fall out after a volcanic eruption.

Down

1 A state that consists of a series of volcanoes.
2 In addition to molten rock, these are released in an eruption.
3 Liquid rock inside the earth.
4 The outermost layer of the earth.
6 The deformation of a volcano when pressure pushes the surface out.
7 An instrument that measures earth movements.
9 The process of molten rock and gases flowing out of a volcano.
11 An ancient Italian volcano that is still active.
12 A volcano in the Phillipines that changed the world's weather.
13 The force that causes volcanoes to erupt.
14 The bowl at the top of a volcano, sometimes filled with water.
16 The hole left behind when a volcano erupts.

Volcanoes

Unscramble the letters into words and write them in the boxes to the left. Now unscramble the letters in the boxes with circles to find the last word.

VUSEIVSU

UEGLB

STLBA

EESRRSPU

BTUIAONP

The kind of movement produced by earthquakes and volcanic eruptions.

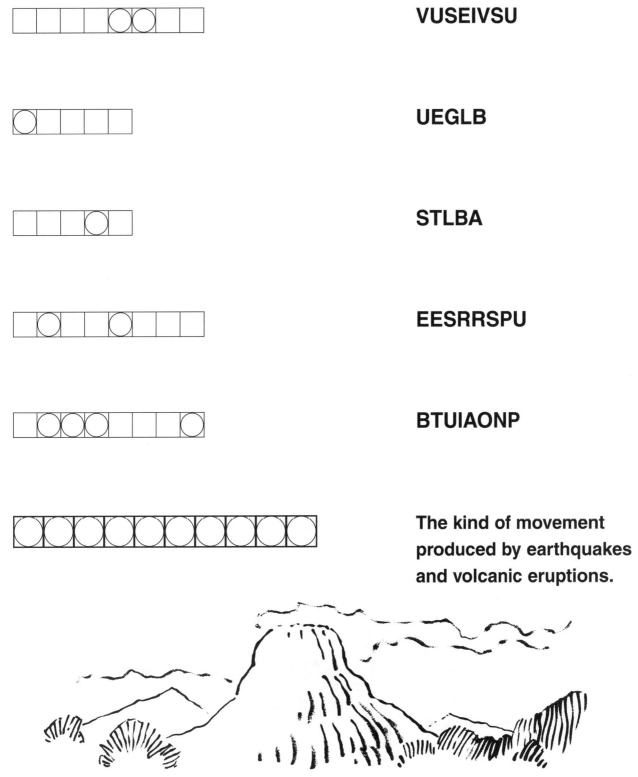

Weather

This puzzle has two lists—words and definitions. Match the words with their definition by drawing a line between them.

cumulonimbus	The form of energy that drives all weather systems.
temperature	The process of changing from a gas to a liquid.
front	A measurement of how warm or cold it is.
heat	Water in liquid or gaseous form.
condensation	The area where two air masses meet.
thunder	A large, spinning storm that originates in an Asian ocean.
moisture	A loud noise created when lightning rapidly heats the atmosphere.
typhoon	A type of cloud that is tall and dark and a source of thunderstorms.

Weather

This puzzle contains hidden words. They can go up and down, across, at an angle, forward, or back. All the hidden words are in the list below the puzzle. When you find one, circle it and look for another.

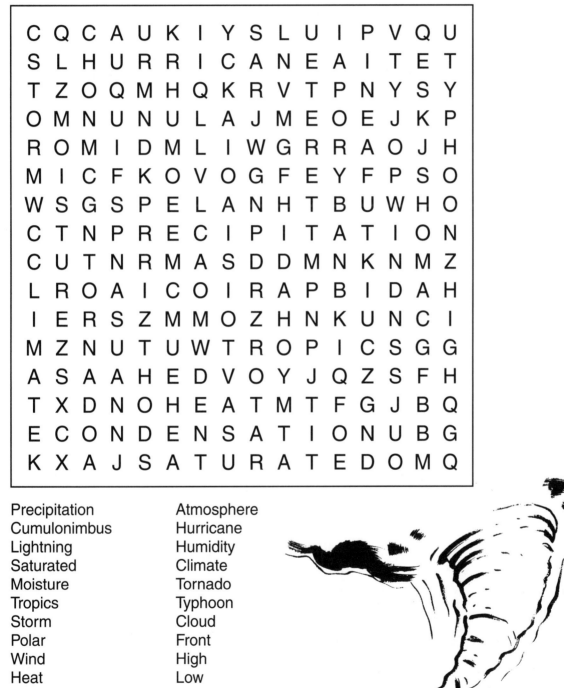

C Q C A U K I Y S L U I P V Q U
S L H U R R I C A N E A I T E T
T Z O Q M H Q K R V T P N Y S Y
O M N U N U L A J M E O E J K P
R O M I D M L I W G R R A O J H
M I C F K O V O G F E Y F P S O
W S G S P E L A N H T B U W H O
C T N P R E C I P I T A T I O N
C U T N R M A S D D M N K N M Z
L R O A I C O I R A P B I D A H
I E R S Z M M O Z H N K U N C I
M Z N U T U W T R O P I C S G G
A S A A H E D V O Y J Q Z S F H
T X D N O H E A T M T F G J B Q
E C O N D E N S A T I O N U B G
K X A J S A T U R A T E D O M Q

Precipitation
Cumulonimbus
Lightning
Saturated
Moisture
Tropics
Storm
Polar
Wind
Heat
Condensation

Atmosphere
Hurricane
Humidity
Climate
Tornado
Typhoon
Cloud
Front
High
Low

Weather

Using the words in the list, you can build your own crossword puzzle. Start with the letter printed at the top and count the number of letters in its word. Now you know what letter that word begins with and how many letters it has. Look at the list and find the word. Write it in and build from there.

Low	Moisture	Heat	Humidity
Wind	Saturated	Storm	Lightning
Cloud	Hurricane	Tornado	Atmosphere
Tropics	Temperature	Typhoon	Cumulonimbus
Thunder	Condensation	Climate	Precipitation

L

Weather

Across

3 Collections of water vapor, ice crystals or both floating in the air.
4 An area where the atmospheric pressure is low.
5 A measurement of how warm or cold it is.
6 The area where two air masses meet.
9 The envelope of air around the earth.
12 A rapidly spinning storm, usually over land, whose winds may reach 300 mph.
14 A type of cloud that is tall and dark and a source of thunderstorms.
17 Water falling from the air.

Down

1 The process of changing from a gas to a liquid.
2 The regions farthest north and south on the earth.
7 A loud noise created when lightning rapidly heats the atmosphere.
8 A disturbed state in the atmosphere.
10 A large, rapidly spinning storm that originates over an ocean in the Northern Hemisphere.
11 Water in any of its three forms.
13 Water in the air.
15 A large, rapidly spinning storm that originates over an ocean in the Southern Hemisphere.
16 Rapidly moving air caused by differences in pressure.

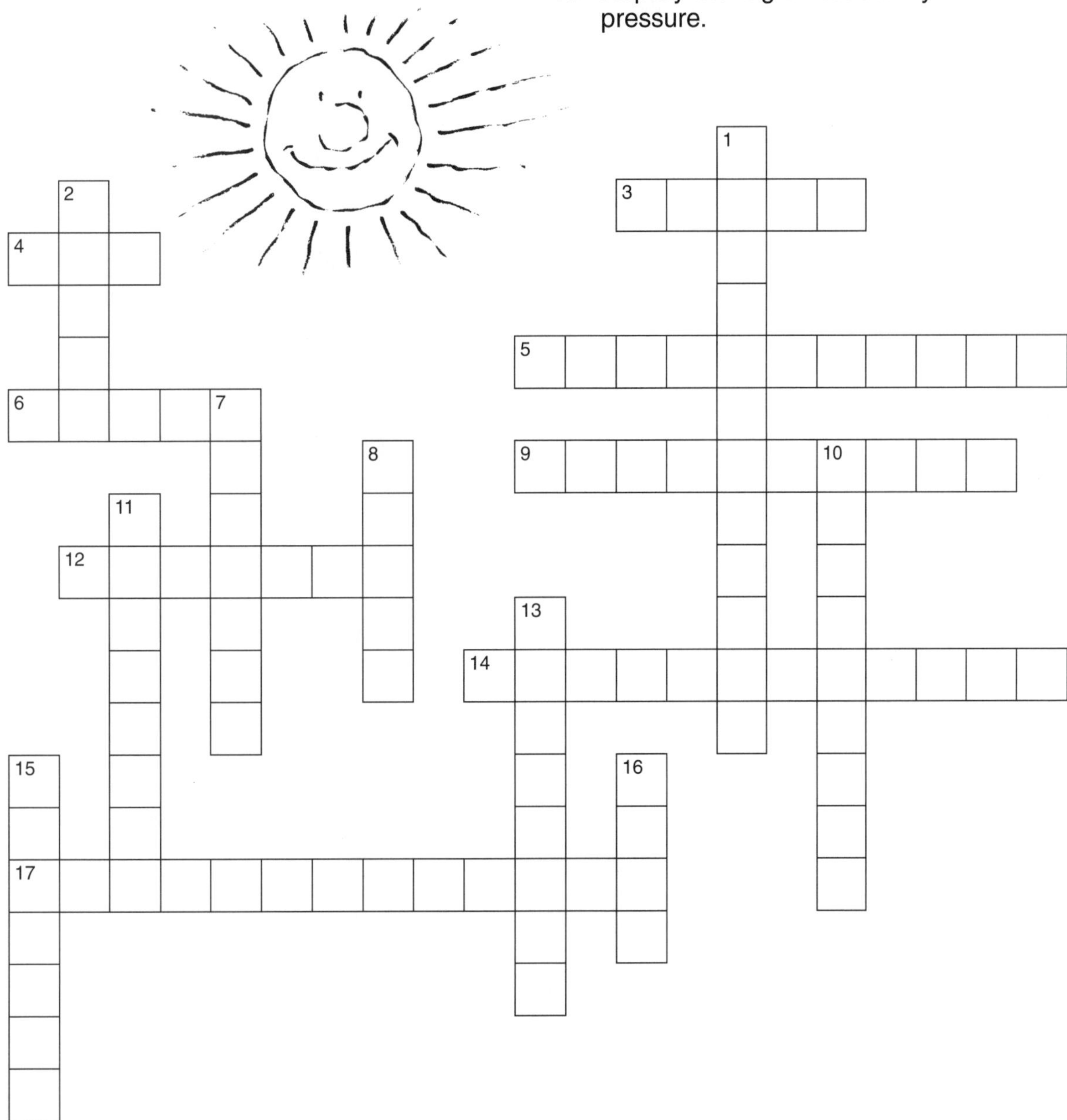

Weather

Unscramble the letters into words and write them in the boxes to the left. Now unscramble the letters in the boxes with circles to find the last word.

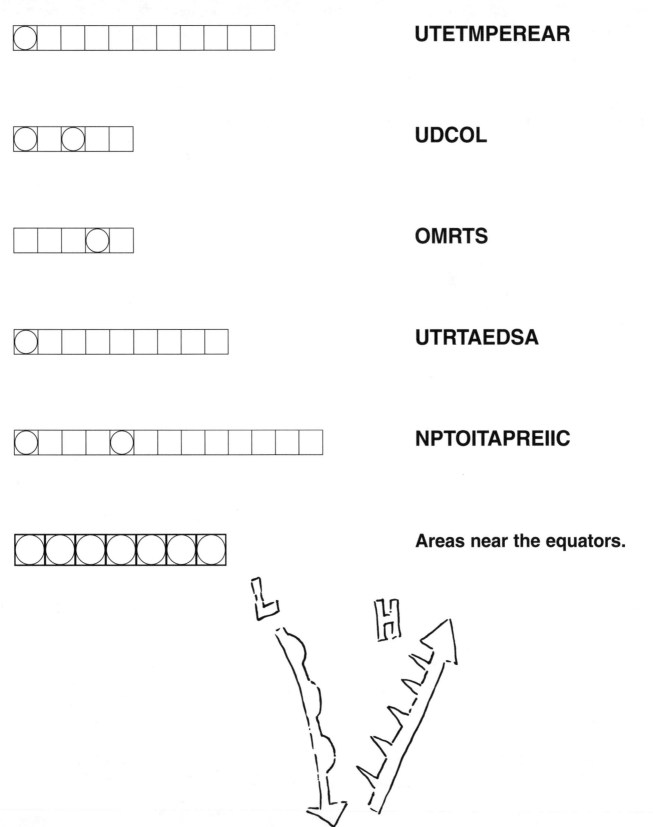

UTETMPEREAR

UDCOL

OMRTS

UTRTAEDSA

NPTOITAPREIIC

Areas near the equators.

L

H

Earth SCIENCE

Weathering and Erosion

This puzzle has two lists—words and definitions. Match the words with their definition by drawing a line between them.

dissolve	Flowing water that is confined to a narrow depression in the earth.
gully	A process of rapid combustion.
river	A long, narrow cut in the earth made by running water.
glaciers	Solid material washed away upstream and deposited downstream.
silt	A liquid compound that contains two hydrogen atoms and one oxygen atom.
water	Rivers of flowing ice.
fire	A series of events that repeat themselves.
cycle	Become equally distributed in a liquid.

Earth SCIENCE

Weathering and Erosion

This puzzle contains hidden words. They can go up and down, across, at an angle, forward, or back. All the hidden words are in the list below the puzzle. When you find one, circle it and look for another.

G	E	T	W	A	V	E	M	J	R	C	N	E	F	Y	Q
U	U	R	E	N	S	T	F	K	O	H	F	P	K	V	J
M	P	L	L	F	I	R	I	V	E	R	R	A	I	N	G
T	X	T	L	I	L	Z	V	T	Z	T	A	C	I	D	R
M	Z	O	C	Y	T	O	A	P	H	X	C	F	K	A	A
F	Z	W	W	Y	P	J	O	G	V	Z	T	N	Z	B	V
F	I	A	A	M	C	L	I	D	N	W	U	A	G	M	E
W	B	R	T	Q	G	L	A	C	I	E	R	S	R	G	L
I	N	S	E	T	N	S	E	N	V	N	E	T	E	I	K
N	U	N	R	U	G	Y	L	L	T	U	G	L	T	X	M
D	D	H	S	A	N	D	O	S	T	S	O	I	L	K	D
U	W	I	C	E	X	S	O	V	E	R	N	R	O	T	E
Y	L	B	Q	G	S	R	C	C	P	P	O	O	J	N	H
Z	R	M	G	I	F	Q	B	R	Z	W	B	R	W	L	M
L	B	M	D	X	S	K	Q	P	T	F	U	J	F	L	B
L	R	I	O	N	V	X	Y	I	A	P	E	Y	B	X	H

Glaciers
Sunlight
Dissolve
Gravel
River
Water
Dust
Soil
Silt
Wind
Fire
Ice

Fracture
Flooding
Plants
Gully
Frost
Cycle
Rain
Sand
Snow
Wave
Acid

Weathering and Erosion

Using the words in the list, you can build your own crossword puzzle. Start with the letter printed at the top and count the number of letters in its word. Now you know what letter that word begins with and how many letters it has. Look at the list and find the word. Write it in and build from there.

Ice
Silt
Wave
Acid
Cycle

Water
Gravel
Glaciers
Dissolve
Sunlight

Rain
Soil
Fire
River
Gully

Frost
Plants
Flooding
Fracture

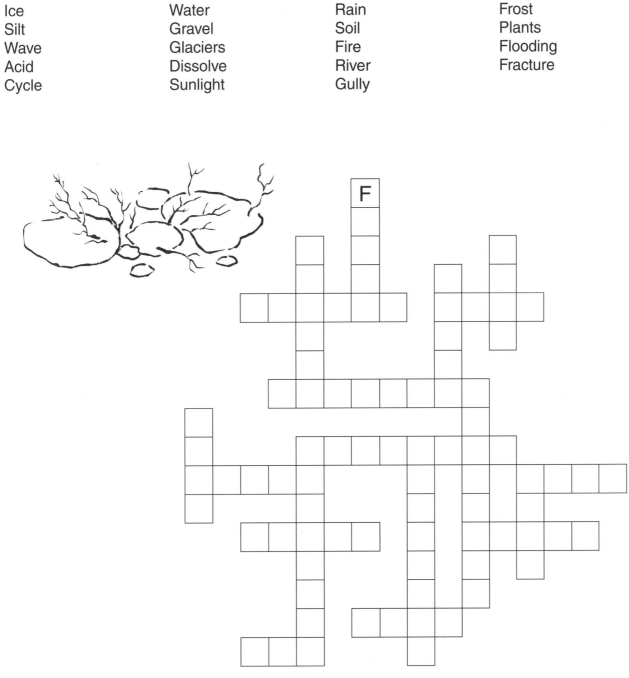

F

Weathering and Erosion

Across

2 A process of rapid combustion.
6 A liquid compound that contains two atoms of hydrogen and one of oxygen.
7 Liquid water falling from the atmosphere.
8 Crystalline water that falls out of the cold atmosphere.
10 A long, narrow cut in the earth caused by running water.
14 Rivers of flowing ice.
15 A disturbance on the surface of water, usually caused by wind.
19 Solid material washed away upstream and deposited downstream.
20 Solid water.
21 The source of almost all energy on earth.
22 Small fragments of minerals or rocks, usually deposited as sediment.
23 Become equally distributed in a liquid.

Down

1 The process of water covering a normally dry area.
3 Flowing water that is confined to a narrow depression in the earth.
4 Pebbles and rock fragments.
5 The way a rock cracks or breaks.
9 A series of events that repeat themselves.
11 A general term applied to fine-grained material that plants can grow in.
12 These organisms have roots that can crack rocks.
13 A thin layer of ice that has condensed out of the air.
16 A corrosive chemical that releases hydrogen ions in water.
17 Small solid particles that can float in the air.
18 The flow of air from an area of high pressure to an area of low pressure.

Earth SCIENCE

Weathering and Erosion

Unscramble the letters into words and write them in the boxes to the left. Now unscramble the letters in the boxes with circles to find the last word.

LSIT

ASND

AVLRGE

SFRTO

OILS

Become equally distributed in a liquid.

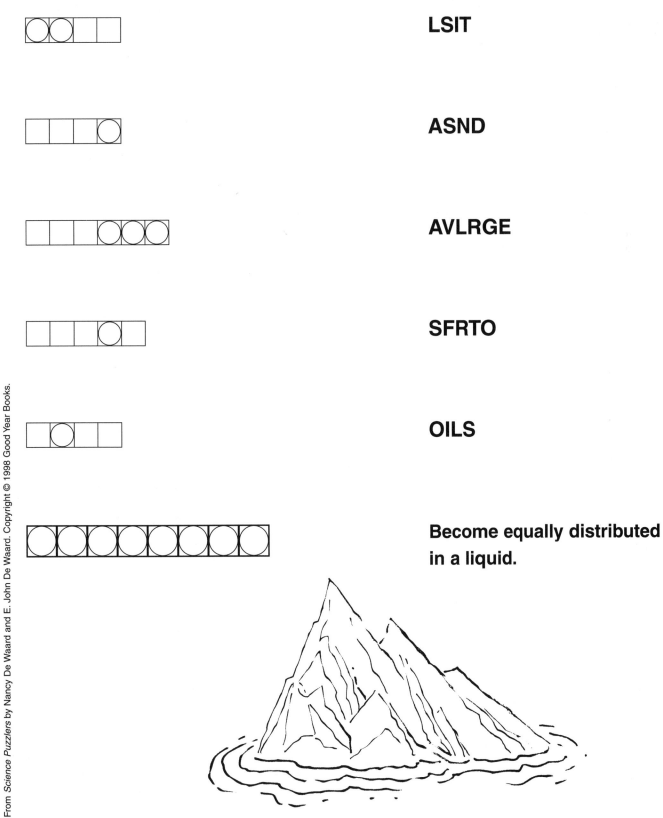

Physical SCIENCE

Atoms and Matter

This puzzle has two lists—words and definitions. Match the words with their definitions by drawing a line between them.

reaction	The central part of the atom, consisting of protons and neutrons.
Mendeleev	A particle, smaller than the atom, that carries a positive charge.
Thomson	A chemical combination of two or more dissimilar atoms.
compound	One of the first to arrange all elements into families.
neutron	A British scientist who discovered the electron.
periodic	A particle, smaller than the atom, that carries no charge.
proton	Repeats at set intervals.
nucleus	Chemicals combining or breaking down into different compounds.

Physical SCIENCE

Atoms and Matter

This puzzle contains hidden words. They can go up and down, across, at an angle, forward, or back. All the hidden words are in the list below the puzzle. When you find one, circle it and look for another

R	O	O	A	C	O	M	P	O	U	N	D	S	S	A	M	E	O
P	R	O	T	O	N	S	F	I	O	N	U	E	B	E	A	A	A
T	E	A	S	E	E	T	T	L	O	T	E	K	S	O	D	P	L
H	W	C	D	T	U	U	T	I	I	E	C	T	R	P	H	R	P
O	U	C	D	D	T	I	T	R	E	I	S	E	I	N	A	R	E
M	E	E	A	M	S	C	C	D	W	I	H	P	A	P	T	M	C
S	M	L	T	O	A	O	O	D	M	D	N	A	E	E	O	E	V
O	A	E	D	E	M	D	A	E	E	N	U	L	A	X	M	N	W
N	U	R	R	E	A	H	H	H	S	E	C	E	H	B	I	D	E
O	N	A	D	E	C	C	T	L	U	U	L	L	H	Y	C	E	B
O	M	T	R	A	L	R	E	J	E	T	E	E	O	E	N	L	H
T	O	O	E	A	L	E	A	A	R	R	U	C	O	A	U	E	H
N	L	R	U	S	I	T	M	A	Y	O	S	T	T	G	M	E	E
H	E	F	T	I	C	O	O	E	L	N	T	R	F	A	B	V	A
T	C	R	L	D	A	Y	I	N	N	S	I	O	T	A	E	N	S
H	U	P	E	R	I	O	D	I	C	T	T	N	F	T	R	A	E
T	L	A	S	Y	M	B	O	L	S	H	O	S	B	I	R	S	O
A	E	N	A	E	N	H	R	U	T	H	E	R	F	O	R	D	F

Accelerator
Alchemist
Bohr
Chadwick
Compound
Dalton
Democritus
Electrons
Element
Mendeleev
Molecule
Neutrons
Nucleus
Periodic
Protons
Reaction
Rutherford
Symbols
Thomson
Atomic Number

Atoms and Matter

Using the words in the list, you can build your own crossword puzzle. Start with the letter printed at the top and count the number of letters in its word. Now you know what letter that word begins with and how many letters it has. Look at the list and find the word. Write it in and build from there.

Bohr	Compound	Dalton	Alchemist
Proton	Mendeleev	Neutron	Rutherford
Thomson	Democritus	Reaction	Atomic Number
Nucleus	Accelerator	Periodic	
Chadwick	Symbol	Molecule	

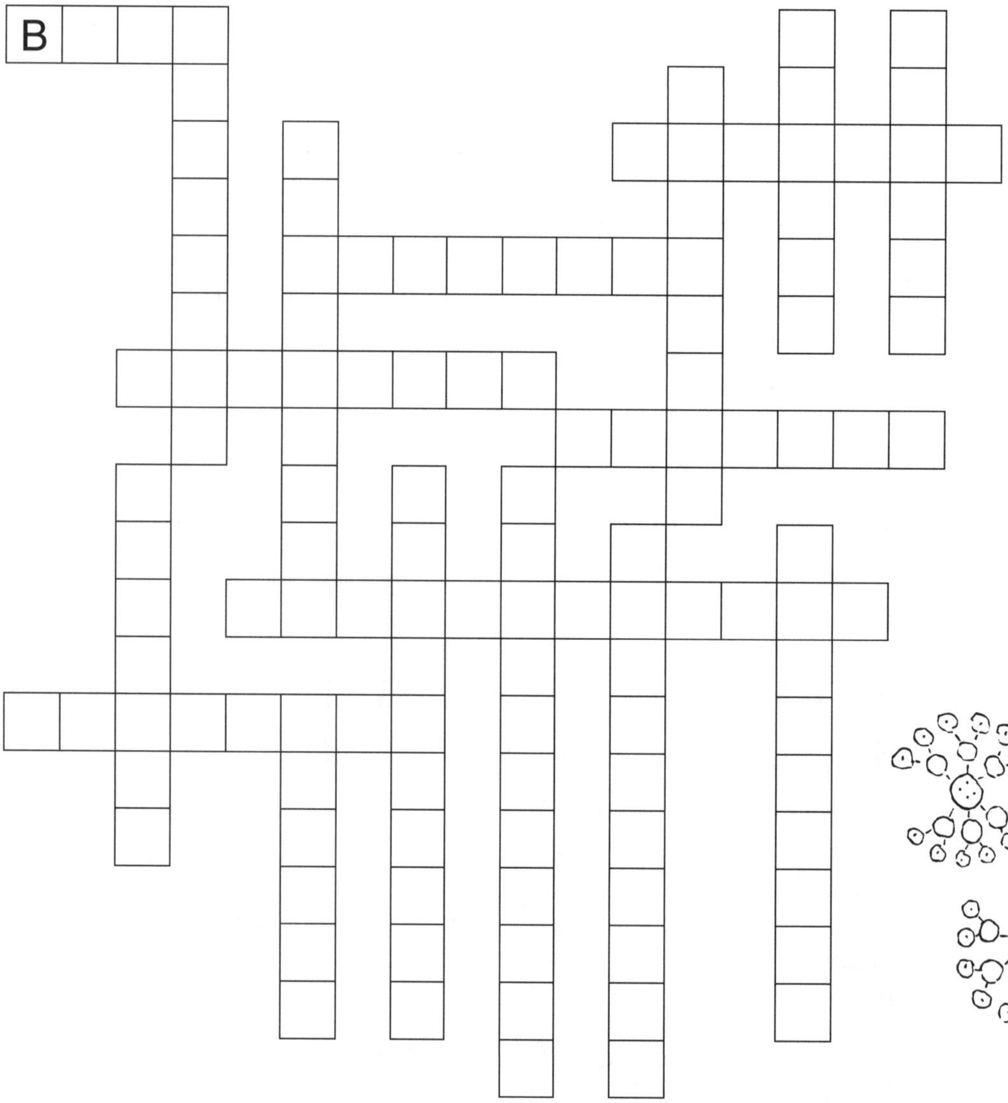

B

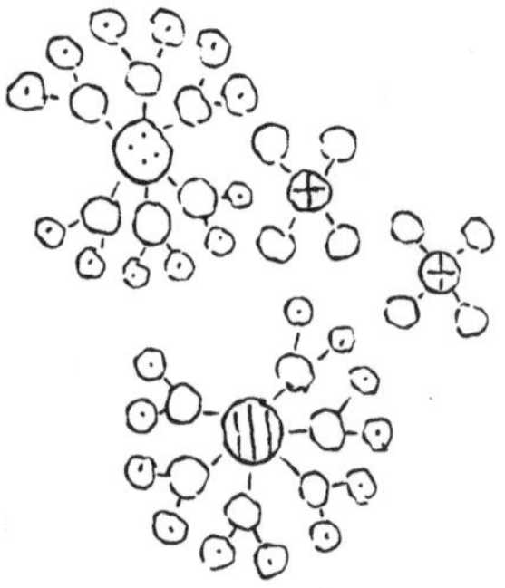

Atoms and Matter

Across

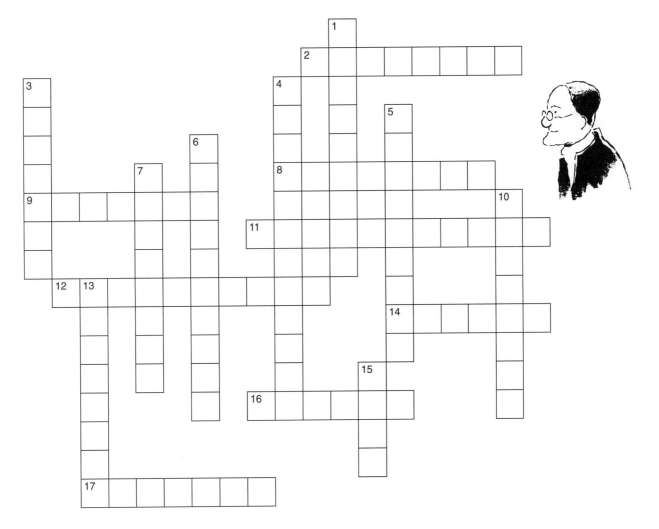

2 Chemicals combining or breaking down into different compounds.
8 The smallest particle of a substance.
9 One of about a hundred basic chemicals that make up the universe.
11 A machine that speeds up atomic particles.
12 An ancient philosopher, one of the first to propose the atomic theory.
14 Letter or picture used to stand for something else.
16 A particle, smaller than the atom, that carries a positive charge.
17 A particle, smaller than the atom, that carries no charge.

Down

1 One of the first to arrange all elements into families.
3 The central part of the atom, consisting of protons and neutrons.
4 The number of protons in an element's nucleus (two words).
5 Ancient scholar who tried to convert other heavy elements into gold.
6 A British scientist who first discovered that atoms had a nucleus.
7 Repeats at set intervals.
10 A chemical combination of two or more dissimilar atoms.
13 A particle, smaller than the atom, that carries a negative charge.
15 A Danish scientist; one of the first to describe the atom's structure.

Atoms and Matter

Unscramble the letters into words and write them in the boxes to the left. Now unscramble the letters in the boxes with circles to find the last word.

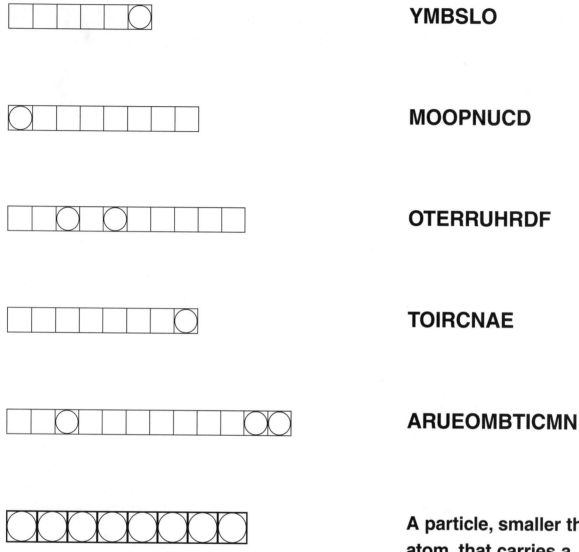

YMBSLO

MOOPNUCD

OTERRUHRDF

TOIRCNAE

ARUEOMBTICMN

A particle, smaller than the atom, that carries a negative charge.

Physical SCIENCE

Matter and Its Changes

This puzzle has two lists—words and definitions. Match the words with their definitions by drawing a line between them.

combustion	A common compound consisting of two atoms of hydrogen and one of oxygen.
conservation	The process of two atoms merging into one.
water	A substance, such as litmus, that signals the presence of something.
indicator	Symbol that represents the atoms in a compound or reaction.
formula	The law of _____ of energy, which says that no energy is lost in a reaction.
fission	A compound that changes blue litmus paper to red and neutralizes bases.
fusion	Rapid oxidation, usually with the release of heat and light.
acid	The process of an atom splitting into pieces.

Physical SCIENCE — Matter and Its Changes

This puzzle contains hidden words. They can go up and down, across, at an angle, forward, or back. All the hidden words are in the list below the puzzle. When you find one, circle it and look for another.

C E A C I D R A I N F H G S E P R L
F R T C L R D C O A B E E T F O C L
O B Y G E E H I L O S I I V P A L I
R O F S M E T J A W T X H S D Y D N
M N C I T S L P I R U G E L H O N D
U D B A U A E S E A N S Y P E N I I
L K P B E N L P B T A N O P O L R C
A E M U P O O S O B O R E I S E M A
C O N S E R V A T I O N S C T U O T
C A E E P E D N T L I S P A I O M O
E O R L R N A A H A I A W C A I F R
M A E B W G R C O F U U L L T H U M
A C E E O E Y A P I T A I T E F E A
T I E N N N I N C H C F T R O U L S
N D G I P H O T O S Y N T H E S I S
E S C B A L D D L A L E I T I I T U
E N A L S M O G A S T B E E A O N A
I S A D O X I D A T I O N L P N R M

Indicator
Formula
Acids
Bases
Properties
Bauxite
Calcium
Gypsum
Carbon
Bond
Conservation
Fusion
Crystals
Energy
Fission
Fuel
Incineration
Mass
Chlorophyll
Oxidation
Photosynthesis
Acid Rain
Smog
Combustion
Water

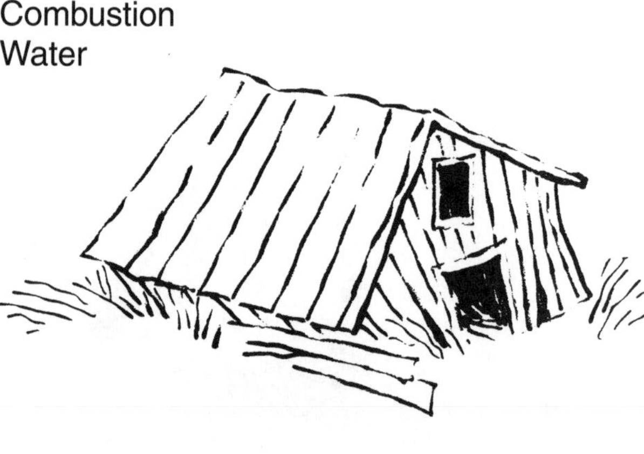

Matter and Its Changes

Using the words in the list, you can build your own crossword puzzle. Start with the letter printed at the top and count the number of letters in its word. Now you know what letter that word begins with and how many letters it has. Look at the list and find the word. Write it in and build from there.

Base	Fission	Mass	Indicator
Acid	Oxidation	Fusion	Combustion
Water	Properties	Carbon	Incineration
Energy	Chlorophyll	Crystal	Photosynthesis
Formula	Conservation	Calcium	
Bauxite	Bond	Acid Rain	

A

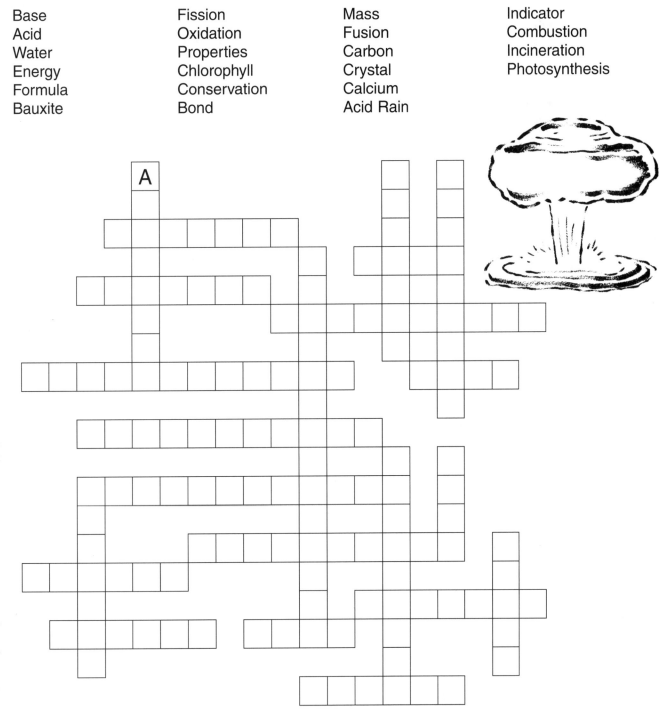

Matter and Its Changes

Across

3 A compound that changes red litmus paper blue and neutralizes acids.
4 The process of an atom splitting into pieces.
9 The catalyst in photosynthesis.
10 The process of burning, commonly used to dispose of trash.
11 The law of _____ of energy, which says that no energy is lost in a reaction.
12 Rapid oxidation, usually with the release of heat and light.
14 The ability to do work; stored in chemical compounds, notably fuels.
16 The characteristics of matter in an object.
17 The amount of matter in an object.
18 Industrial pollution returned to earth in precipitation (two words).

Down

1 The force that holds atoms together in a molecule.
2 A common compound consisting of two atoms of hydrogen and one of oxygen.
4 A compound that can be used as a source of energy.
5 A substance, such as litmus, that signals the presence of something.
6 A silver-white metal that is used to build strong bones and teeth.
7 The reaction that stores the energy of sunlight in carbohydrates.
8 When oxygen combines with another element such as iron or carbon.
12 A solid form of a substance that has an orderly internal arrangement.
13 The ore that is the source of aluminum.
15 A soft mineral that is mined and used to make plaster.

Matter and Its Changes

Unscramble the letters into words and write them in the boxes to the left. Now unscramble the letters in the boxes with circles to find the last word.

SYGMUP

TWREA

NCIATRHNNE

ACCMULI

NBAROC

A solid form of a substance that has an orderly internal arrangement.

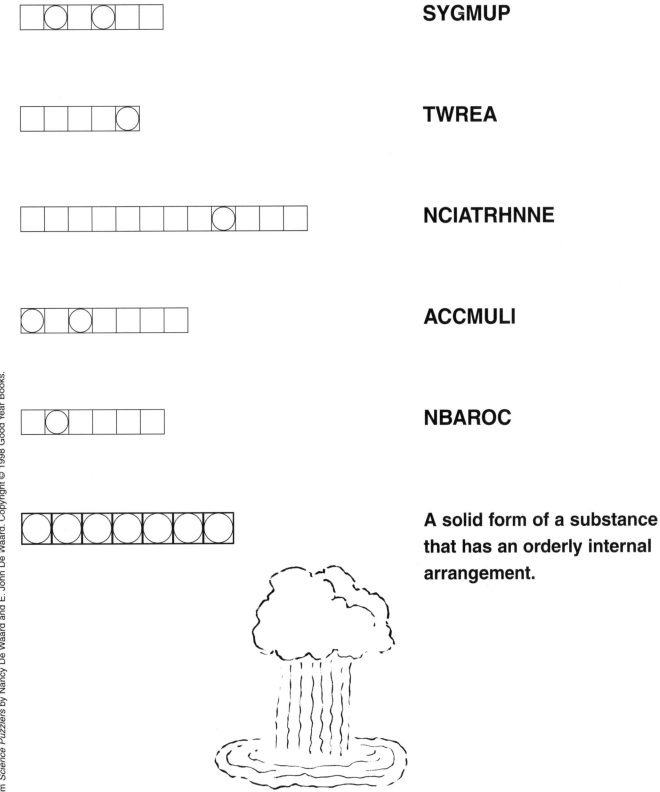

Electricity and Magnetism

This puzzle has two lists—words and definitions. Match the words with their definitions by drawing a line between them.

parallel

series

field

alnico

electron

coil

iron

accelerator

Natural magnets contain this element.

A particle, smaller than the atom, that carries a negative charge.

A circular electrical circuit that produces a magnetic field.

A machine that speeds up atomic particles.

A circuit in which electricity can flow through two or more paths.

A circuit in which all current is restricted to one path.

A magnetic alloy that contains aluminum, nickel, and cobalt.

The area of influence around a magnet.

Physical SCIENCE Electricity and Magnetism

This puzzle contains hidden words. They can go up and down, across, at an angle, forward, or back. All the hidden words are in the list below the puzzle. When you find one, circle it and look for another.

D E A L S D H G S E H I R T L O D N
A L L N N A N S E S T F N E E T T E
E E N M V Y A R A N A H L D I T O F
E C I R I P C N U H E L O U P Y E N
D T C C M N O P D C A R C M R R M Y
T R O O O S N F A R U R A O S J A H
M O C R W D D R A R I R T T C O G E
B N I N T A U P P C T A R S O O N R
T S S B D S C C C R R I I E A R I O
D T I I L T T O C E O S C T N B T L
N S T N A E O B L H G T R L I T I U
R E R A A U R E C E A E O E E E T E
S R O A T E C N E U T R O N S S E A
L I T E S C E S O E D H G D S I O D
S E V O A N R C P E L B I E C D B D
D S A A T M K I L O W A T T S E N O
O L I G H T N I N G E O T E E S F H
R C S T W P U U E Y E O C C A C E N

Accelerator
Circuit
Coil
Conductor
Current
Electrons
Generator
Kilowatts
Lightning
Magnetite
Neutrons
Parallel
Particles
Protons
Thomson
Charge
Series
Iron
Alnico
Compass

Physical SCIENCE

Electricity and Magnetism

Using the words in the list, you can build your own crossword puzzle. Start with the letter printed at the top and count the number of letters in its word. Now you know what letter that word begins with and how many letters it has. Look at the list and find the word. Write it in and build from there.

Coil	Electron	Alnico	Lightning
Charge	Conductor	Compass	Magnetite
Series	Generator	Circuit	Accelerator
Current	Attraction	Thomson	
Neutron	Iron	Particle	

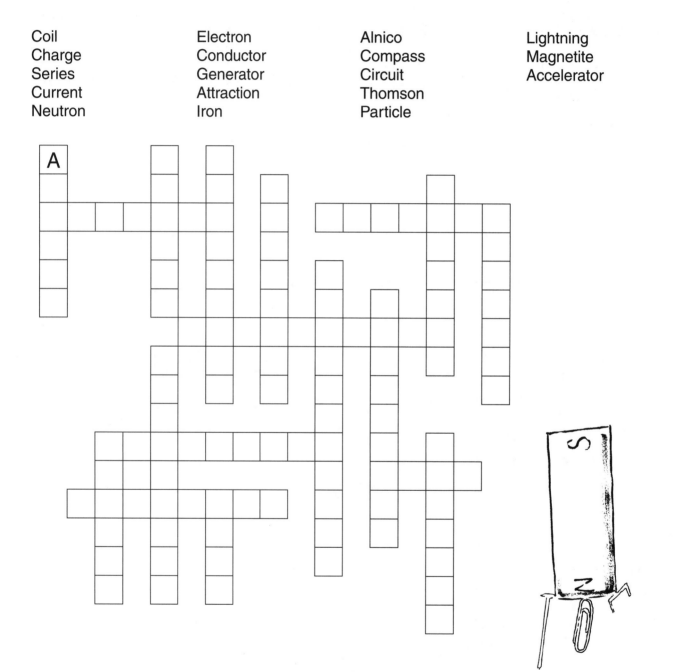

A

Electricity and Magnetism

Across

3 A measure of electricity used to calculate your electricity bill.
4 A particle, smaller than the atom, that carries no charge.
5 A circuit in which electricity can flow through two or more paths.
8 A substance that will carry an electrical current.
9 A circular electrical circuit that produces a magnetic field.
13 A machine that speeds up atomic particles.
14 A particle, smaller than the atom, that carries a positive charge.
15 Natural magnets contain this element.
16 The path that electricity takes from its source to a load and back.
17 The amount and kind of electrical potential of an object.
18 The flow of energy in an electrical circuit.

Down

1 A particle, smaller than the atom, that carries a negative charge.
2 A circuit in which all current is restricted to one path.
6 A force that draws bodies together.
7 A huge flow of electrical current from clouds to earth.
10 A very small piece of matter.
11 A natural ore that is magnetic.
12 A machine that converts mechanical energy into electrical energy.

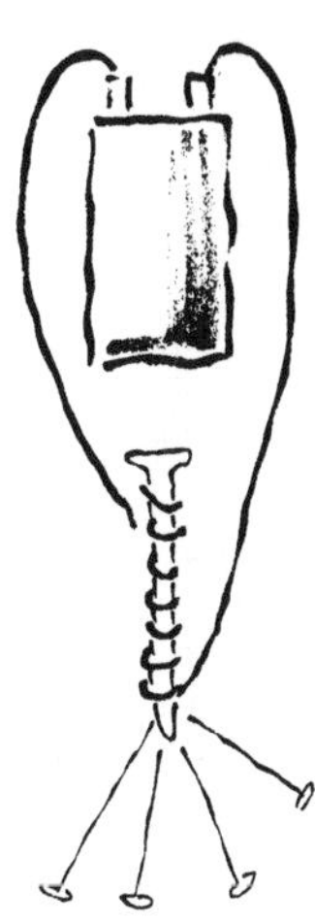

Physical SCIENCE

Electricity and Magnetism

Unscramble the letters into words and write them in the boxes to the left. Now unscramble the letters in the boxes with circles to find the last word.

NPTOOR

ICTRICU

RTPCAEIL

CSAMPSO

NRIO

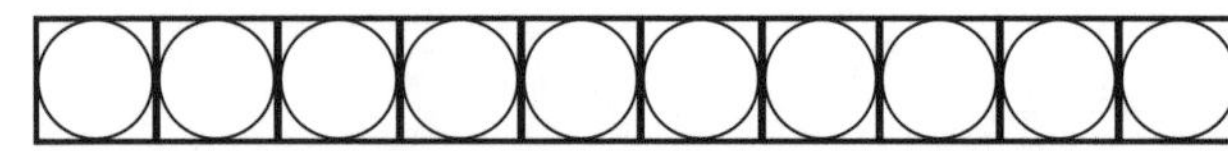

A force that draws bodies together.

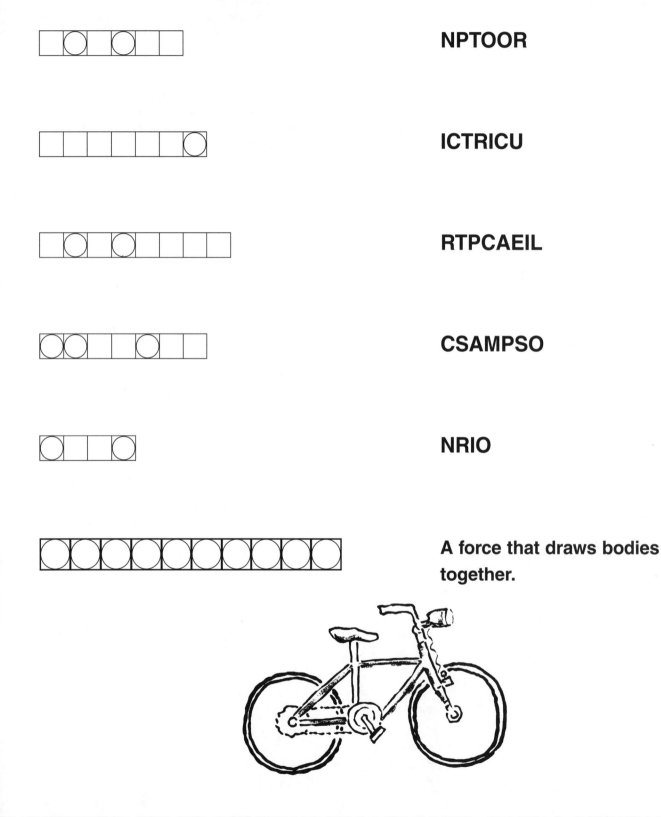

Elements

This puzzle has two lists—words and definitions. Match the words with their definitions by drawing a line between them.

carbon	One of the lightest elements, used in blimps and balloons.
tungsten	A reddish brown metal used to conduct electricity.
helium	A device that analyzes the light given off when an element is burned.
spectrometer	One of the first to arrange elements into families.
chlorine	A very heavy metal used as source of energy in nuclear power plants.
Mendeleev	Chains of atoms of this element are basic to living things.
copper	This element is used to purify water.
uranium	A gray metal with a high melting point; used in incandescent lights.

Physical SCIENCE

Elements

This puzzle contains hidden words. They can go up and down, across, at an angle, forward, or back. All the hidden words are in the list below the puzzle. When you find one, circle it and look for another.

```
R N H S V L V C H Y D R O G E N E L
E T H M P C O P P E R S E U H A T R
S N E W E E E U E E E E B R E T E T
N D E C E N C T N H A H Z A L N A U
O R E I P S D T A F L E S N I S O N
T O I P S C W E R X N Y B I U I M G
P F X I N A E A L O O S F U M L E S
L S E Y R C A N E E M R H M E I R T
A E O R G O D R C Y E E T W N C C E
T S G D A E N E H M E V T O E O U N
I N R H I L N S L E S R B E S N R C
N I S S L U U I O V W R L E R D Y H
U T H S A E M M R A A Y L A T T W O
M R G H D R O A I C A L C I U M T E
E O B T D F L I N N L N I N E O N F
S G K T W L C E E Y U S C R A M E S
E E T A E D F E A E T M E N H E T T
O N D M S S H E D D C E D E T E S A
```

Nitrogen
Calcium
Uranium
Copper
Helium
Iron
Lead
Mercury
Carbon
Neon

Oxygen
Platinum
Mendeleev
Silicon
Hydrogen
Sodium
Aluminum
Spectrometer
Tungsten
Chlorine

Elements

Using the words in the list, you can build your own crossword puzzle. Start with the letter printed at the top and count the number of letters in its word. Now you know what letter that word begins with and how many letters it has. Look at the list and find the word. Write it in and build from there.

Iron	Aluminum	Neon	Nitrogen
Carbon	Tungsten	Sodium	Hydrogen
Copper	Chlorine	Oxygen	Platinum
Mercury	Mendeleev	Silicon	Spectrometer

Elements

Across

1 A silver-white metal that can be extracted from table salt.
2 A silver-white metal that is essential to strong bodies and teeth.
5 This element is used to purify water.
8 A device that analyzes the light given off when an element is burned.
12 The lightest element, very common throughout the universe.
13 A precious metal, used in pollution control devices.
14 An element that glows when electricity passes through it.
15 A very heavy metallic element that used to be used in plumbing.
16 Chains of atoms of this element are basic to living things.

Down

1 This element is found in sand and is essential to modern electronics.
3 A common gas in our atmosphere; essential for plant growth.
4 A reddish brown metal used to conduct electricity.
6 One of the first to arrange elements into families.
7 One of the lightest elements, used in blimps and balloons.
9 A gray metal with a high melting point; used in incandescent lights.
10 A very heavy metal used as source of energy in nuclear power plants.
11 An element attracted to magnets.

Elements

Unscramble the letters into words and write them in the boxes to the left. Now unscramble the letters in the boxes with circles to find the last word.

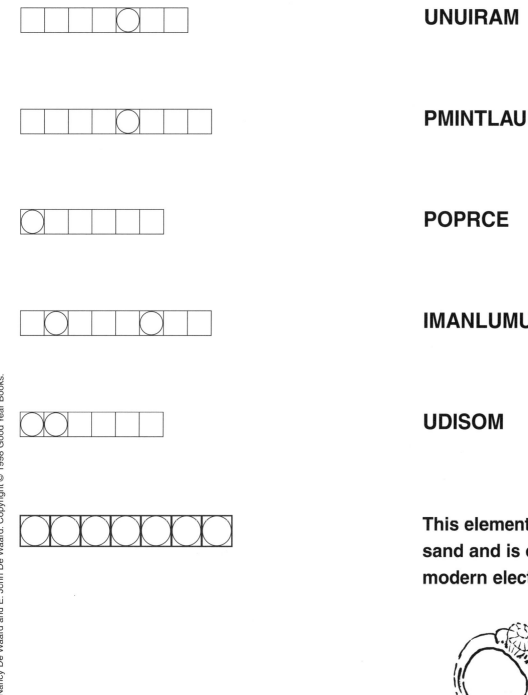

☐☐☐☐◯☐☐ **UNUIRAM**

☐☐☐☐◯☐☐☐ **PMINTLAU**

◯☐☐☐☐☐ **POPRCE**

☐◯☐☐◯☐☐☐ **IMANLUMU**

◯◯☐☐☐☐ **UDISOM**

◯◯◯◯◯◯◯ **This element is found in sand and is essential to modern electronics.**

Physical SCIENCE — Light and Heat

This puzzle has two lists—words and definitions. Match the words with their definitions by drawing a line between them.

convex	Part of the spectrum with long wavelengths, easily converted to heat.
sunlight	Electromagnetic waves that carry energy, arranged by wavelength.
radiation	Lenses with thick centers and thin edges are called _____.
energy	Light travels in waves; the color of light is determined by _____.
spectrum	The ability to do work.
reflection	The ultimate source of almost all the energy on earth.
infrared	The process of radiated energy bouncing off a surface.
wavelength	Light travels through the vacuum of space as electromagnetic _____.

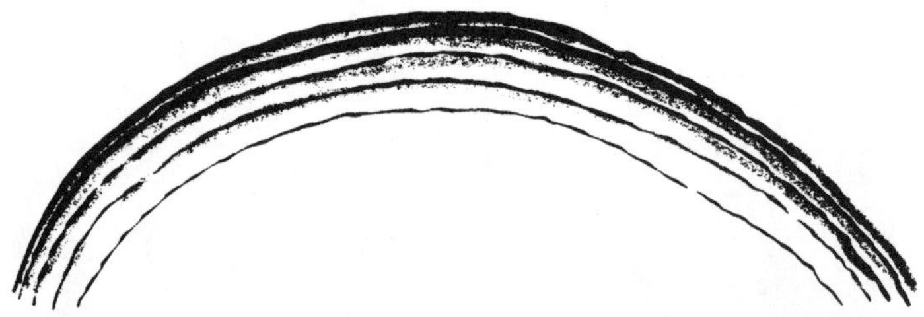

Light and Heat

This puzzle contains hidden words. They can go up and down, across, at an angle, forward, or back. All the hidden words are in the list below the puzzle. When you find one, circle it and look for another.

```
I R Y E E S R T O S I E A O L P O E
D N C O N C A V E U C U P H E T U E
Y S R U D A S O E N H G R E R S E D
M L L A A R E R H L E L R U N E T E
O B A S D M E I T I A E I S S E E S
X D O P A I I E Y G T H M N L G S S
Y E E E N T A T E H O U O O N A T H
G B L C H A H T R T E I I A M E L I
E L E T E W L O I H S V H H E L E U
N Y G R R U I B T O A C H I L A E R
I A T U E C I G L R N V I S I B L E
E N A M I A N P T S A S E N N Y X F
R L F H L E X L M N I C E A G E D L
D O O R L E U P T N I E A R V H O E
S F R E A D N E I H O I E N E D Z C
N E V C E R T S A L L N O E O W O T
W A C I N F E E T A E C E R N E N E
W D N R E S A D N I O H O O A Y E S
```

Change
Energy
Explosion
Heat
Infrared
Mass
Oxygen
Ozone
Radiation

Reflect
Spectrum
Sunlight
Ultraviolet
Visible
Wavelength
Convex
Concave
Lens

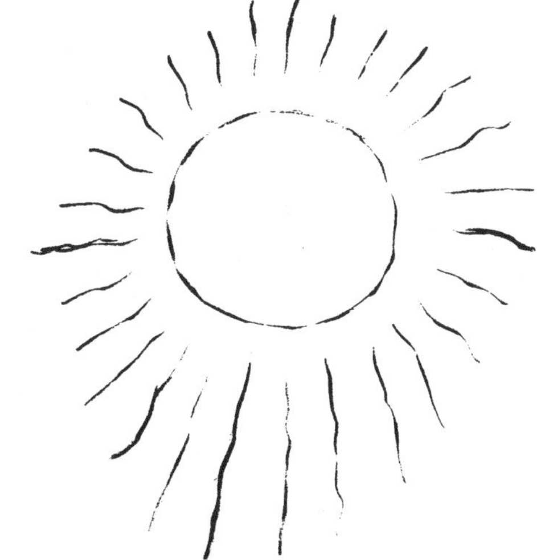

Physical SCIENCE

Light and Heat

Using the words in the list, you can build your own crossword puzzle. Start with the letter printed at the top and count the number of letters in its word. Now you know what letter that word begins with and how many letters it has. Look at the list and find the word. Write it in and build from there.

Heat	Sunlight	Change
Mass	Explosion	Concave
Oxygen	Wavelength	Infrared
Convex	Lens	Radiation
Visible	Ozone	Reflection
Spectrum	Energy	Ultraviolet

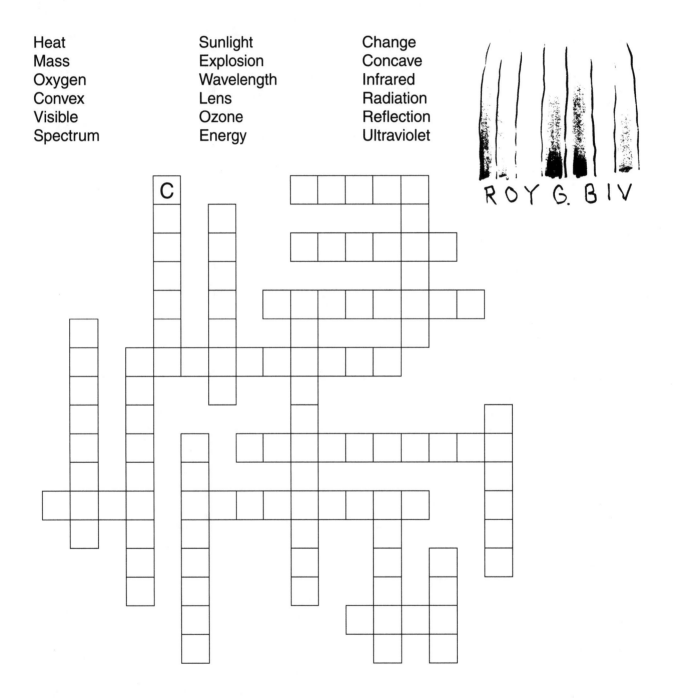

ROY G. BIV

C

Physical SCIENCE

Light and Heat

Across

1 Light travels through the vacuum of space as electromagnetic _____.

6 Part of the spectrum with long wavelengths, easily converted to heat.

7 Energy cannot be created or destroyed; it can only ______ form.

8 A rapid expansion of matter accompanied by heat and light.

10 The ultimate source of almost all the energy on earth.

12 A type of sunlight with wavelengths too short to be seen.

15 Lenses with thin centers and thick edges are called ______ .

16 The ability to do work.

17 The amount of matter in an object.

Down

2 Atmospheric element that, combined with fuel, releases heat and light.

3 Light travels in waves; the color of light is determined by its _____.

4 The process of radiant energy bouncing off a surface.

5 A piece of glass or other transparent material that bends light.

7 Lenses with thick centers and thin edges are called _____.

9 Light energy that can be seen is called _____ light.

11 Electromagnetic waves that carry energy; arranged by wavelength.

13 Molecule in the upper atmosphere that screens out harmful ultraviolet light.

14 A form of energy that makes molecules vibrate faster.

Light and Heat

Unscramble the letters into words and write them in the boxes to the left. Now unscramble the letters in the boxes with circles to find the last word.

OAECVNC

ONZOE

EDWNVLEAHT

ENYCOX

IBSLEVI

Lenses with thick centers and thin edges are called ______.

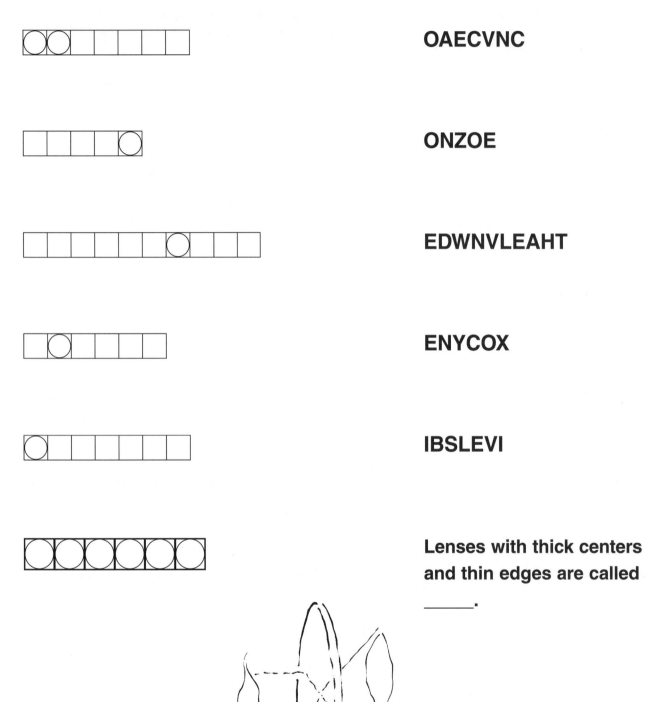

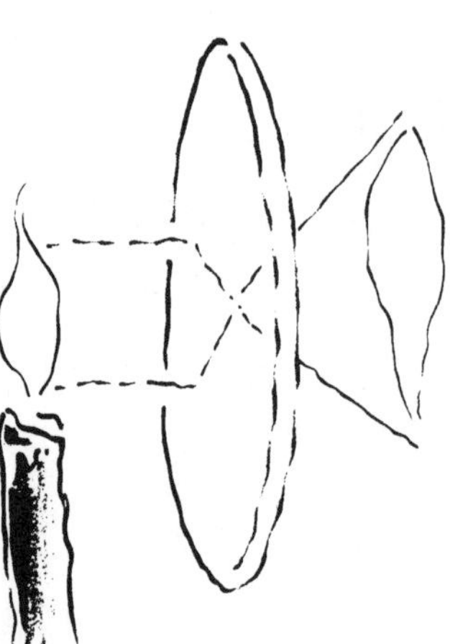

Physical SCIENCE

Simple Machines

This puzzle has two lists—words and definitions. Match the words with their definitions by drawing a line between them.

Words	Definitions
screw	A wheel that changes the direction of force in a rope around it.
inertia	A circular simple machine that has an axle at its center.
friction	A toothed wheel used to transmit energy.
fulcrum	A push or a pull that can move an object.
force	An inclined plane wrapped around a cylinder.
gear	The support point around which a lever moves.
pulley	The tendency of an object to resist a change in motion.
wheel	A force that resists one object's sliding over another.

Simple Machines

This puzzle contains hidden words. They can go up and down, across, at an angle, forward, or back. All the hidden words are in the list below the puzzle. When you find one, circle it and look for another.

```
M H N S T Y E A X L E A E N T S R A
E E C A B I F R S S U T E E O U N S
O P D M I T E A E T U P I H R B H E
R E U L W N F O A E S F M E N P C D
H A D L I N E R T I A R T F M H S D
N K O I L R N D R D O I T A S I A L
P L R I A E W R R M E C R P I R I E
Y H E I D F Y E E K A T S M D A O E
O T M N E L U R D D R I A L R T B T
D U N C E U E L T G O O O S S I T D
T R N O A B T A C C E N E T E O N E
R B F E E R E D A R H D I R I U A E
P I W M T I R F E H U N F D O R A B
R N L E W C F I O C H M E P A O M W
R E H R H A E T R R H A M E H B E A
T E H H E N U T N A C O G S Y R A R
W E E H E T L H T I C E D F C S T T
S R E N L T L E V E R D N S R R T E
```

Compound
Force
Friction
Fulcrum
Gear
Inertia
Lever
Lubricant
Pulley
Ramp
Ratio
Screw
Turbine
Wedge
Wheel
Axle

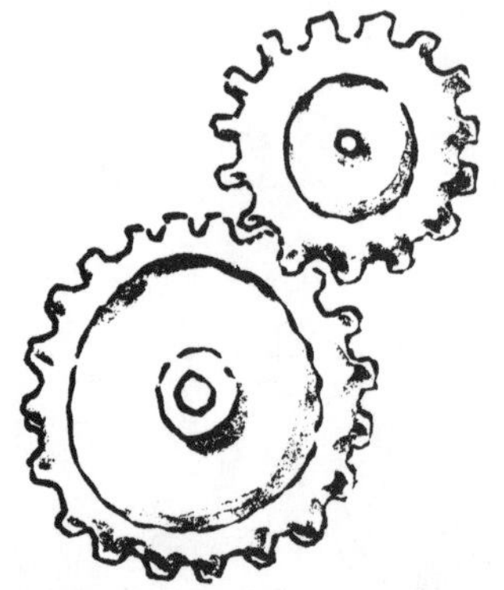

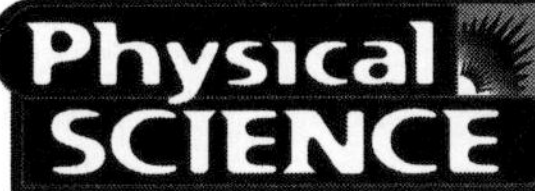

Simple Machines

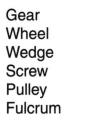

Using the words in the list, you can build your own crossword puzzle. Start with the letter printed at the top and count the number of letters in its word. Now you know what letter that word begins with and how many letters it has. Look at the list and find the word. Write it in and build from there.

Gear
Wheel
Wedge
Screw
Pulley
Fulcrum
Compound
Lubricant
Axle
Lever
Ratio
Force
Inertia
Turbine
Friction

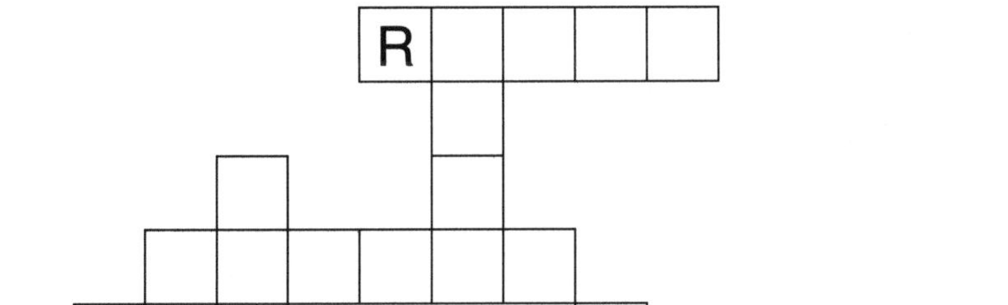

R

Simple Machines

Across

1 The number of times one gear turns another is called its _____.
3 A wheel that changes the direction of force in a rope around it.
5 A circular disk of blades that is moved by a moving fluid.
7 A force that resists one object's sliding over another.
12 A machine that contains two or more simple machines is a _____ machine.
13 A toothed wheel used to transmit energy.
14 A circular simple machine that has an axle at its center.

Down

2 The shaft upon which a wheel rotates.
4 A slippery substance that allows objects to slide easily.
6 The support point around which a lever moves.
8 The tendency of an object to resist a change in motion.
9 An inclined plane used to move objects from one height to another.
10 A push or a pull that can move an object.
11 A long bar that pivots on a fulcrum and can be used to move objects.

Physical SCIENCE

Simple Machines

Unscramble the letters into words and write them in the boxes to the left. Now unscramble the letters in the boxes with circles to find the last word.

IBETRNU

EGRA

FNCRITIO

POOUNDCM

CURUMFL

A slippery substance that allows objects to slide easily.

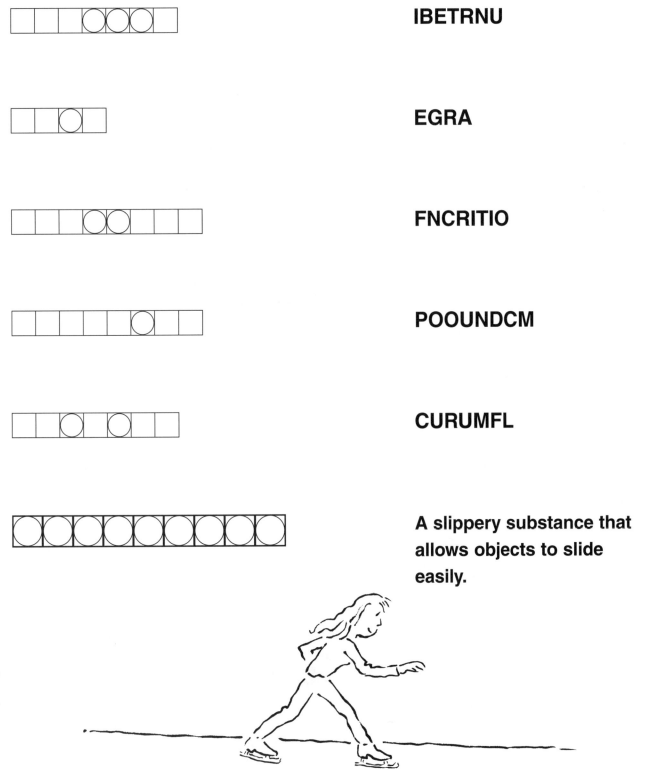

Motion

This puzzle has two lists—words and definitions. Match the words with their definitions by drawing a line between them.

reaction	The process of changing velocity.
kinetic	Work done per unit of time.
pull	Energy that is moving is called _____ energy.
acceleration	A force away from a source.
power	A force toward the source.
inertia	A body that is not moving is said to be at _____.
push	The resistance of a body to changes in motion.
rest	A force that is opposite to an action.

Motion

This puzzle contains hidden words. They can go up and down, across, at an angle, forward, or back. All the hidden words are in the list below the puzzle. When you find one, circle it and look for another.

F S E N E R G Y M H A L L E T E N A

K X R C A N R O L L I N G A T R I L

L I T H S L I D I N G H L E O T E O

H O N E A P T E A R T A C B R V I R

O D E E F M O E M T F N E E E C E C

O P E P T H R T S A A P N G E W N F

R E A U E I T A E T E I S E O M E M

L T R S I D C G S N R H T P D A W D

S E E H E S D I R I T A A E T N T E

T A A N L S D C S A R I E T O N O T

R J C P E L N N S E V P A I V E N D

E E T E O E I S L A S I T L E N R H

A H I R E R M E L F S C T T L H E E

M L O O N R C A O H I E H Y O D S E

L E N E L C E A S R E E G T C R T S

I V T L A A A H F S A A N A I E H R

N S U R E S I S T A N C E E T E L V

E P L O Q M H E F O R C E T Y E I O

Accelerate
Distance
Energy
Force
Friction
Gravity
Inertia
Kinetic
Mass
Newton
Power
Pull
Push
Reaction
Resistance
Rest
Rolling
Sliding
Speed
Streamline
Velocity
Potential

Motion

Using the words in the list, you can build your own crossword puzzle. Start with the letter printed at the top and count the number of letters in its word. Now you know what letter that word begins with and how many letters it has. Look at the list and find the word. Write it in and build from there.

Push	Sliding	Force	Velocity
Power	Distance	Speed	Reaction
Energy	Friction	Newton	Potential
Kinetic	Resistance	Gravity	Streamlining
Rolling	Acceleration	Inertia	

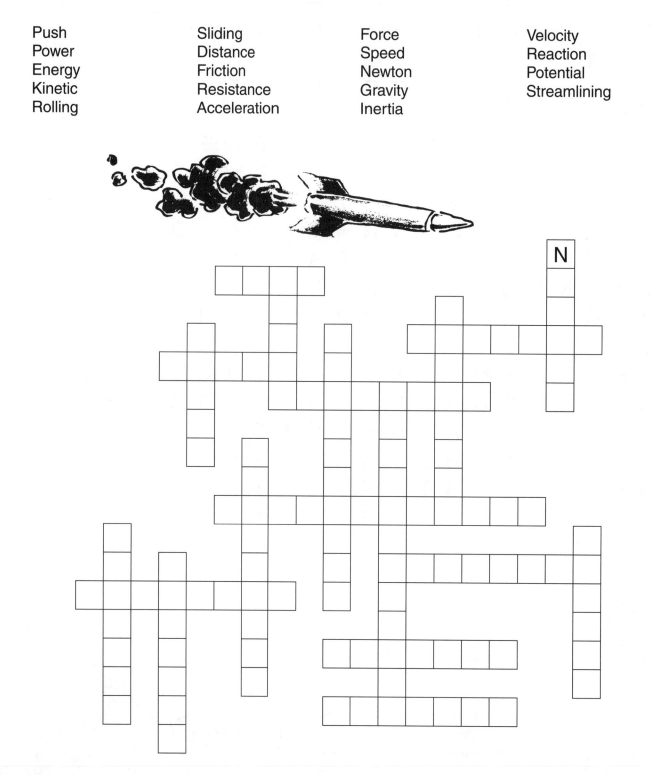

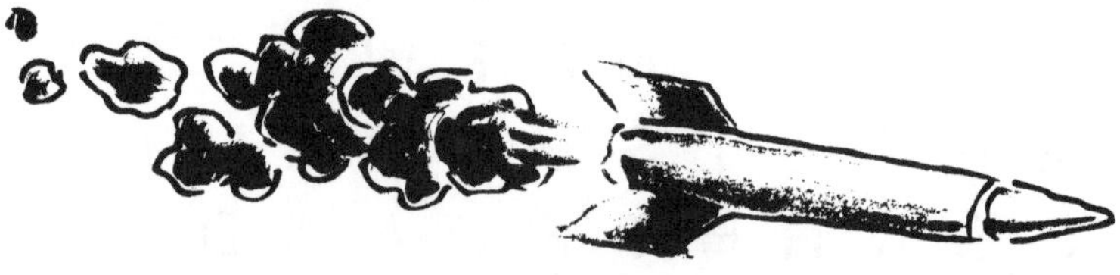

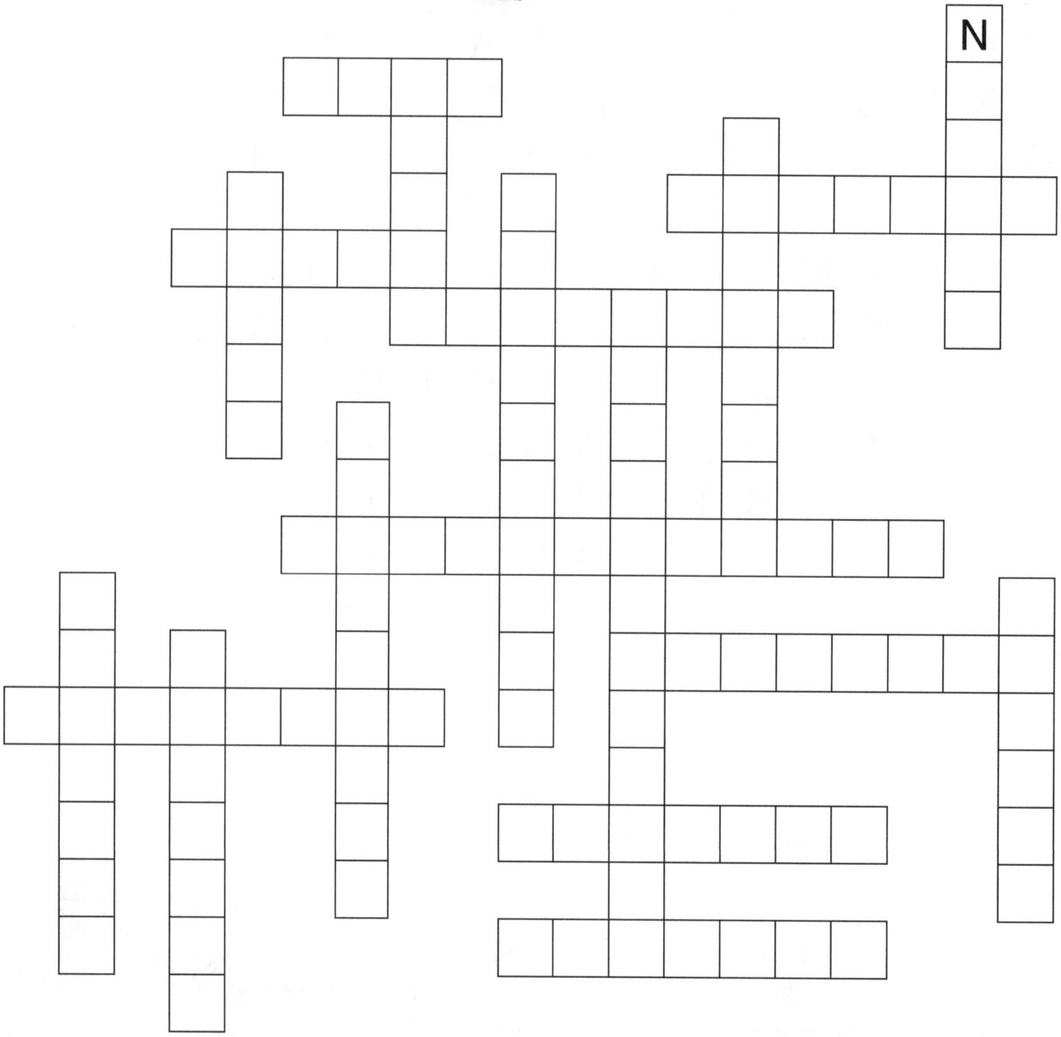

N

Physical SCIENCE Motion

Across

1 A force away from a source.
6 The force of attraction between two bodies.
7 A force that resists one object moving over another.
8 The kind of friction between a wheel and the road.
10 A force that opposes the movement of energy.
13 The process of changing velocity.
15 The British scientist who first described gravity.
16 Energy that is stored is called _____ energy.
17 A push or a pull.
19 Change in position per unit time in a particular direction.
20 The ability to do work.

Down

2 What kind of friction will a car skidding on an icy road show?
3 The amount of space between two points.
4 Work done per unit of time.
5 A force that is opposite to an action.
9 Smoothing an object so that it will move easily through a fluid.
11 The resistance of a body to changes in motion.
12 Energy that is moving is called _____ energy.
14 A measure of motion defined as distance traveled per unit of time.
18 A body that is not moving is said to be at _____.

Motion

Unscramble the letters into words and write them in the boxes to the left. Now unscramble the letters in the boxes with circles to find the last word.

PTEOILATN

IKETICN

FICRINOT

REGEYN

AEIRNTCO

The process of changing velocity.

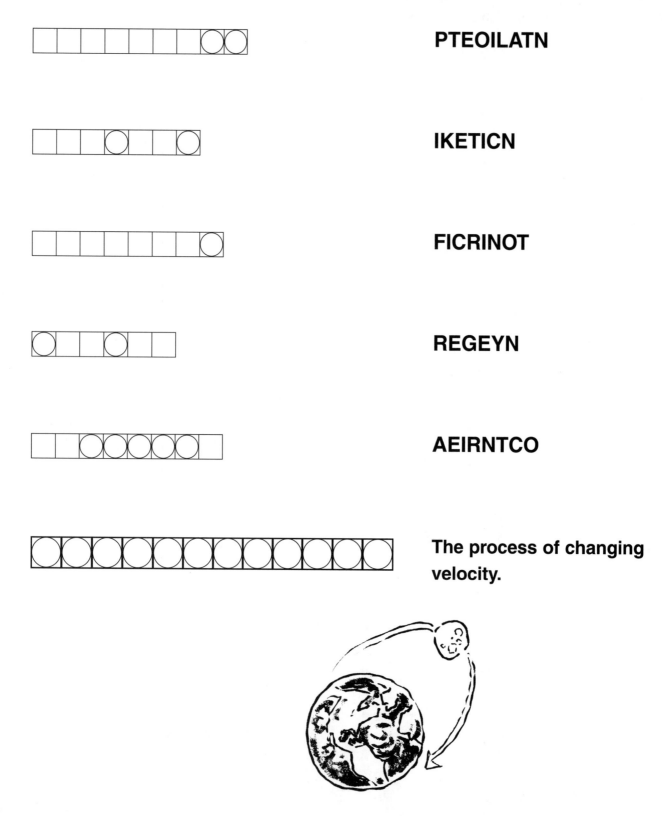

Sound

This puzzle has two lists—words and definitions. Match the words with their definitions by drawing a line between them.

note	The human organ used to detect sound.
pitch	The name given to very low musical notes.
frequency	A musical sound of one frequency
acoustics	The number of times an object vibrates per second.
bass	An object vibrating in response to sound is _____.
ear	How high or low the frequency of a sound is.
resonating	When a sound can be heard it is called _____.
audible	The study of how sound behaves.

Sound

This puzzle contains hidden words. They can go up and down, across, at an angle, forward, or back. All the hidden words are in the list below the puzzle. When you find one, circle it and look for another.

```
T D H S J P O P H U R T A D M I S L
P L D D C R E J F F D N I T T N O M
O J R H E E M Z E S A F E L O D D N
E C D D E U O H V R T T O I E J H A
F R E Q U E N C Y O C R T I E E M D
F H A S K O T E R R L A E D S E T I
A I F R H E R T Z S R U U B G O S U
D S D B H S R B E B P T M O L M R D
S N O A P E E C I B I I E E Y E O E
V O O S I T S V R L X V C O R H Q T
D H R S L L O E P N A P L E M E C A
E T T H I I N M T W W I L P E X D R
C E E V W O A I S E I B O P T E W H
I Q N C D T T Z N L I E E J I E T U
B A O I P S E O U D O E E E T T I G
E T D I W P X Q U A C O U S T I C S
L G B S H N D A O M O E C R I F I H
S E F T E W O N O T E U E L E A R T
```

Amplitude
Audible
Bass
Deaf
Decibels
Ear
Frequency
Hertz
Pitch
Resonate
Vibrations
Wave
Acoustics
Note
Anvil
Volume
Treble

Sound

Using the words in the list, you can build your own crossword puzzle. Start with the letter printed at the top and count the number of letters in its word. Now you know what letter that word begins with and how many letters it has. Look at the list and find the word. Write it in and build from there.

Ear	Vibrates	Hertz
Wave	Frequency	Treble
Pitch	Resonating	Audible
Anvil	Deaf	Amplitude
Volume	Bass	Acoustics

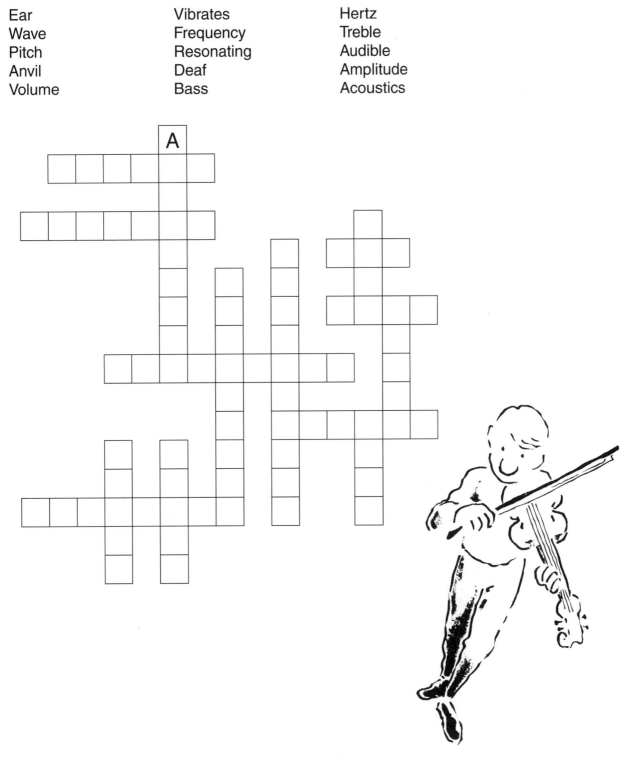

Sound

Across

2 Unable to hear; hearing impaired.
3 The middle ear has three bones—the hammer, the _____, and stirrup.
8 The unit used to measure the frequency of sound.
9 A measure of the amount of energy in a sound.
12 An object vibrating in response to a sound is _____.
14 The name given to the higher musical notes.
16 Units used to measure sound, equal to one-tenth of a bel.

Down

1 How high or low the frequency of a sound is.
3 The study of how sound behaves.
4 When a sound can be heard, it is called _____.
5 A musical sound of one frequency.
6 The loudness of a sound.
7 The number of times an object vibrates per second.
10 When an object _____ it creates a sound.
11 Sound travels in the form of a _____.
13 The human organ used to detect sound.
15 The name given to very low musical notes.

Sound

Unscramble the letters into words and write them in the boxes to the left. Now unscramble the letters in the boxes with circles to find the last word.

CDESLBEI

PTCHI

ASSB

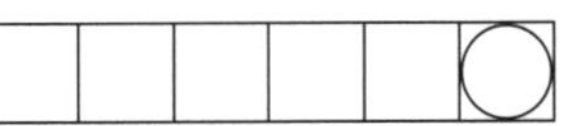

OVEMLU

BTRSIVEA

The name given to the higher musical notes.

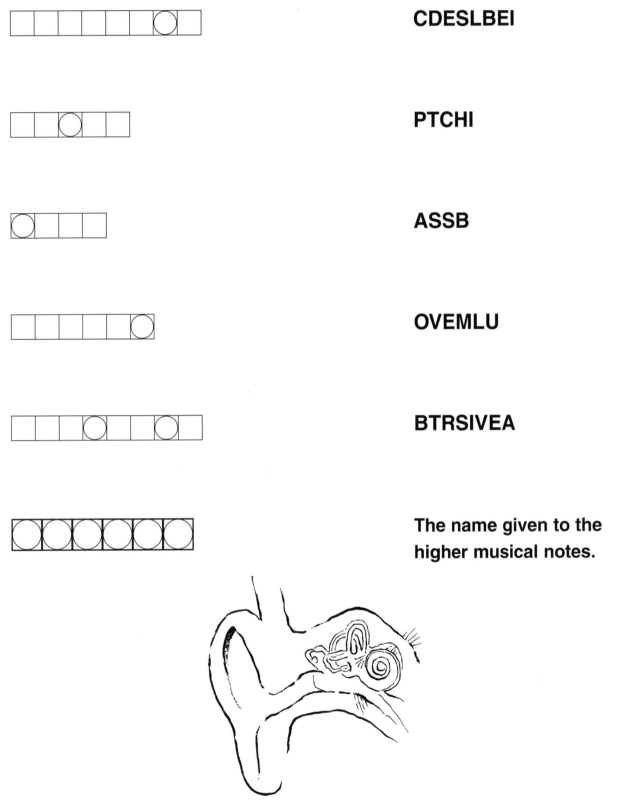

The Human BODY

Digestion

This puzzle has two lists—words and definitions. Match the words with their definition by drawing a line between them.

energy	A large organ that secretes bile.
intestines	A measure of the energy content of food.
villi	A long tube where food and water are absorbed into the blood.
food	Fingerlike projections in the small intestine, where food is absorbed.
stomach	End product made available to the body by digestion and respiration.
omnivore	A nourishing substance that provides nutrients to the body.
liver	A large muscular organ that thoroughly mixes food with enzymes.
calories	An organism that eats both plants and animals.

Human Body | # Digestion

This puzzle contains hidden words. They can go up and down, across, at an angle, forward, or back. All the hidden words are in the list below the puzzle. When you find one, circle it and look for another.

```
E C L R U S M I V E P T M S F S O E
G R E J S I I V R H R A U E E Y T V
A I C S A L I F Y E E G N I F S Y A
S A I T L A E N V R A R R C A O G A
T H E I I I N I T H T O E W R L O A
R E V W V S L S P D L E F O E E U D
I A I L A M D O A A S B I L E A A I
C D S X P O S T C W E H H R I R Y S
P S F U O E I N T E S T I N E S I I
W O T L G M B L R D S S D W F E E S
P X B E E A N W L O I E N Z Y M E S
R Y S T E C R I T E A O E H S P Y T
O G T L C L N R V T S N O N N S E E
T E O X T C A R B O H Y D R A T E N
E N M M E N M A N T R H I A R T E E
I W A S O T S N Q S N E N H M O C R
N E C H E W J F A T A C I D C A T G
T E H I R F O A E N U T R I E N T Y
```

Gastric
Bile
Saliva
Calories
Energy
Stomach
Esophagus
Bloodstream

Fat
Chew
Food
Intestines
Liver
Carbohydrate
Nutrient
Enzymes

Omnivore
Acid
Oxygen
Pancreas
Protein
Sugar
Villi
Waste

Digestion

Using the words in the list, you can build your own crossword puzzle. Start with the letter printed at the top and count the number of letters in its word. Now you know what letter that word begins with and how many letters it has. Look at the list and find the word. Write it in and build from there.

Fat	Chewing	Blood	Calories
Food	Nutrient	Saliva	Esophagus
Oxygen	Pancreas	Gastric	Carbohydrates
Energy	Intestines	Stomach	
Protein	Acid	Omnivore	

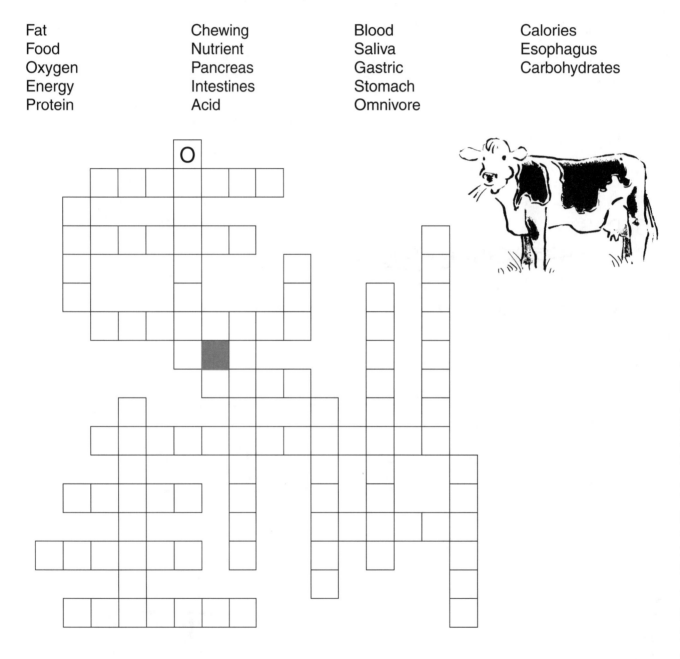

Digestion

Across

4 A sweet carbohydrate.
5 One of the three main classes of food. It contains amino acids.
7 Having to do with the stomach.
8 An organism that eats both plants and animals.
9 One of the three main classes of foods. It is in many oils.
11 A muscular tube that connects the throat with the stomach.
12 A measure of energy content of food.
15 A long tube where food is absorbed into the blood.
16 A large muscular organ that thoroughly mixes food with enzymes.
17 A gas from the atmosphere necessary for getting energy out of food.

Down

1 A substance that provides nourishment to an organism.
2 A large gland that secretes stomach enzymes and hormones to the blood.
3 Contains the enzyme used in the first step in digestion.
6 A class of foods that includes sugars and starches.
10 Chemicals that are essential in the digestion of certain foods.
12 The first step in digestion.
13 Made available to the body through digestion and respiration.
14 The liquid tissue that carries nutrients from digestion to the body.

Human Body

Digestion

Unscramble the letters into words and write them in the boxes to the left. Now unscramble the letters in the boxes with circles to find the last word.

NIROMVOE

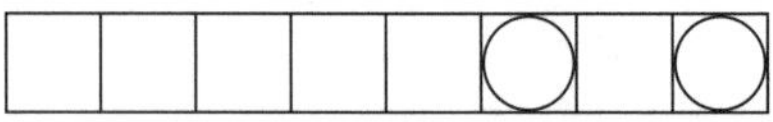

INERUNTT

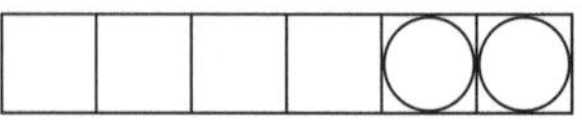

OEACRISL

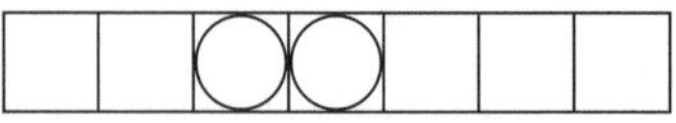

OYNEXG

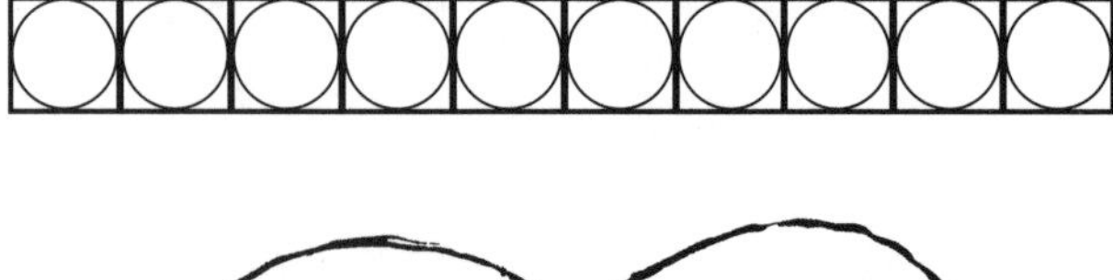

TRAGCSI

A long tube where food and water are absorbed into the blood.

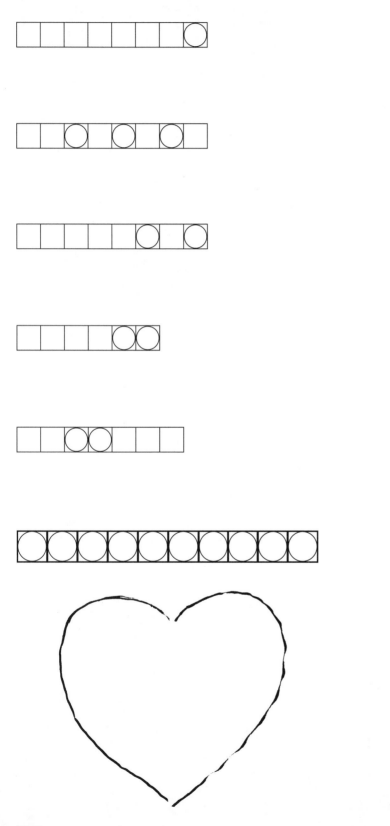

Circulation

This puzzle has two lists—words and definitions. Match the words with their definition by drawing a line between them.

cilia

blood

waste

muscle

heart

artery

venule

atrium

A blood vessel that carries blood away from the heart.

Tiny hairs that sweep dust and dirt out of the respiratory system.

A muscular organ that pumps blood through the body.

The only liquid tissue in the body.

What the blood carries away from the cells.

A tissue that can contract and relax.

The chamber of the heart that receives blood from the body.

The smallest branch of a vein.

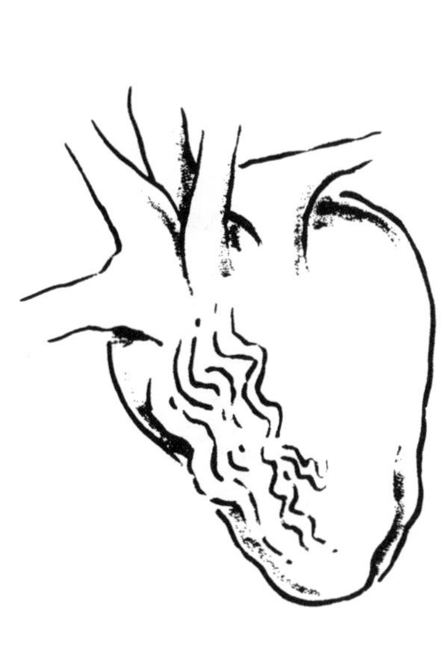

Circulation

This puzzle contains hidden words. They can go up and down, across, at an angle, forward, or back. All the hidden words are in the list below the puzzle. When you find one, circle it and look for another.

```
G R C B G V Y E Z W C X R E P E
C B C O A K G Y R O I L U Z C Y
G B E X W A D I U G L P L E A Y
E L L Q J A R T E R I O L E P L
I C C O Y Z P T H L A C L N I D
V K I X O X Y G E N I C Y K L W
L O K W U D B A O R S R T O L J
O L B X T X E H T U Y O S D A V
H S W R R V H N M R Y N P J R E
R W A V D F E O E D I J D Z Y N
N E S O L V L H H E H U B L T U
H S T X R F R V V R R S M S X L
Q A E K A T V K R Z J V G Z P E
E C O N T R A C T I O N S H F B
W B R E A T H I N G U W D J Y V
G K A D L D D H G L S G B H X B
```

Contraction
Capillary
Arteriole
Artery
Muscle
Blood
Lungs
Heart
Vein

Breathing
Ventricle
Venule
Oxygen
Atrium
Cilia
Aorta
Waste

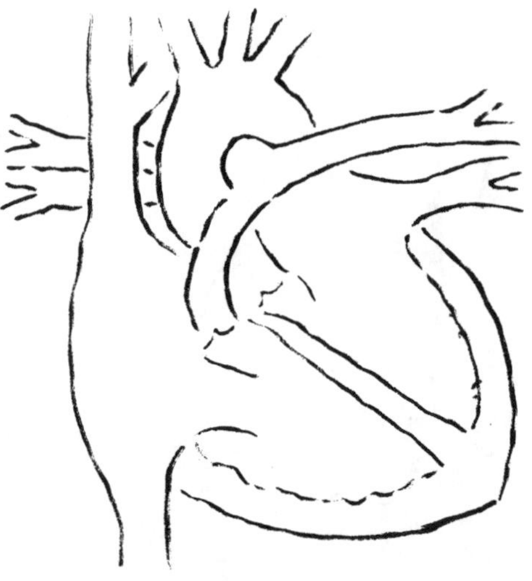

Circulation

Using the words in the list, you can build your own crossword puzzle. Start with the letter printed at the top and count the number of letters in its word. Now you know what letter that word begins with and how many letters it has. Look at the list and find the word. Write it in and build from there.

Vein
Blood
Aorta
Atrium
Oxygen
Artery
Capillary
Breathing
Vein
Waste
Heart
Lungs
Venule
Muscle
Ventricle
Arteriole
Contraction

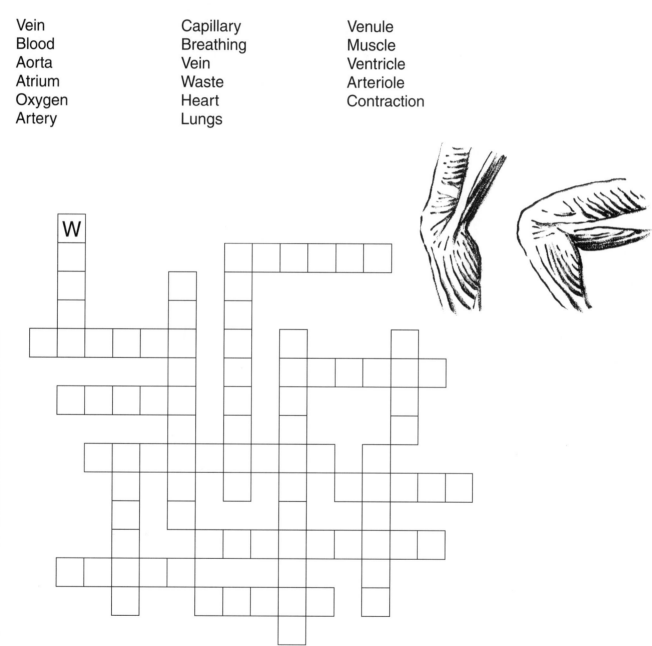

W

Circulation

Across

3 The only liquid tissue in the body.
6 What the blood carries away from the cells.
8 An element in the air that is essential for respiration.
9 A muscular organ that pumps blood through the body.
10 A tiny blood vessel that connects an arteriole to a venule.
13 Sack-shaped respiratory organs where blood picks up oxygen.
14 Tiny hairs that sweep dust and dirt out of the respiratory system.
15 The chamber in the heart that pumps blood out to parts of the body.
16 A blood vessel that carries blood toward the heart.

Down

1 The main artery leading from the heart.
2 A blood vessel that carries blood away from the heart.
4 The smallest branch of an artery.
5 The process of inhaling and exhaling air.
7 A muscle shortening, such as when the heart forces blood into arteries.
11 The chamber of the heart that receives blood from the body.
12 A tissue that can contract and relax.
15 The smallest branch of a vein.

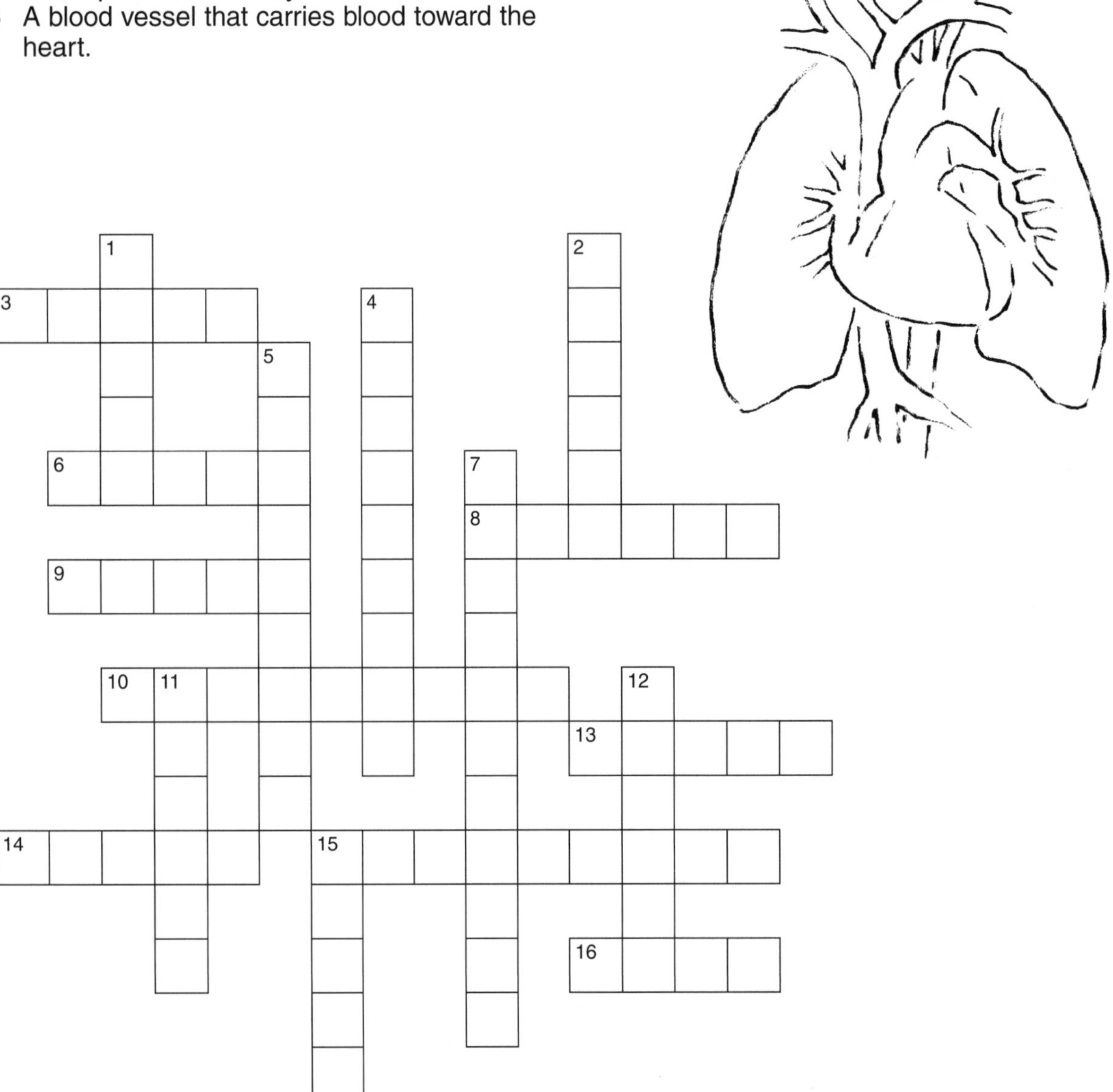

Circulation

Unscramble the letters into words and write them in the boxes to the left. Now unscramble the letters in the boxes with circles to find the last word.

RCOCITTNONA

AYCIALRPL

IENV

ORATA

IEHTBNRAG

The smallest branch of an artery.

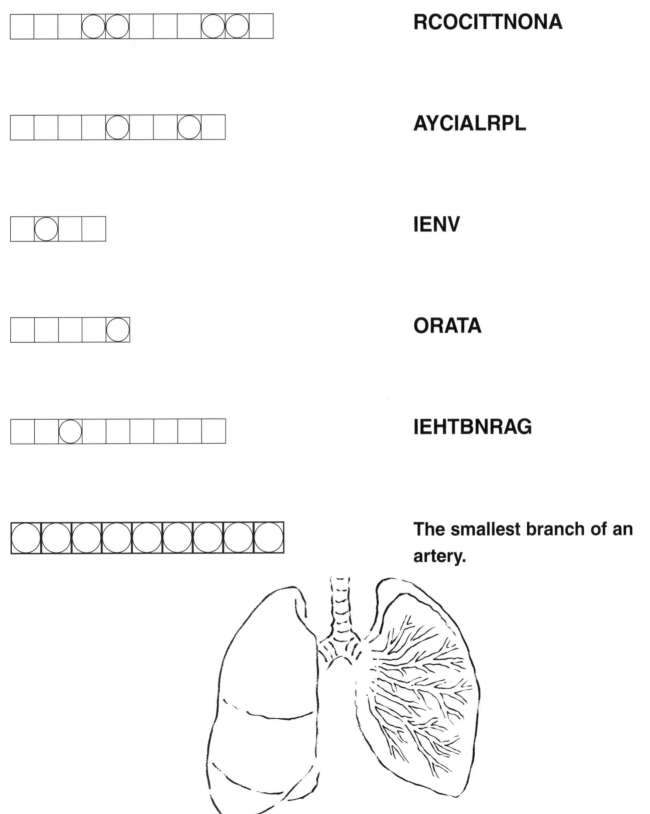

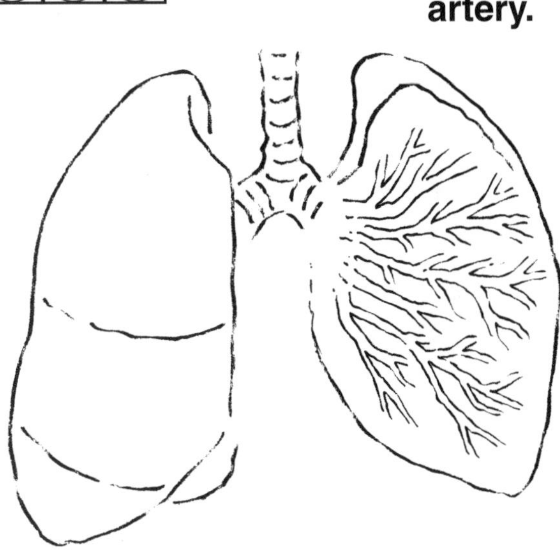

Human Heredity

This puzzle has two lists—words and definitions. Match the words with their definition by drawing a line between them.

radiation	A thin covering over a cell part, such as the nucleus.
membrane	An individual whose heredity prevents the production of skin pigment.
evolution	The part of a cell that contains most of its DNA.
inheritance	Energy from outside the cell that is responsible for many mutations.
gene	The characteristics transmitted from parent to offspring.
nucleus	The name of the American on the team that explained the structure of the DNA molecule.
albino	A change in the genes of a species over a long period of time.
Watson	The part of a chromosome that provides instructions for a trait.

Human Heredity

This puzzle contains hidden words. They can go up and down, across, at an angle, forward, or back. All the hidden words are in the list below the puzzle. When you find one, circle it and look for another.

M	O	R	A	E	N	P	Q	D	D	D	M	D	Y	N
B	N	I	B	C	U	L	K	R	B	I	J	B	C	U
R	U	H	P	J	E	Y	C	A	L	R	H	Y	U	O
C	F	A	B	M	E	N	D	E	L	O	G	T	R	P
L	E	M	D	M	O	P	A	R	Y	T	A	X	E	I
E	E	Q	E	I	N	H	E	R	I	T	A	N	C	E
U	O	M	U	T	A	T	I	O	N	D	F	E	D	S
B	C	X	O	O	T	G	V	D	V	E	G	S	R	E
S	E	L	E	C	T	I	O	N	N	X	E	S	W	I
T	R	E	F	B	N	S	O	A	A	S	Y	I	K	P
U	J	I	I	D	A	B	R	N	A	L	S	V	E	F
I	M	F	I	N	Y	B	K	E	R	G	B	E	I	G
I	C	H	R	O	M	O	S	O	M	E	W	I	C	S
T	E	N	H	E	L	I	X	U	M	N	Z	D	N	G
M	Q	Q	M	A	D	D	W	J	M	E	T	Z	C	O

Inheritance
Recessive
Selection
Membrane
Nucleus
Mendel
Helix
Radiation
Copied
DNA
Chromosome
Disease
Mutation
Albino
Gene
RNA

Human Heredity

Using the words in the list, you can build your own crossword puzzle. Start with the letter printed at the top and count the number of letters in its word. Now you know what letter that word begins with and how many letters it has. Look at the list and find the word. Write it in and build from there.

RNA	Diseases	Helix	Radiation
Gene	Selection	Mendel	Evolution
Copied	Recessive	Mutation	Inheritance
Nucleus	Chromosome	Dominant	
Membrane	DNA	Reproduce	

Human Heredity

Across

1 The body inside a cell that contains most of its DNA.
4 A permanent change in the DNA of a cell.
6 Children resemble parents because DNA molecules can ______ .
7 The part of a chromosome that provides instructions for a trait.
8 A gene that does not express itself when paired with a dominant gene.
11 The characteristics transmitted from parent to offspring.
15 The process that determines which genes survive.
16 Energy from outside the cell that is responsible for many mutations.
17 Initials of the chemical deoxyribonucleic acid.
18 Cystic fibrosis and sickle cell anemia are genetic _______ .

Down

2 A change in the genes of a species over a long period of time.
3 A medieval monk who first published the laws that govern inheritance.
5 A thin covering over a cell part such as the nucleus.
9 A long, threadlike molecule that includes genes.
10 Initials of the chemical ribonucleic acid.
12 An individual whose heredity prevents the production of skin pigment.
13 Traits are passed along when chromosomes are _______ .
14 The spiral shape of the DNA molecule is called a _______ .

Human Body

Human Heredity

Unscramble the letters into words and write them in the boxes to the left. Now unscramble the letters in the boxes with circles to find the last word.

GEEN

NELMED

EOMROCOHSM

NSUUECL

ILUOVETNO

The process that determines which genes survive.

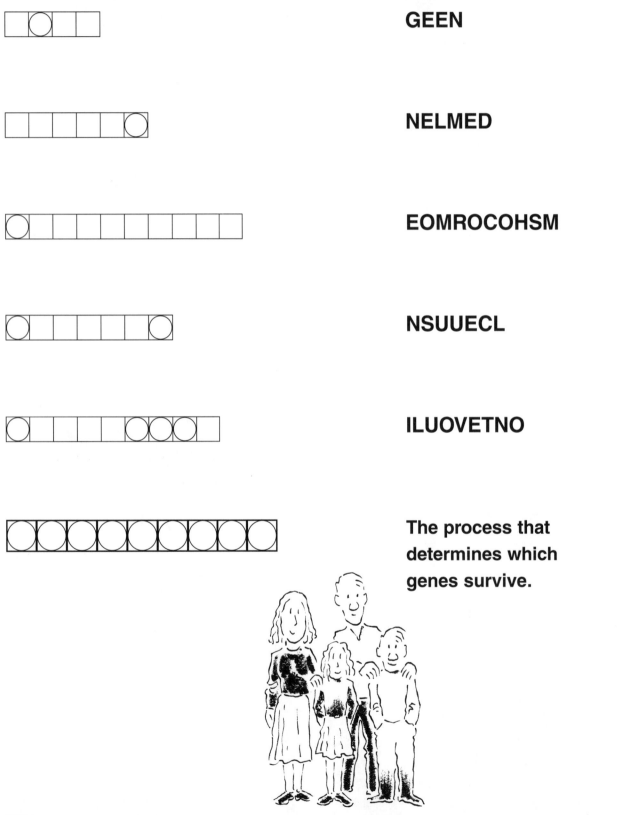

Hygiene

This puzzle has two lists—words and definitions. Match the words with their definition by drawing a line between them.

germs	A condition of poor health.
vaccination	A disease or disorder caused by disease germs in the body.
disease	The foods usually eaten by a person.
immune	Microorganisms that cause disease.
infection	Protected from disease.
exercise	Chemicals used to alter the way the body works.
diet	Protecting people from disease by inoculating with a vaccine.
drugs	A process that requires activity; usually used to develop fitness.

Human Body

Hygiene

This puzzle contains hidden words. They can go up and down, across, at an angle, forward, or back. All the hidden words are in the list below the puzzle. When you find one, circle it and look for another.

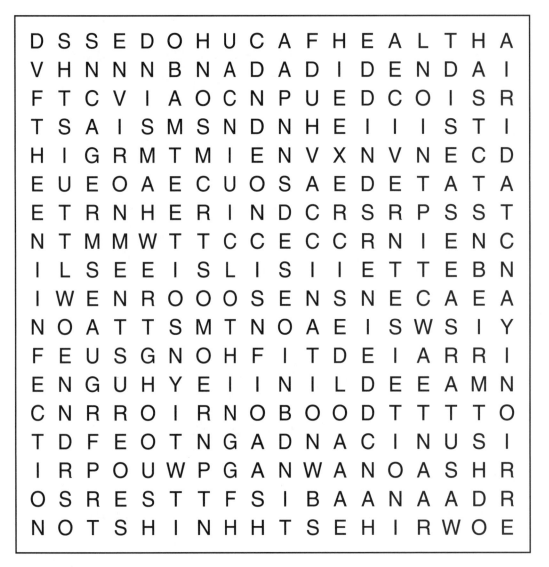

```
D S S E D O H U C A F H E A L T H A
V H N N N B N A D A D I D E N D A I
F T C V I A O C N P U E D C O I S R
T S A I S M S N D N H E I I I S T I
H I G R M T M I E N V X N V N E C D
E U E O A E C U O S A E D E T A T A
E T R N H E R I N D C R S R P S S T
N T M M W T T C C E C C R N I E N C
I L S E E I S L I S I I E T T E B N
I W E N R O O O S E N S N E C A E A
N O A T T S M T N O A E I S W S I Y
F E U S G N O H F I T D E I A R R I
E N G U H Y E I I N I L D E E A M N
C N R R O I R N O B O O D T T T T O
T D F E O T N G A D N A C I N U S I
I R P O U W P G A N W A N O A S H R
O S R E S T T F S I B A A N A A D R
N O T S H I N H H T S E H I R W O E
```

Adolescent
Washing
Vaccination
Drugs
Bones
Clothing
Disease
Bacteria
Exercise
Germs
Diet
Growth
Health
Immune
Environment
Infection
Nutrition
Rest
Sanitary

Hygiene

Using the words in the list, you can build your own crossword puzzle. Start with the letter printed at the top and count the number of letters in its word. Now you know what letter that word begins with and how many letters it has. Look at the list and find the word. Write it in and build from there.

Rest	Bacteria	Health
Germs	Nutrition	Disease
Immune	Vaccination	Exercise
Bathing	Soap	Infection
Clothing	Drugs	Environment

Hygiene

Across

2 The foods usually eaten by a person.
4 Protected from disease.
6 Coverings that protect the body and keep it warm.
7 The process of taking in and using food.
10 Protecting people from disease by inoculating with a vaccine.
11 The process of removing dirt and germs from the skin.
12 A process that requires activity; usually used to develop fitness.
14 A condition of poor health.
15 A substance that can remove dirt and bacteria.

Down

1 Microorganisms that cause disease.
3 A disease or disorder caused by disease germs in the body.
5 The conditions surrounding an individual or place.
8 Tiny organisms, some of which can cause infectious disease.
9 Clean, free from dirt.
13 A period of inactivity, such as sleep.

Hygiene

Unscramble the letters into words and write them in the boxes to the left. Now unscramble the letters in the boxes with circles to find the last word.

□□□□□◯ **IUMEMN**

□□□□◯ **MGSRE**

□◯□□◯□□ **HIGNASW**

◯□◯□ **IEDT**

□□□□◯ **UDSGR**

A condition of poor health.

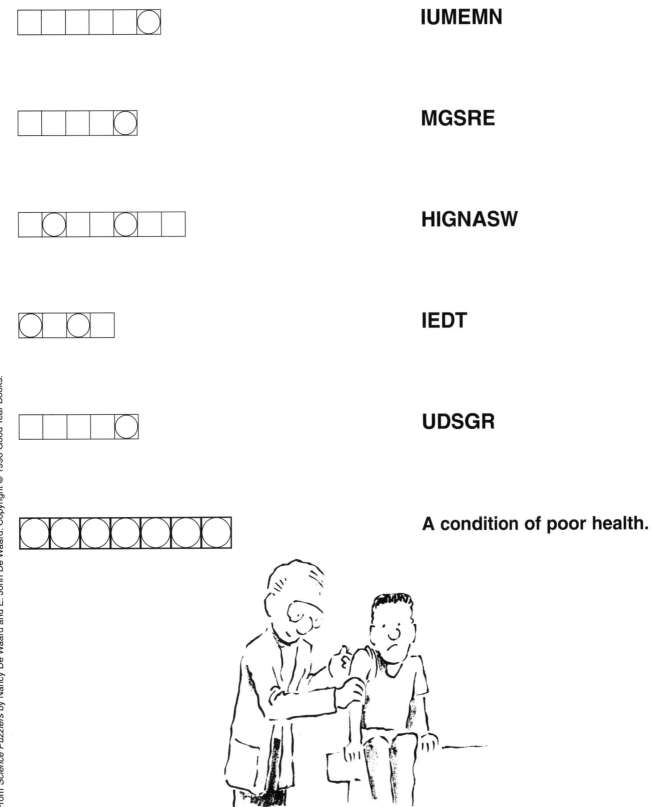

Nutrition and Health

This puzzle has two lists—words and definitions. Match the words with their definition by drawing a line between them.

water	The first meal of the day.
kidneys	Chemicals that are required in small quantities for good health.
metabolism	All the processes necessary to keep an organism alive.
vitamins	A large organ that provides bile and is essential to digestion.
liver	A large muscular organ that mixes food and enzymes during digestion.
heart	A pair of organs that clean your blood of waste.
breakfast	A liquid that makes up most of the body and must be drunk regularly.
stomach	A muscular organ that powers the system that carries food to your body.

Nutrition and Health

This puzzle contains hidden words. They can go up and down, across, at an angle, forward, or back. All the hidden words are in the list below the puzzle. When you find one, circle it and look for another.

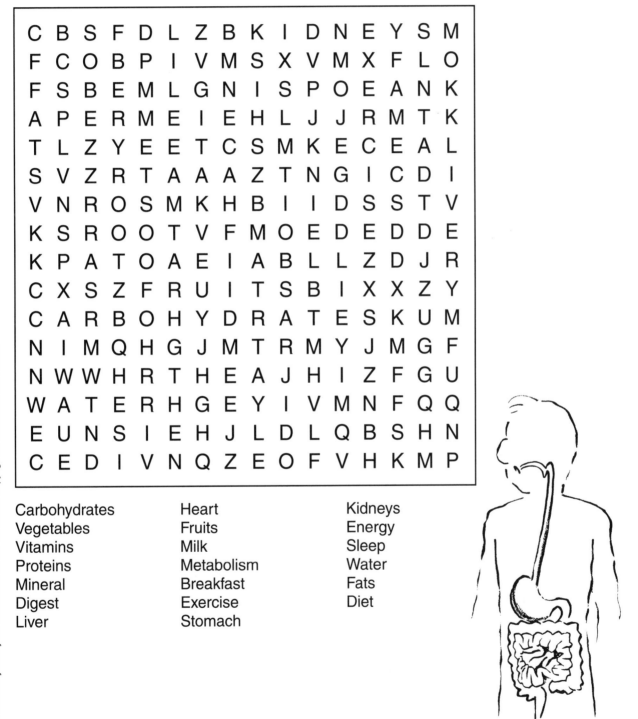

C	B	S	F	D	L	Z	B	K	I	D	N	E	Y	S	M
F	C	O	B	P	I	V	M	S	X	V	M	X	F	L	O
F	S	B	E	M	L	G	N	I	S	P	O	E	A	N	K
A	P	E	R	M	E	I	E	H	L	J	J	R	M	T	K
T	L	Z	Y	E	E	T	C	S	M	K	E	C	E	A	L
S	V	Z	R	T	A	A	A	Z	T	N	G	I	C	D	I
V	N	R	O	S	M	K	H	B	I	I	D	S	S	T	V
K	S	R	O	O	T	V	F	M	O	E	D	E	D	D	E
K	P	A	T	O	A	E	I	A	B	L	L	Z	D	J	R
C	X	S	Z	F	R	U	I	T	S	B	I	X	X	Z	Y
C	A	R	B	O	H	Y	D	R	A	T	E	S	K	U	M
N	I	M	Q	H	G	J	M	T	R	M	Y	J	M	G	F
N	W	W	H	R	T	H	E	A	J	H	I	Z	F	G	U
W	A	T	E	R	H	G	E	Y	I	V	M	N	F	Q	Q
E	U	N	S	I	E	H	J	L	D	L	Q	B	S	H	N
C	E	D	I	V	N	Q	Z	E	O	F	V	H	K	M	P

Carbohydrates
Vegetables
Vitamins
Proteins
Mineral
Digest
Liver

Heart
Fruits
Milk
Metabolism
Breakfast
Exercise
Stomach

Kidneys
Energy
Sleep
Water
Fats
Diet

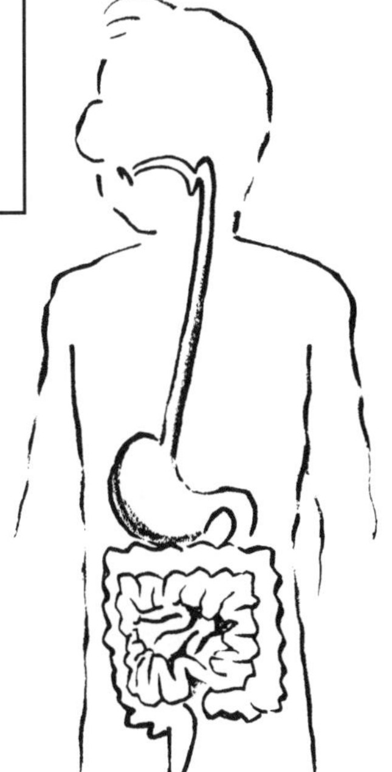

Nutrition and Health

Using the words in the list, you can build your own crossword puzzle. Start with the letter printed at the top and count the number of letters in its word. Now you know what letter that word begins with and how many letters it has. Look at the list and find the word. Write it in and build from there.

Diet	Proteins	Digest
Fats	Metabolism	Mineral
Liver	Carbohydrates	Vitamins
Water	Milk	Breakfast
Kidneys	Sleep	Vegetables
Exercise	Fruit	

V

Nutrition and Health

Across

4 What is released when you burn food inside your body.
6 The first meal of the day.
10 The types and amount of food and drink you consume.
11 The process of moving your muscles to keep them fit.
12 A large group of foods containing starches and sugars.
14 A large group of foods, including meats and grains, that are essential for growth.
15 A large group of foods found in red meat and oils.
16 A pair of organs that clean your blood of waste.
17 A large muscular organ that mixes food and enzymes during digestion.

Down

1 A natural substance, such as iron, needed to maintain health.
2 What you do to food as it passes through your system.
3 A nutritious fluid produced by mammals, usually to feed their young.
5 Plant parts that do not contain seeds and are eaten for food.
7 A liquid that makes up most of the body and must be drunk regularly.
8 Chemicals that are required in small quantities for good health.
9 All the processes necessary to keep an organism alive.
13 A muscular organ that powers the system that carries food to your body.

Human Body

Nutrition and Health

Unscramble the letters into words and write them in the boxes to the left. Now unscramble the letters in the boxes with circles to find the last word.

YSIKDNE

EEGETSVABL

ACOMHTS

YGRENE

IMKL

A natural substance, such as iron, needed to maintain health.

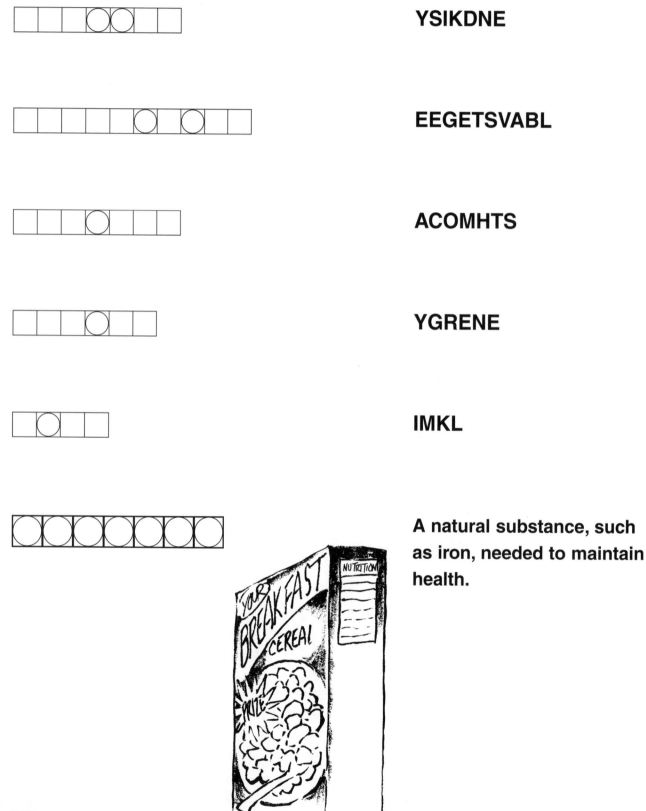

Safety

This puzzle has two lists—words and definitions. Match the words with their definition by drawing a line between them.

hot water	When riding at night, your bike should have one of these in front.
headlight	Each time you ride your bike, what should you test?
poison	The most dangerous chemical in the laboratory (two words).
brakes	When you turn your bike, you should warn others with hand ______.
apron	Your eyes' best friend in the laboratory.
taste	In the laboratory, one of these will protect your clothing.
signals	Unless your teacher tells you to, you should never test for this.
goggles	You should never taste an unknown in the lab because it might be this.

Safety

This puzzle contains hidden words. They can go up and down, across, at an angle, forward, or back. All the hidden words are in the list below the puzzle. When you find one, circle it and look for another.

F	H	T	T	T	C	S	T	A	F	E	H	H	E	R	I	I	H
N	A	F	J	H	L	S	U	E	O	C	E	I	E	I	I	S	S
H	T	T	O	A	E	T	T	E	E	N	E	T	T	E	A	S	T
F	P	E	N	C	O	L	O	D	H	A	A	Q	H	W	Y	G	U
D	B	G	A	O	T	T	M	S	E	W	I	R	T	A	F	O	R
T	I	E	E	H	N	A	T	E	T	E	T	I	W	E	I	G	E
S	A	I	N	E	H	J	R	O	T	I	Y	H	S	E	A	G	S
S	A	S	A	H	H	E	H	E	L	S	T	N	Y	A	E	L	Y
S	A	F	T	N	N	R	A	E	S	O	T	S	M	T	O	E	O
O	R	C	I	E	T	A	P	D	B	D	T	A	B	L	E	S	N
T	R	E	O	S	E	P	N	O	L	D	H	T	O	K	J	O	O
I	F	S	F	C	E	R	F	P	G	I	R	W	L	E	S	H	U
D	B	O	I	L	E	O	E	D	R	E	G	E	S	I	E	R	H
A	F	R	S	O	E	N	F	U	E	C	R	H	O	S	S	I	R
L	E	O	A	N	O	C	A	R	E	E	U	P	T	A	W	A	Y
N	T	E	E	K	S	S	T	P	N	E	E	E	I	F	T	I	L
Y	B	T	N	U	E	P	M	O	E	V	F	E	N	O	E	Y	O
V	G	A	Q	D	I	S	R	S	R	U	R	I	V	I	A	N	H

Helmet
Reflector
Headlight
Goggles
Apron
Poison
Away
Taste
Green
Both Ways
Wash

Brakes
Signals
Symbols
Hot Water

Safety

Using the words in the list, you can build your own crossword puzzle. Start with the letter printed at the top and count the number of letters in its word. Now you know what letter that word begins with and how many letters it has. Look at the list and find the word. Write it in and build from there.

Away
Taste
Green
Helmet
Goggles
Symbols
Both Ways
Reflector
Wash
Apron
Brakes
Poison
Signals
Hot Water
Headlight

Safety

Across

3 You should never taste an unknown in the lab because it might be this.
6 When cutting with a knife you should always cut in this direction.
7 After working in the lab, what should you do with your hands?
9 In the laboratory, one of these will protect your clothing.
10 Never cross a street unless you look ______ (two words).
12 When riding at night, your bike should have one of these on the rear.
13 Your eyes' best friend in the laboratory.
14 Head protection that should always be worn when riding a bike.

Down

1 When you turn your bike, you should warn others with hand ______.
2 The most dangerous chemical in the laboratory (two words).
4 Each time you ride your bike, what should you test?
5 To be safe you should learn the ______ for poison and other dangers.
8 When riding at night, your bike should have one of these in front.
11 Never cross the street unless the traffic light is this color.

Safety

Unscramble the letters into words and write them in the boxes to the left. Now unscramble the letters in the boxes with circles to find the last word.

NARPO

EEGNR

YMBSLOS

ILAHTDHGE

FTRLREOCE

You should never taste an unknown in the lab because it might be this.

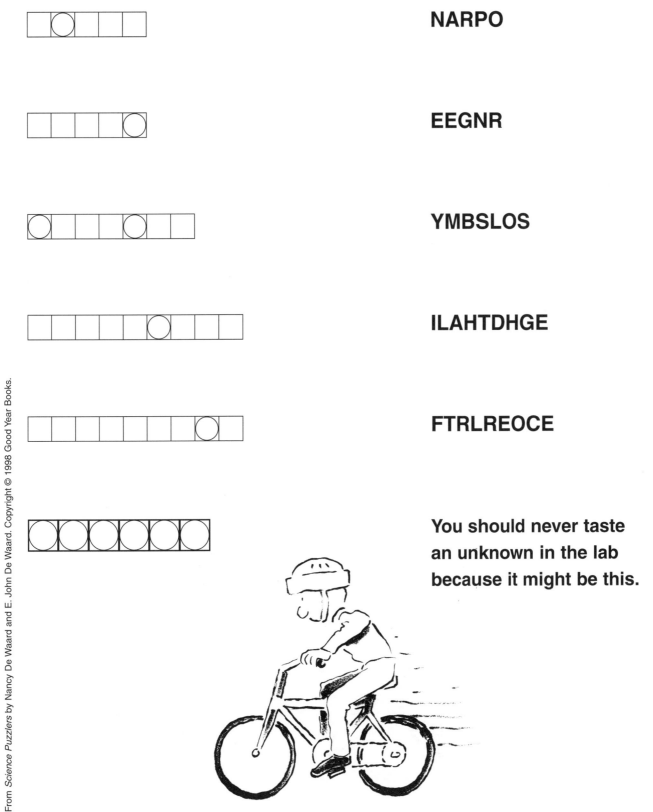

Senses

This puzzle has two lists—words and definitions. Match the words with their definition by drawing a line between them.

inner	The part of the eye where light is focused.
taste	Organs that detect sound waves.
lens	A distinctive smell.
retina	Cells that are responsible for color vision are called ______ cells.
ears	The ear has three main parts: the outer, the middle, and the ______.
cone	The part of the eye that focuses light.
scent	A basic sense that allows you to detect flavors.
iris	The colorful part of the eye.

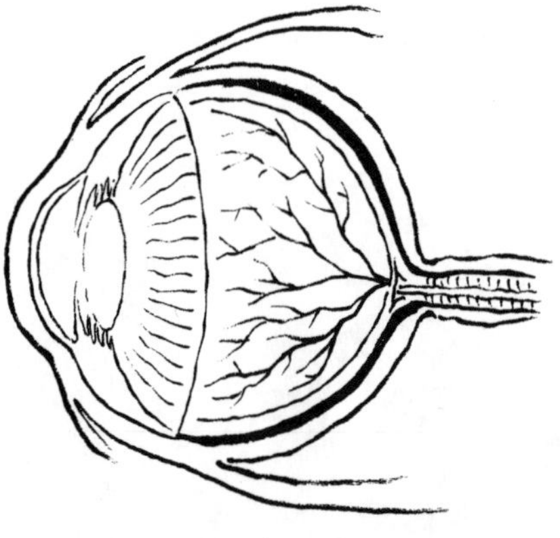

Senses

This puzzle contains hidden words. They can go up and down, across, at an angle, forward, or back. All the hidden words are in the list below the puzzle. When you find one, circle it and look for another.

```
Y E T T A S T E E G A A L C E A T E
C B I T T E R T E I O A I E O E T R
D E A E A E J S C I S T C T E R E N
S I P A O S F S H A P F O L T S O O
A R E T L F S H N O D I L S A I I H
S N B O F O A M S E N T O I S A H A
W A F N A O U D E S R A R I N S A T
E S A G C U T R N L O E V E N N P D
E M O U T C T N R V L N T O H J E T
T O S E O F I H N E V A I I O E L R
I K S E R N B I R I S T H G N A S A
S E E C Y A S A D E A A A R S A O L
N O C G E E Z I L R I E O L S N U T
C E U A E N R E B A P E O G I A N H
R H L R N C T I C S N O E D S G D D
P D A E A A V I R O V C A E O F H R
E W O C N B L A C E E O E O R R E T
O I E A N S E S N T S O T U D C B A
```

Acrid
Balance
Bitter
Canal
Color
Cone
Ears
Inner
Iris
Lens
Light
Nasal
Odor
Olfactory
Optic
Retina
Salt
Scent
Smell
Smoke
Sound
Sour
Sweet
Taste
Tongue
Vibration
Vision

Senses

Using the words in the list, you can build your own crossword puzzle. Start with the letter printed at the top and count the number of letters in its word. Now you know what letter that word begins with and how many letters it has. Look at the list and find the word. Write it in and build from there.

Ears	Optic	Sour	Vision
Lens	Taste	Sweet	Bitter
Scent	Retina	Color	Olfactory
Sound	Balance	Light	
Salty	Vibrations	Inner	
Canal	Iris	Smell	

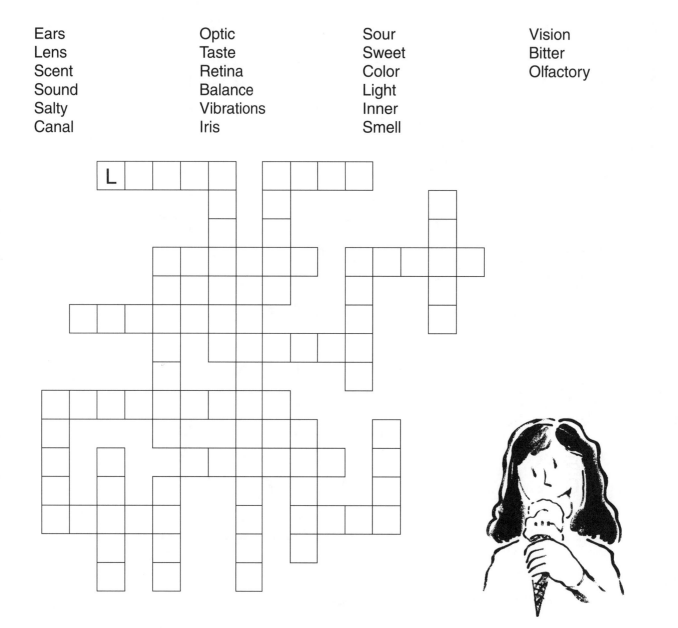

Human Body — Senses

Across

1 One of the four basic tastes: not bitter, salty, or sour.
6 Having to do with the nose.
9 Cells that are responsible for color vision are called ______ cells.
11 Having to do with smell.
14 The process of sensing with the eyes.
15 The part of the eye where light is focused.
17 A distinctive smell.
18 A basic sense, used to detect odors.
21 The colorful part of the eye.
22 One of the four basic tastes: not bitter, salty, or sweet.
23 Vibrations in the air that can be heard.

Down

2 A basic sense that allows you to detect flavors.
3 Periodic movement of matter, sometimes detected as sound.
4 The ear has three main parts: the outer, the middle, and the ______.
5 One of the four basic tastes: not bitter, sweet, or sour.
7 The semicircular canals in your ears are key to this sense.
8 One of the four basic tastes: not sour, sweet, or salty.
10 The nerve that connects the eyes and brain is called the ______ nerve.
12 Visible electromagnetic energy.
13 A passageway from one part of an organ or system to another.
16 Harsh or bitter in smell or taste.
19 Organs that detect vibrations in the atmosphere.
20 The part of the eye that focuses light.

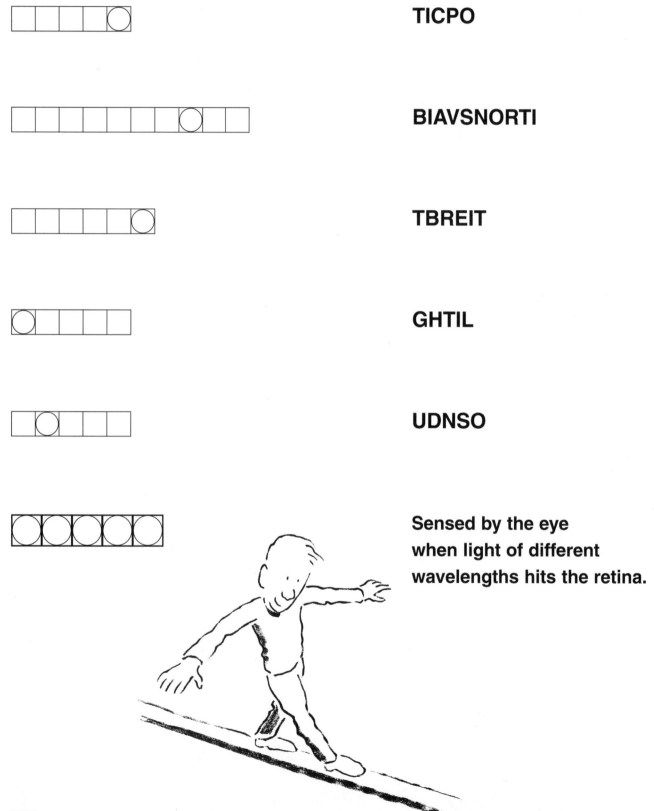

Senses

Unscramble the letters into words and write them in the boxes to the left. Now unscramble the letters in the boxes with circles to find the last word.

TICPO

BIAVSNORTI

TBREIT

GHTIL

UDNSO

Sensed by the eye when light of different wavelengths hits the retina.

Human Body

Skeletal-Muscular System

This puzzle has two lists—words and definitions. Match the words with their definition by drawing a line between them.

ligaments

socket

heart

vertebrae

nerve

triceps

marrow

cartilage

Small circular bones that make up the backbone.

The large muscle on the back of the upper arm.

The flexible part of the nose is supported by this tissue.

A muscle that contracts regularly every day of your life.

The tissue in the center of bones; produces blood cells.

The hip joint is a ball and _______ joint.

The tissue that directs how and when muscles move.

Strong bands of connective tissue that hold bones in place.

Human Body

Skeletal-Muscular System

This puzzle contains hidden words. They can go up and down, across, at an angle, forward, or back. All the hidden words are in the list below the puzzle. When you find one, circle it and look for another.

P O L U T R I C E P S Y H S E R
R V V H V E M G C S P V E O W I
F T H Z M B N Q N L F C A C M J
O Y N C B O C D K Q S U R K M G
O W E H O X A Q O P S U T E W O
G Y W E J N R L E N M C A T B S
S K U L L O T C R E S R U O Z P
Y Q O M I D I R F P B V Z Z L I
J C P H G B L N A E V M G X V N
H R J K A U A M T C U Q M D O E
H P V D M X G R K I T J A V E R
I S W S E W E E C C O H R V N P
P A B I N V O L U N T A R Y X T
K U X D T M A G Q Y M E O L D Q
F D Y Y S C T B N P N O W W W D
W Q N A G I I F O R A K B A J L

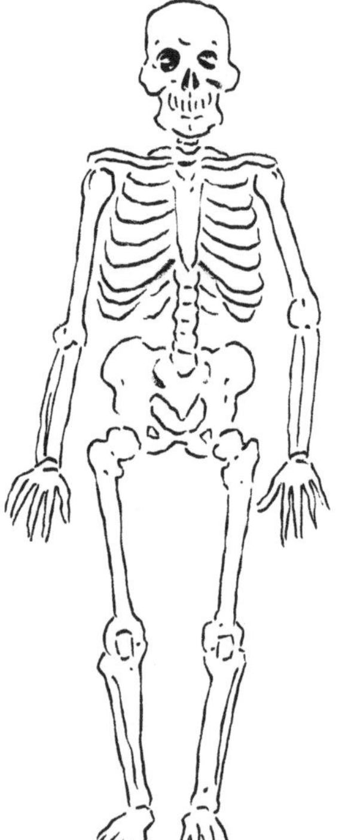

Involuntary
Cartilage
Voluntary
Calcium
Tendons
Biceps

Femur
Spine
Skull
Vertebrae
Ligaments
Contract

Triceps
Marrow
Socket
Heart
Joint
Nerve

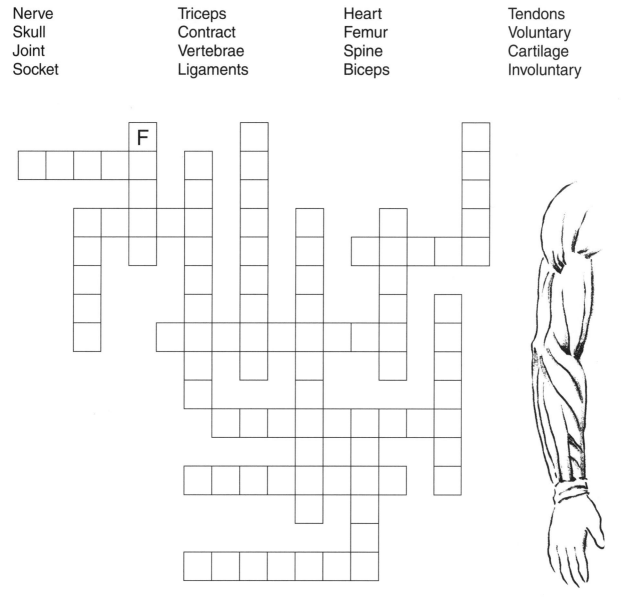

Skeletal-Muscular System

Using the words in the list, you can build your own crossword puzzle. Start with the letter printed at the top and count the number of letters in its word. Now you know what letter that word begins with and how many letters it has. Look at the list and find the word. Write it in and build from there.

Nerve	Triceps	Heart	Tendons
Skull	Contract	Femur	Voluntary
Joint	Vertebrae	Spine	Cartilage
Socket	Ligaments	Biceps	Involuntary

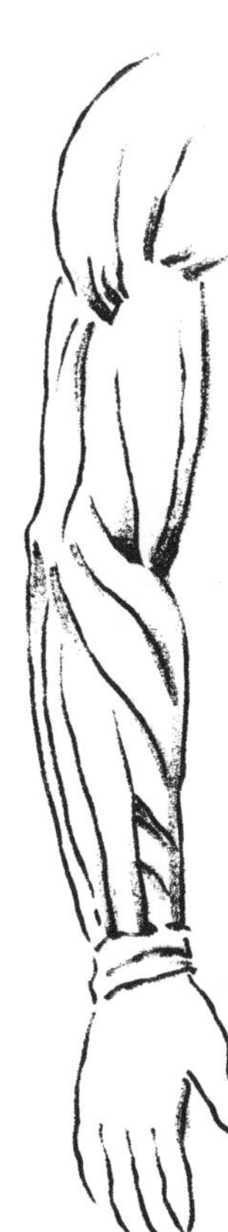

Skeletal-Muscular System

Across

1 Tough tissue that connects a muscle to a bone.
4 The large muscles on your upper arm.
7 A collection of bones fused together that protect the brain.
9 The tissue that directs how and when muscles move.
13 The flexible part of the nose is supported by this tissue.
15 A muscle that contracts regularly every day of your life.
16 The large muscle on the back of the upper arm.
17 The tissue in the center of bones; produces blood cells.

Down

2 Vertebrae stacked on each other make up this.
3 The large bone in your upper leg.
5 Muscles that we can control are called ________ muscles.
6 _________ muscles are those that contract automatically.
8 Strong bands of connective tissue that hold bones in place.
10 Small circular bones that make up the backbone.
11 The point where two bones meet.
12 The hip joint is a ball and _______ joint.
14 A chemical element that is essential to strong bones.

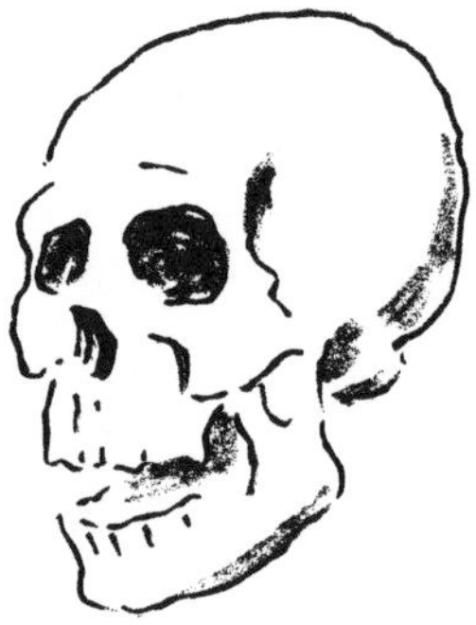

Skeletal-Muscular System

Unscramble the letters into words and write them in the boxes to the left. Now unscramble the letters in the boxes with circles to find the last word.

KULSL

NIPES

IBPSEC

SOENDTN

ACTOCRTN

The hip joint is a ball and _______ joint.

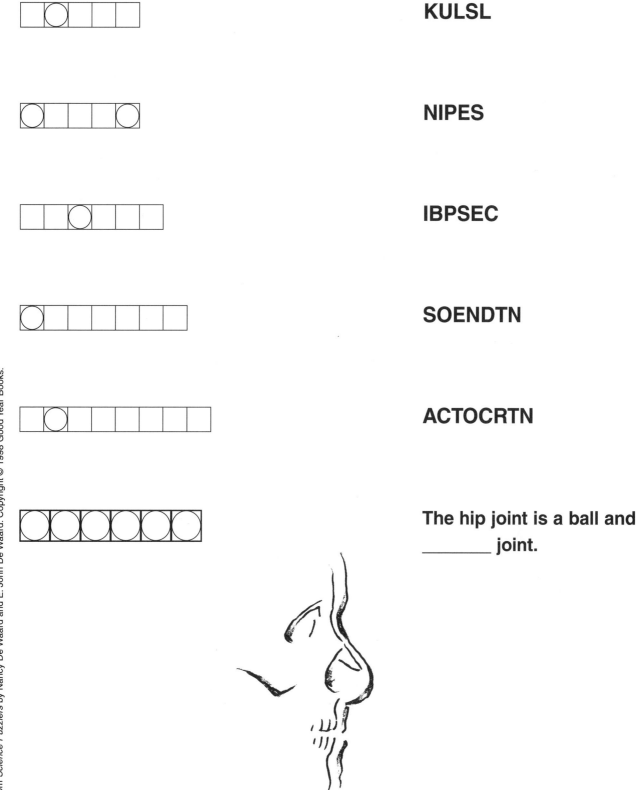

Life SCIENCE Answer Key

Animals

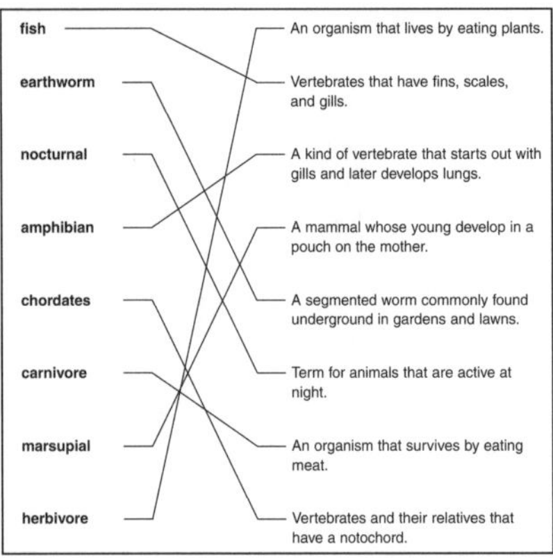

2

PLACENTA
AMPHIBIAN
NOCTURNAL
CHORDATES
TRILOBITE
EARTHWORM
HAIR
CARNIVORE
MARSUPIAL
MATES
HERBIVORE
PREDATOR
VERTEBRATE
FISH
MAMMALS

5

3

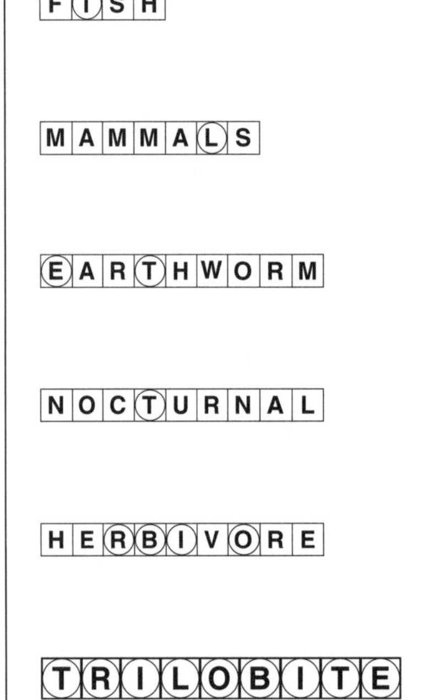

6

HERBIVORE
DINOSAURS
MAMMALS
REPTILE
VERTEBRATE
CARNIVORE
AMPHIBIAN
MARSUPIAL
CHORDATES
EARTHWORM
FISH
SCALES
TRILOBITE

4

Birds

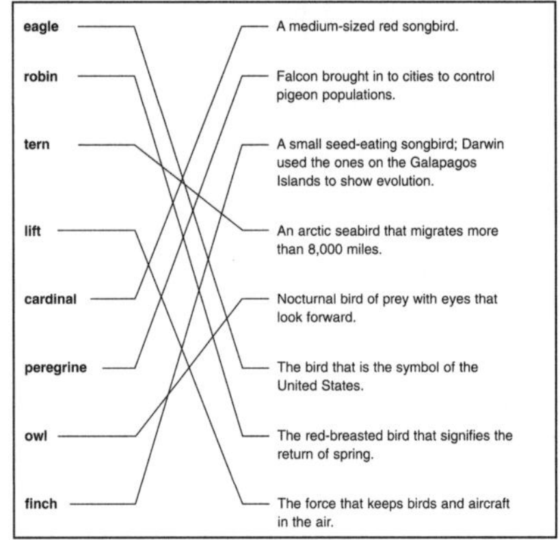

7

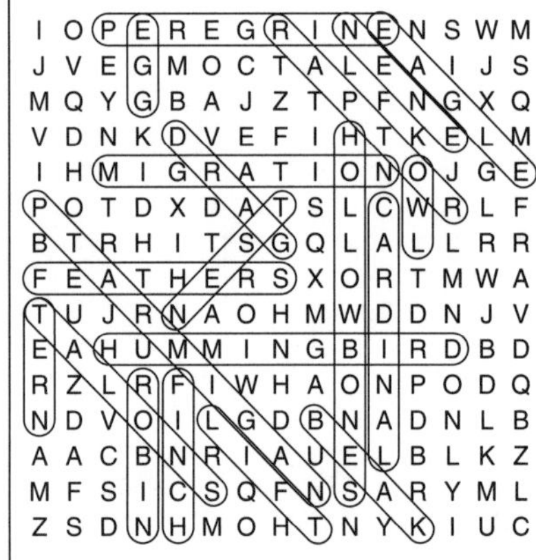

8

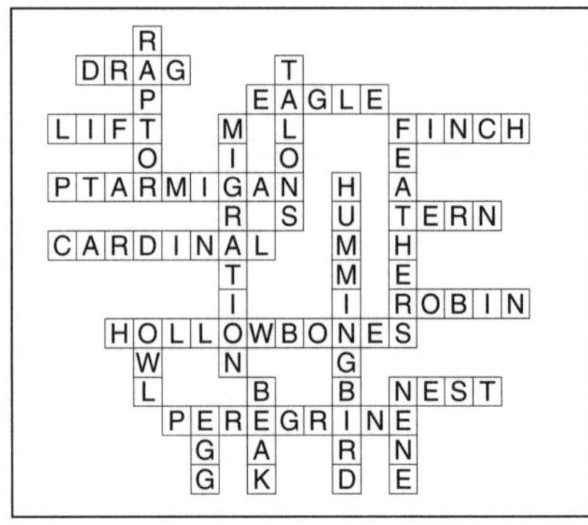

9

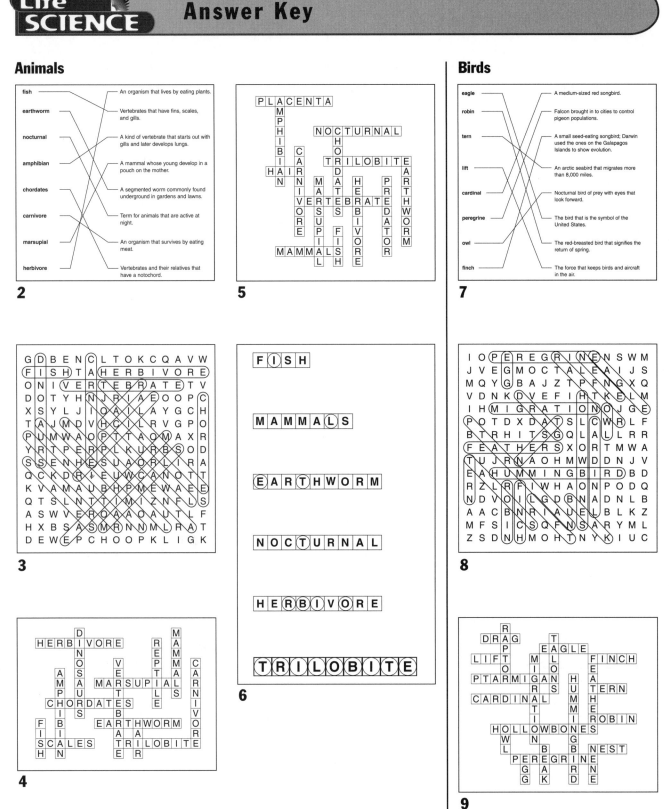

10

11

Plants

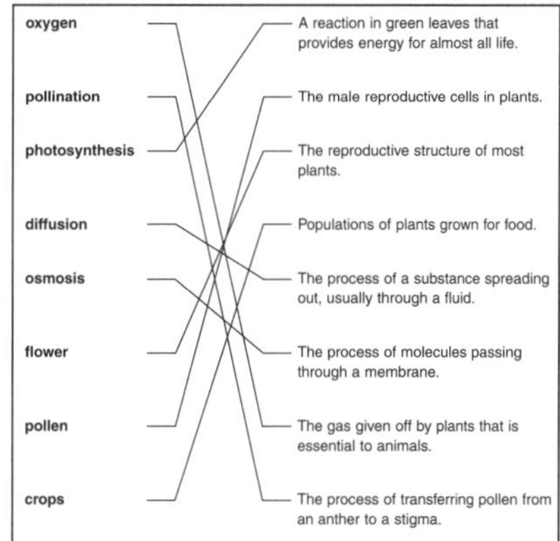

12

13

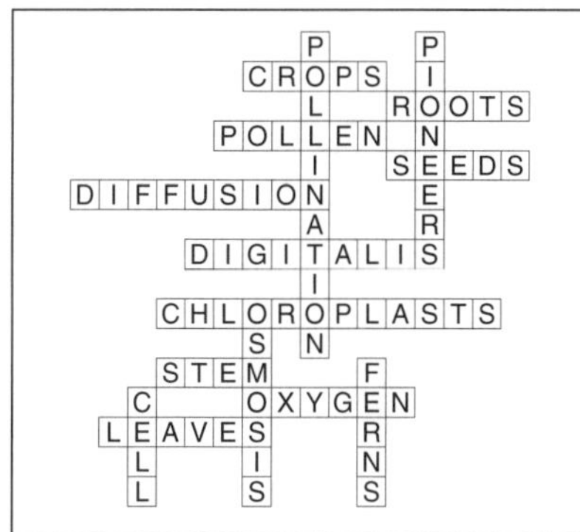

14

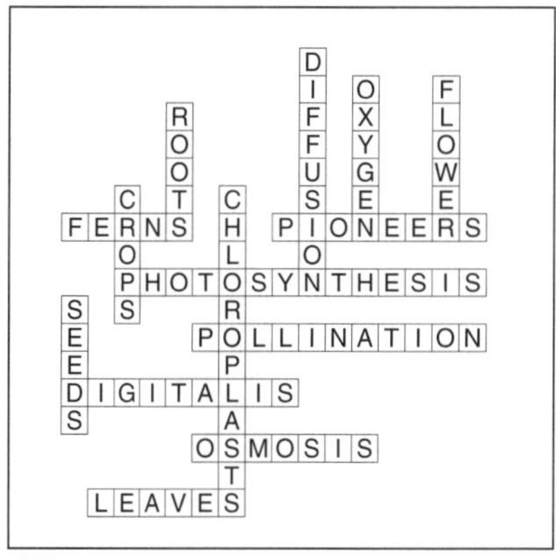

15

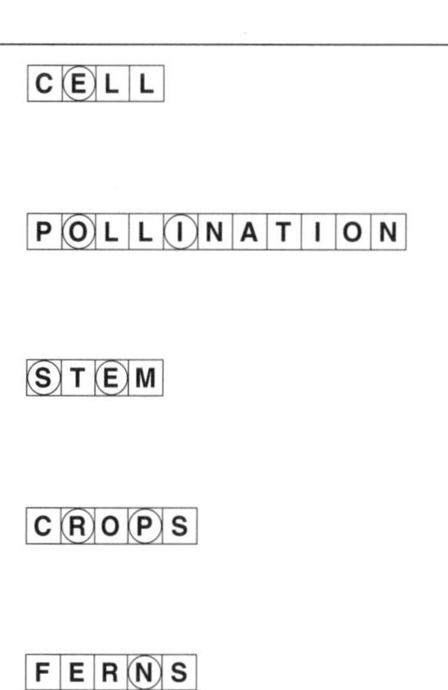

16

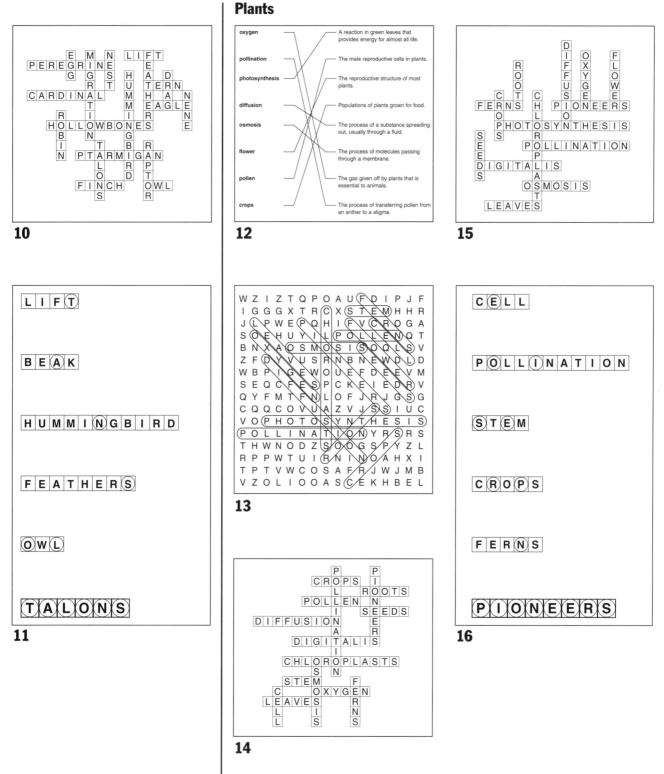

Mammals

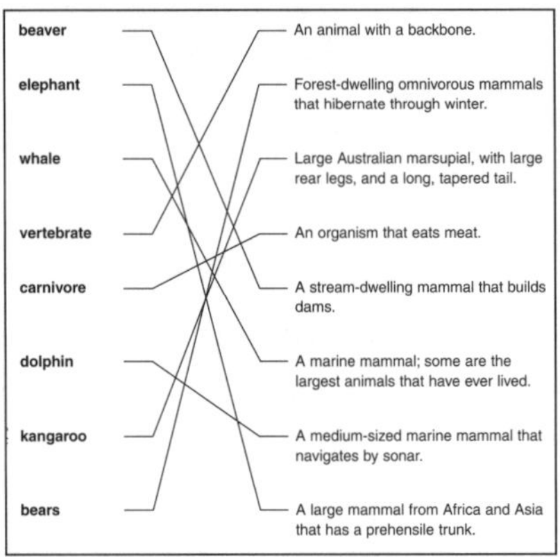

17

20

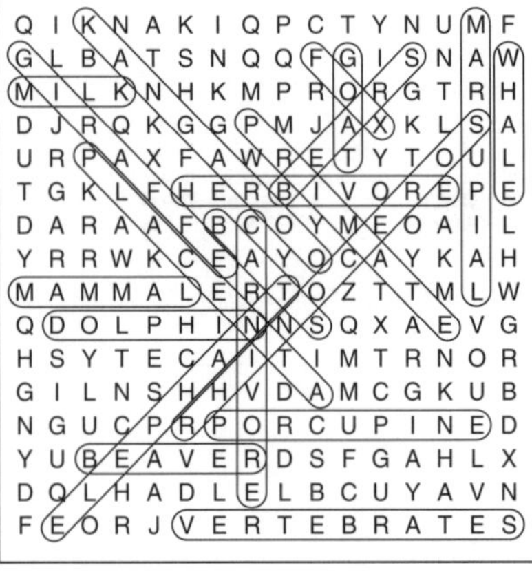

18

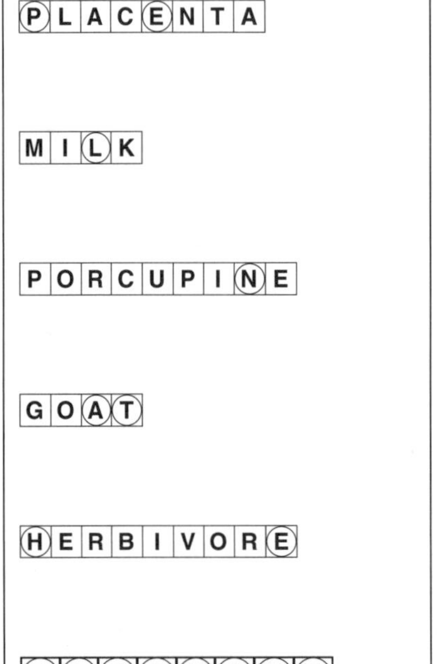

21

19

Insects

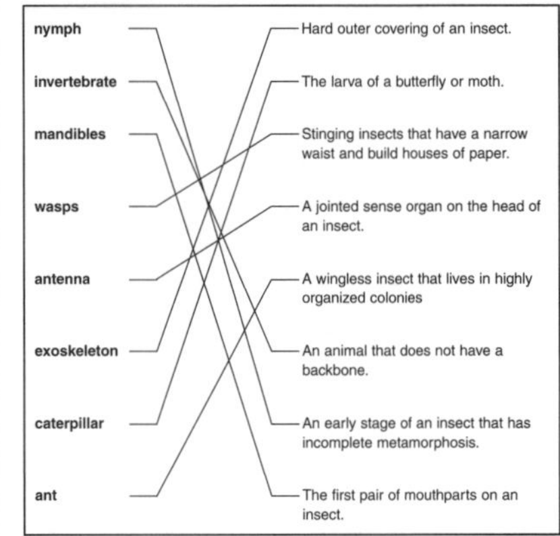

22

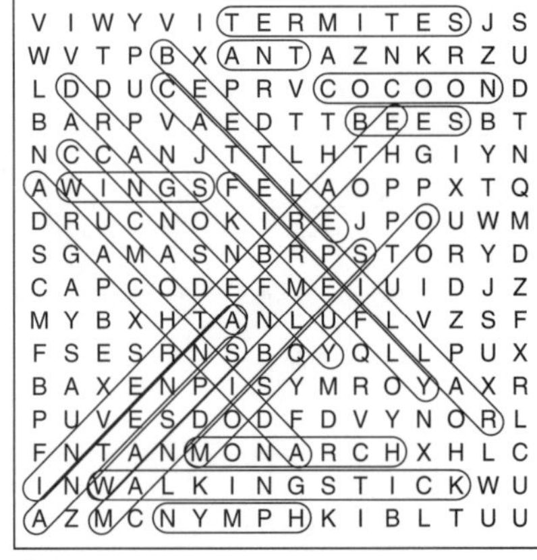

23

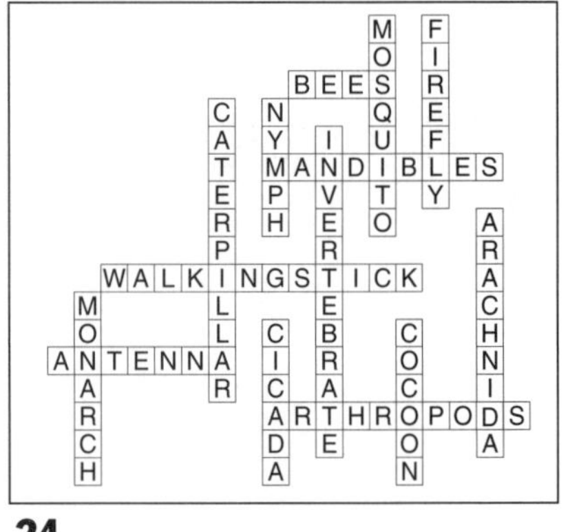

24

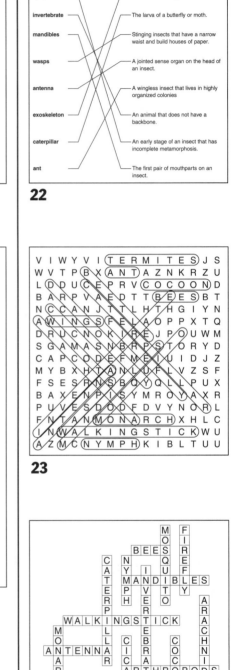

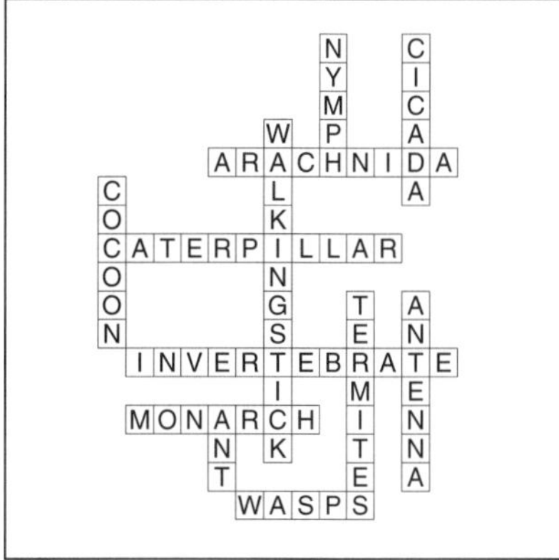

25

Adaptation

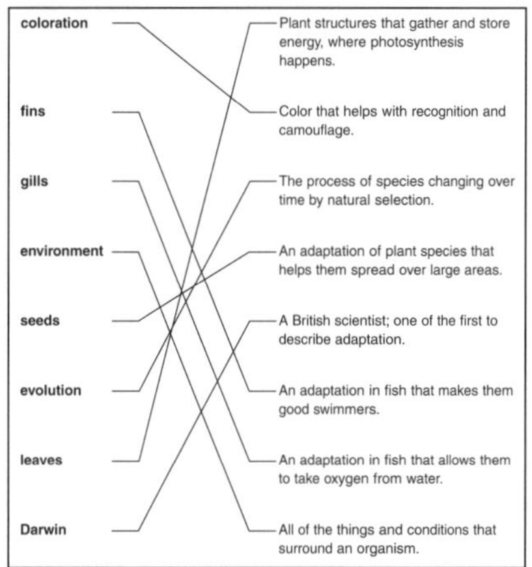

27

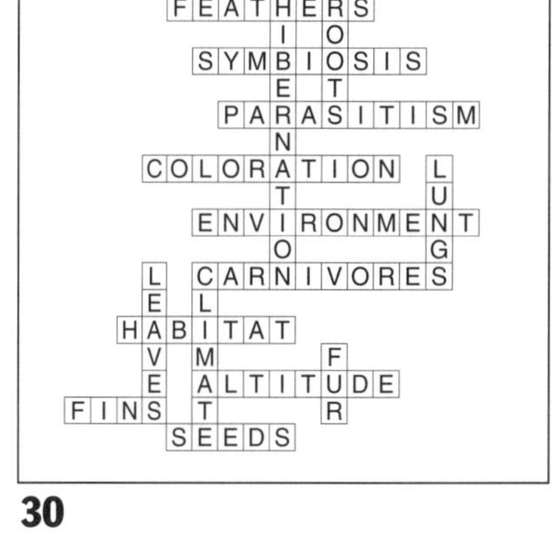

30

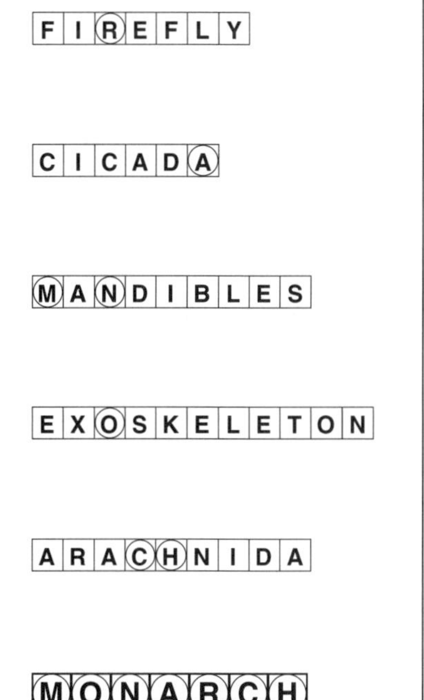

26

28

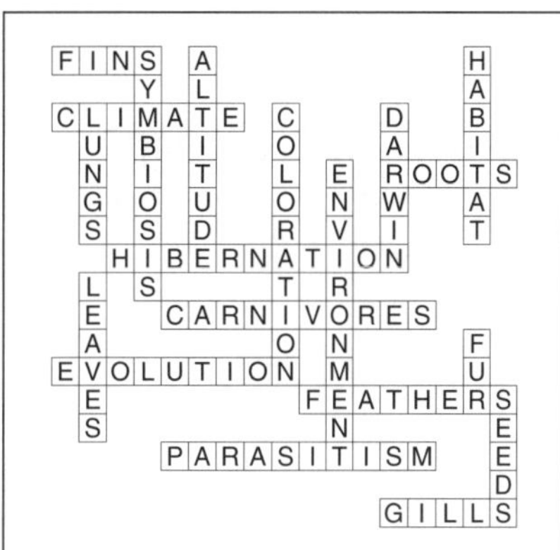

29

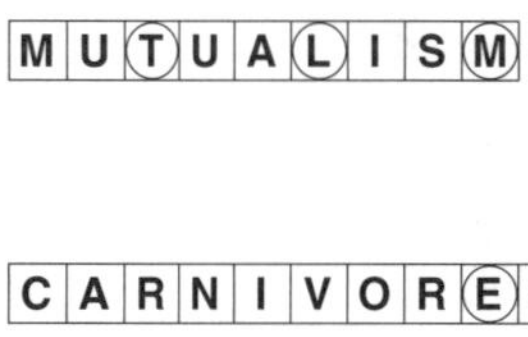

ALTITUDE

DARWIN

COLORATION

CLIMATE

31

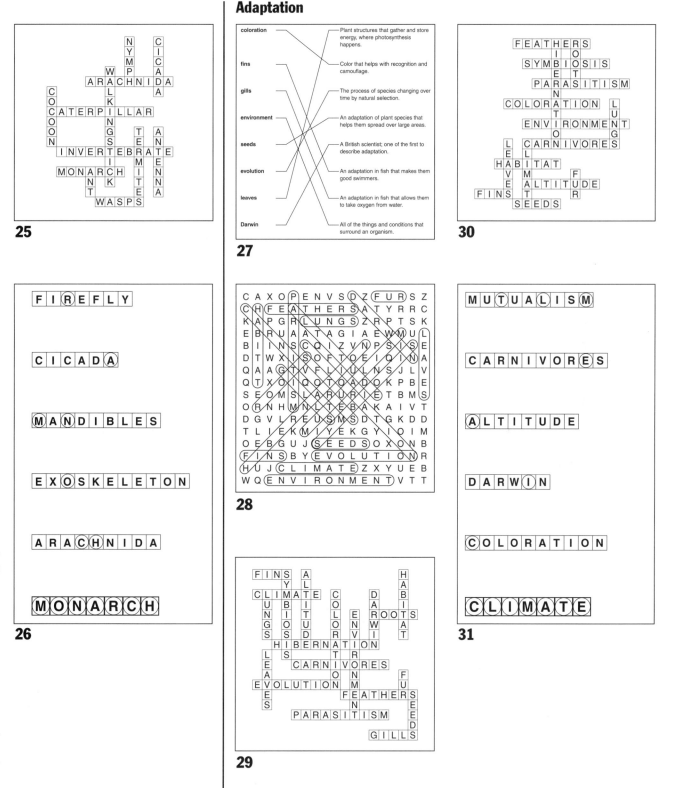

Answer Key

Ecology

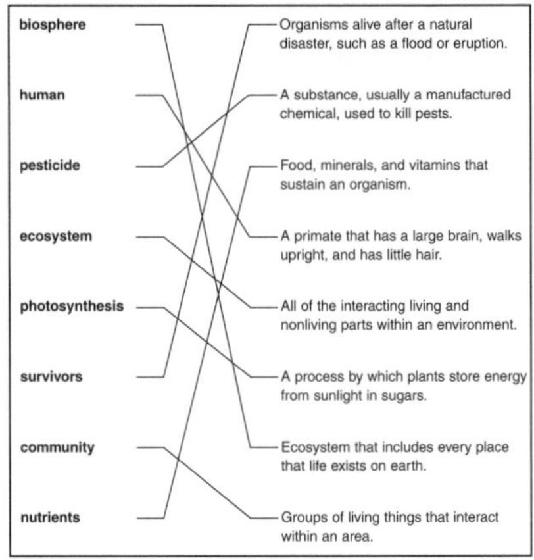

32

33

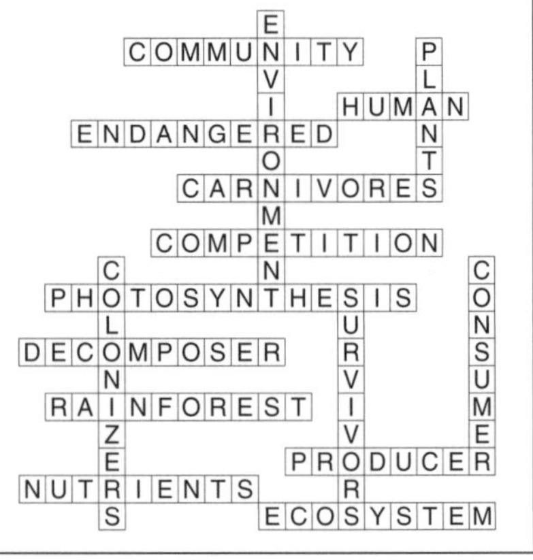

34

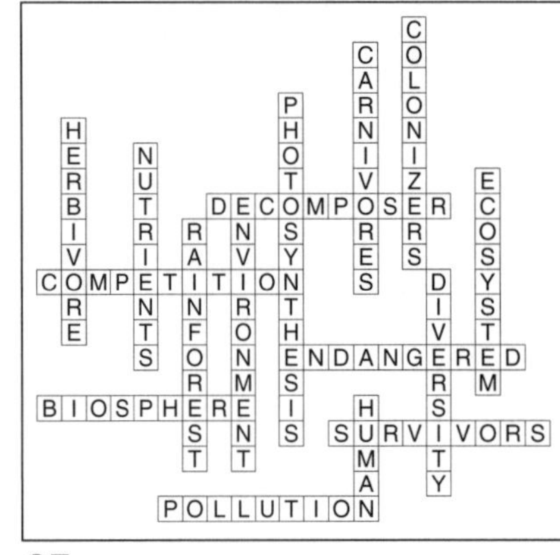

35

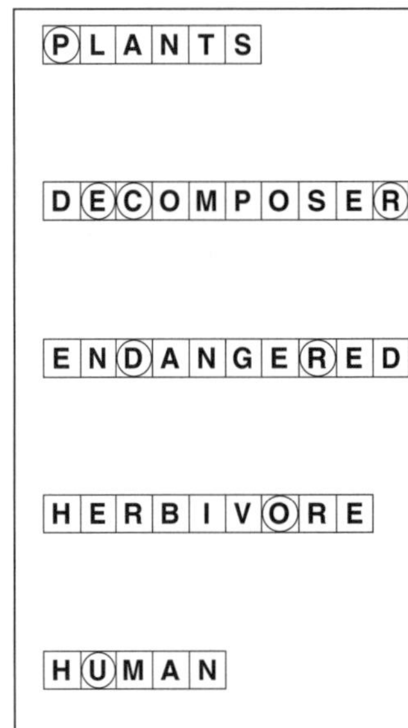

36

Biomes and Habitats

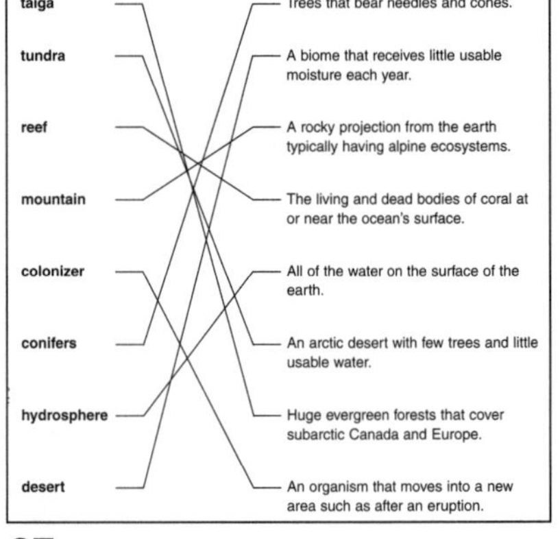

taiga
tundra
reef
mountain
colonizer
conifers
hydrosphere
desert
Trees that bear needles and cones.
A biome that receives little usable moisture each year.
A rocky projection from the earth typically having alpine ecosystems.
The living and dead bodies of coral at or near the ocean's surface.
All of the water on the surface of the earth.
An arctic desert with few trees and little usable water.
Huge evergreen forests that cover subarctic Canada and Europe.
An organism that moves into a new area such as after an eruption.

37

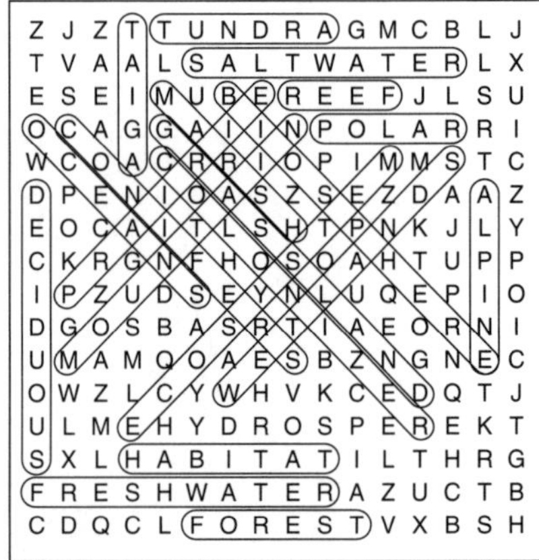

38

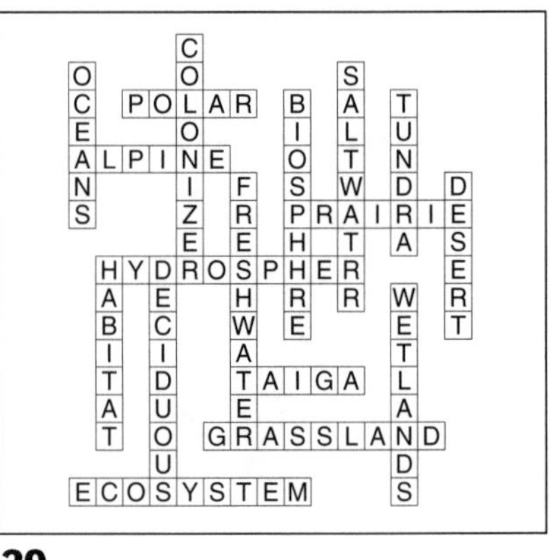

39

Food Chains

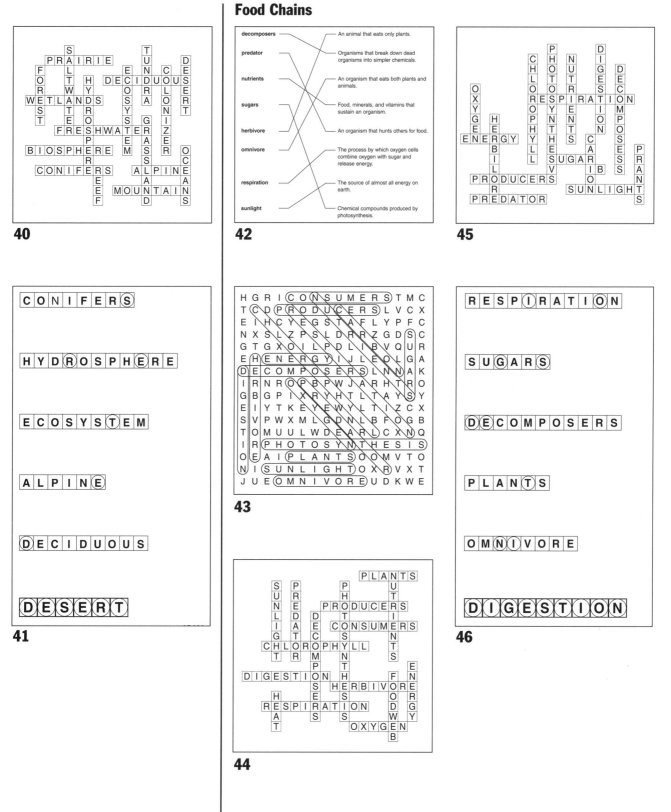

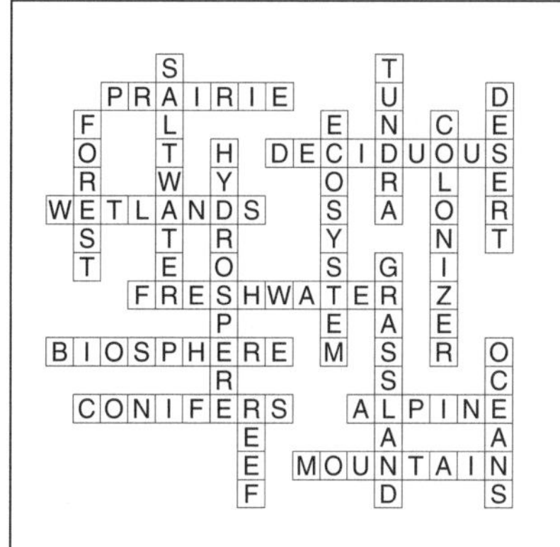

40

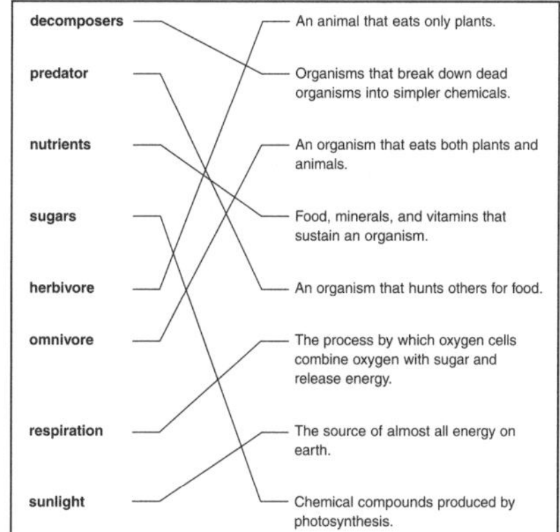

42

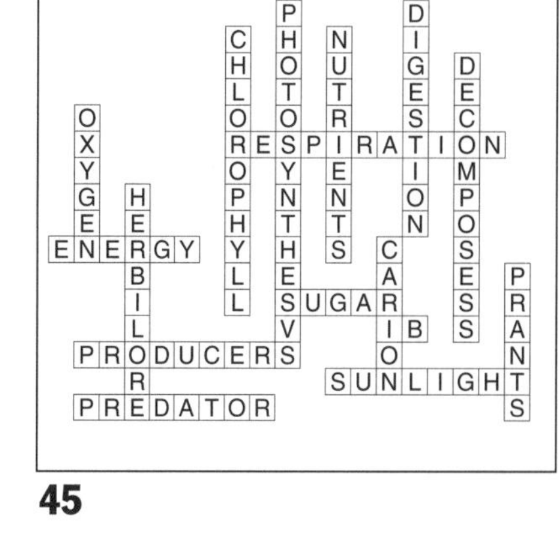

45

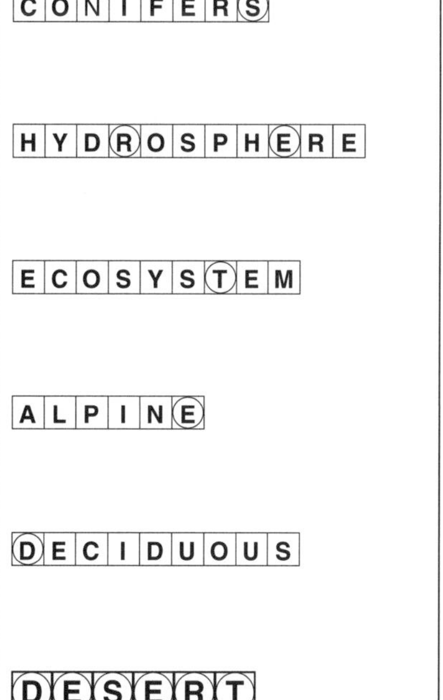

41

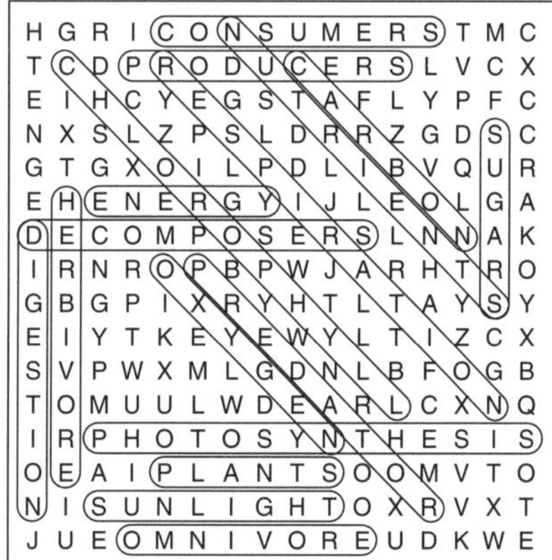

43

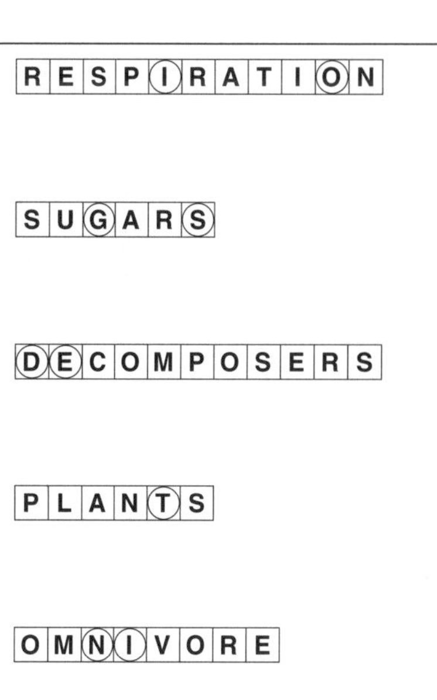

46

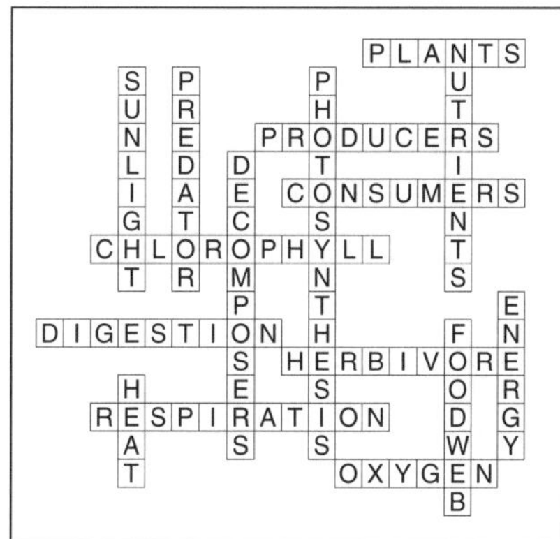

44

Heredity

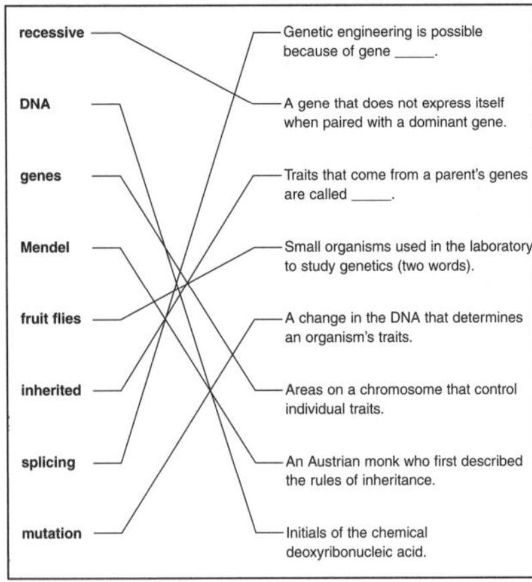

47

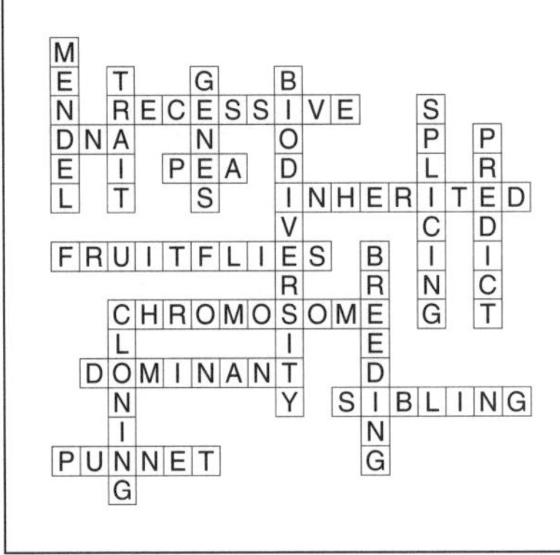

50

48

DNA

GENES

PUNNET

BIODIVERSITY

MENDEL

BREEDING

51

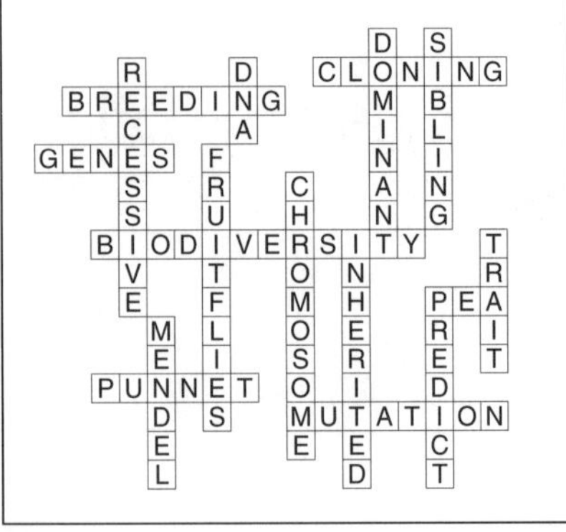

49

Evolution

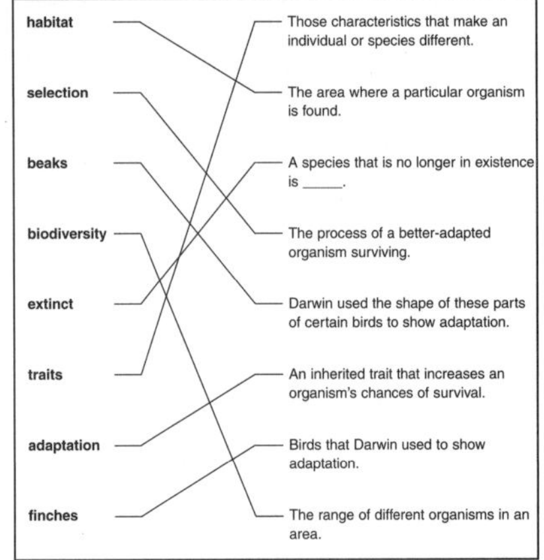

52

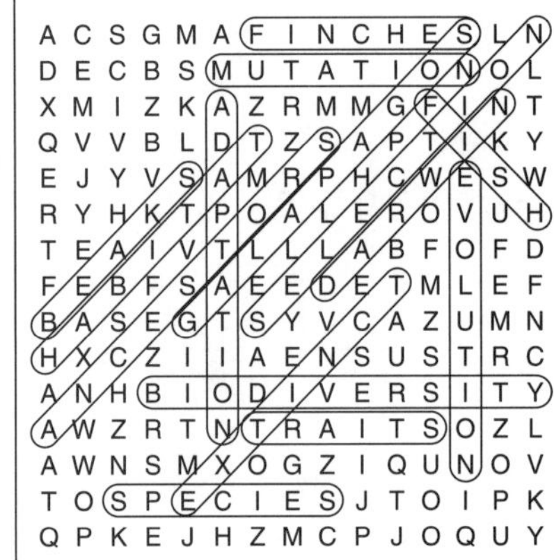

53

54

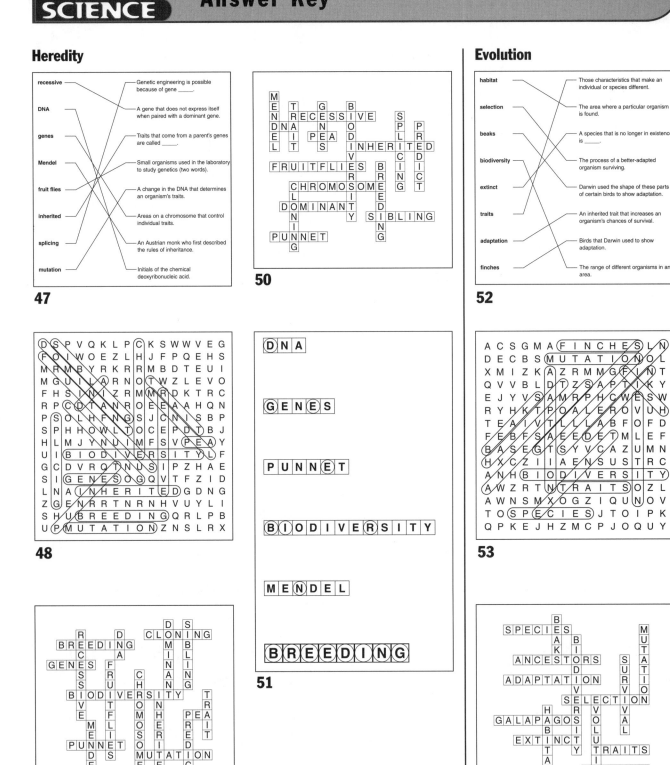

55

S P E C I E S

A D A P T A T I O N

S U R V I V A L

F I N C H E S

S E L E C T I O N

56

Dinosaurs

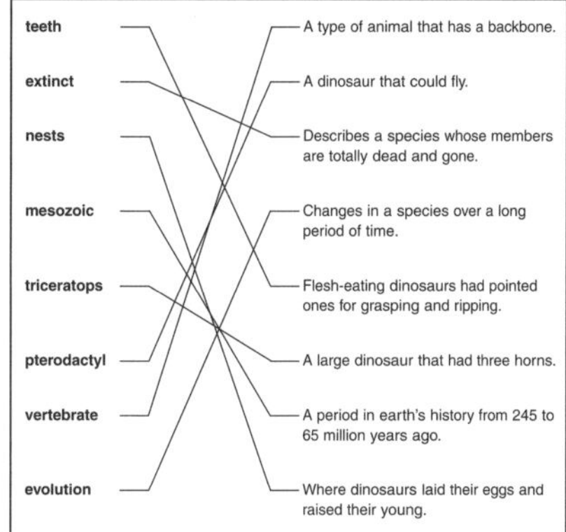

teeth
extinct
nests
mesozoic
triceratops
pterodactyl
vertebrate
evolution
A type of animal that has a backbone.
A dinosaur that could fly.
Describes a species whose members are totally dead and gone.
Changes in a species over a long period of time.
Flesh-eating dinosaurs had pointed ones for grasping and ripping.
A large dinosaur that had three horns.
A period in earth's history from 245 to 65 million years ago.
Where dinosaurs laid their eggs and raised their young.

58

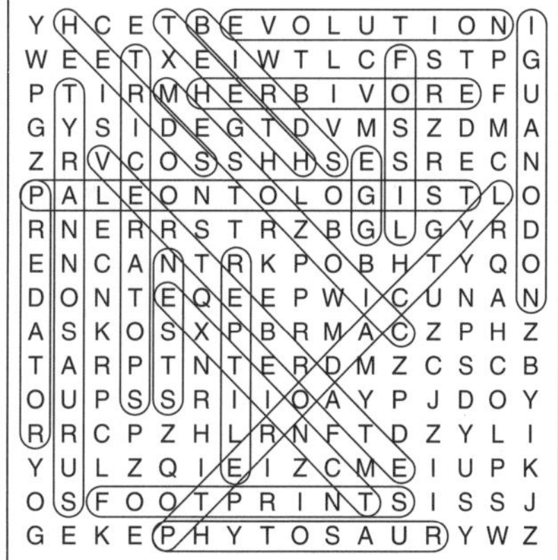

59

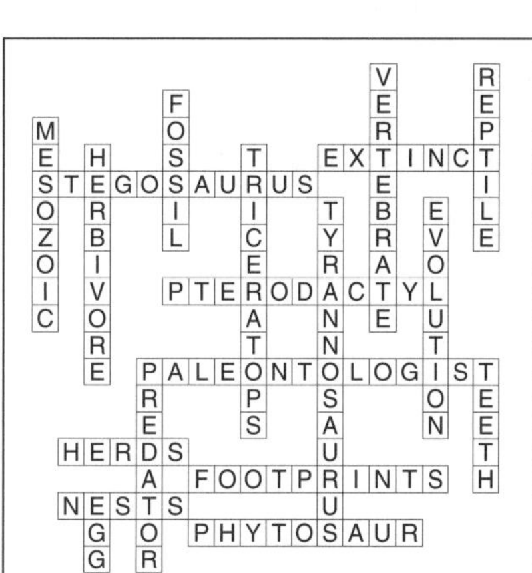

60

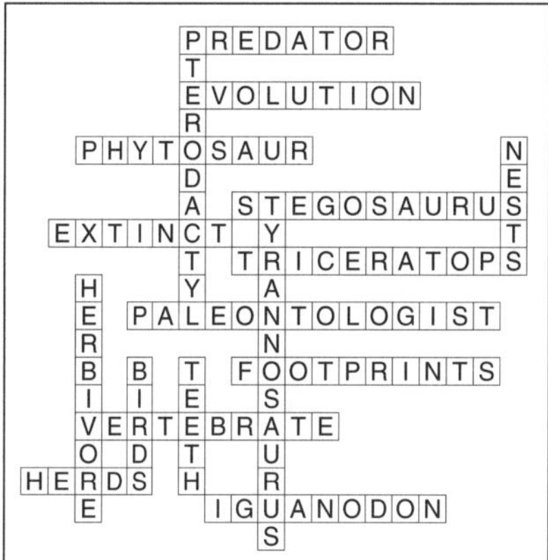

61

F O O T P R I N T S

H E R D S

T E E T H

P T E R O D A C T Y L

M E S O Z O I C

P R E D A T O R

62

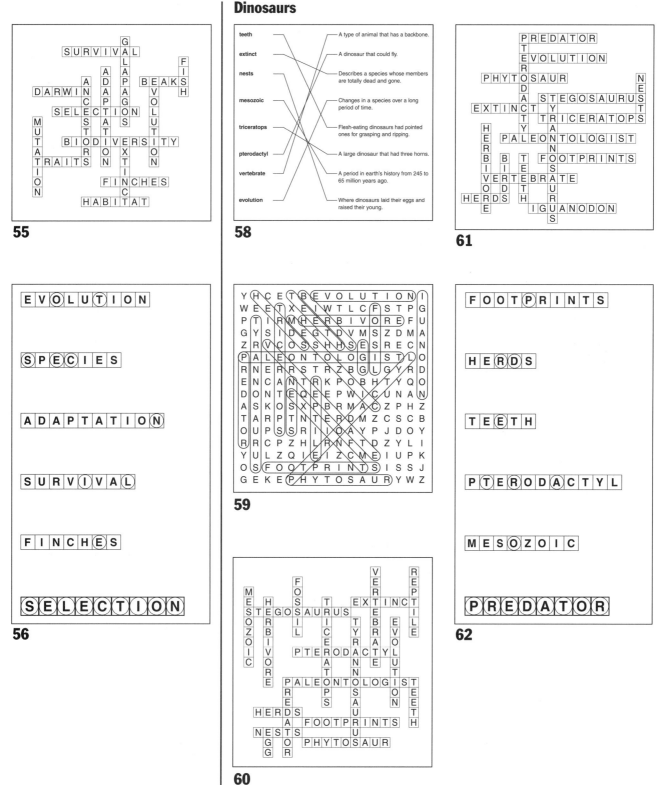

Earth SCIENCE

Answer Key

Earthquakes

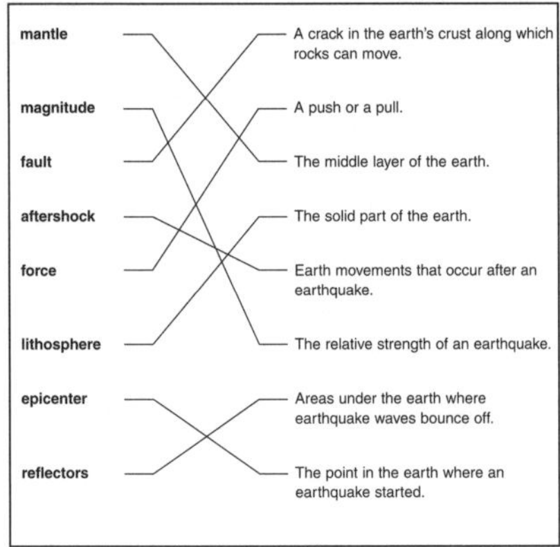

mantle
magnitude
fault
aftershock
force
lithosphere
epicenter
reflectors
A crack in the earth's crust along which rocks can move.
A push or a pull.
The middle layer of the earth.
The solid part of the earth.
Earth movements that occur after an earthquake.
The relative strength of an earthquake.
Areas under the earth where earthquake waves bounce off.
The point in the earth where an earthquake started.

63

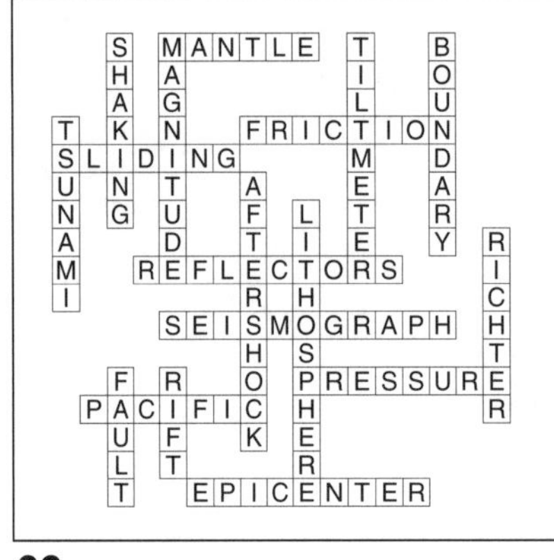

66

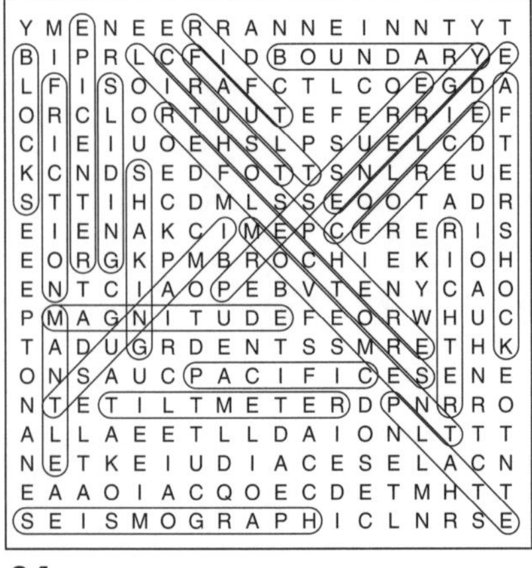

64

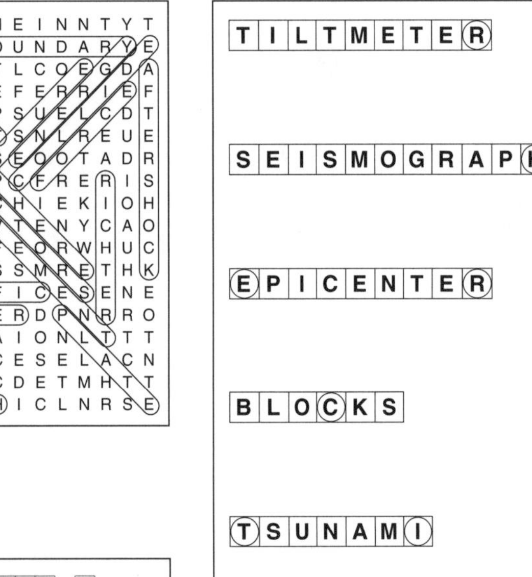

67

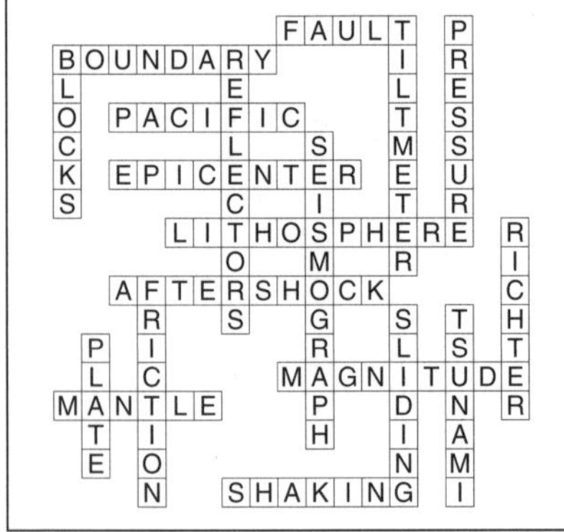

65

The Moon

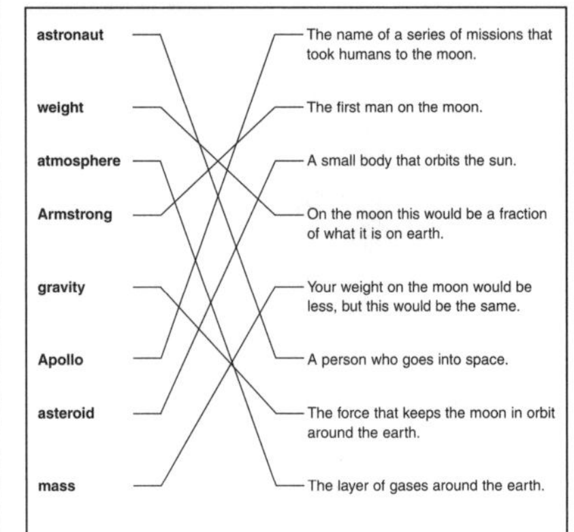

astronaut
weight
atmosphere
Armstrong
gravity
Apollo
asteroid
mass
The name of a series of missions that took humans to the moon.
The first man on the moon.
A small body that orbits the sun.
On the moon this would be a fraction of what it is on earth.
Your weight on the moon would be less, but this would be the same.
A person who goes into space.
The force that keeps the moon in orbit around the earth.
The layer of gases around the earth.

68

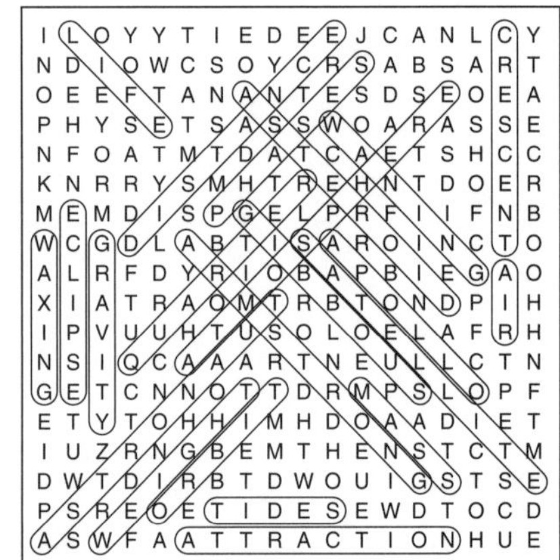

69

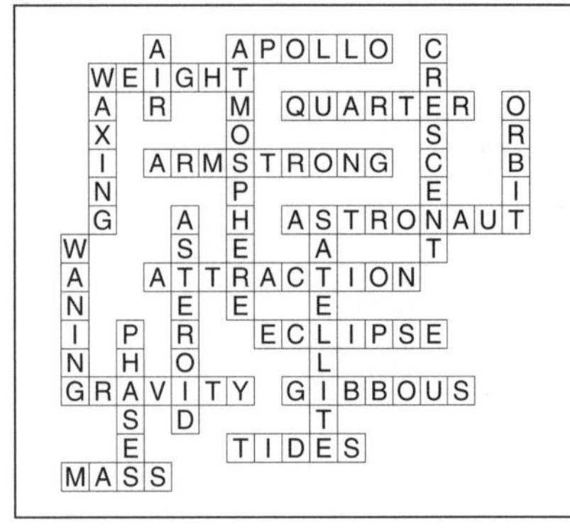

70

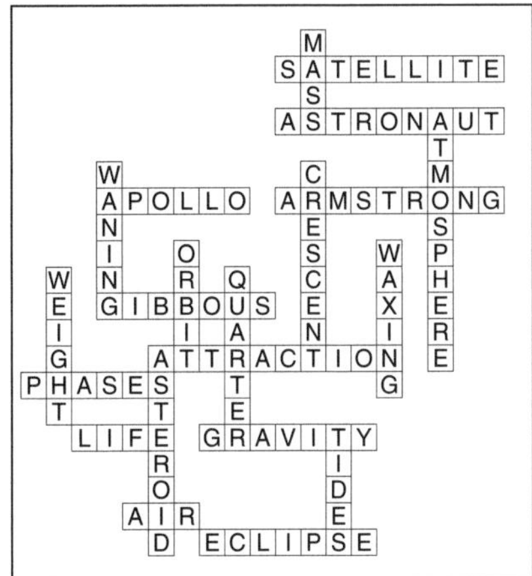

71

QUARTER

ATMOSPHERE

CRESCENT

GIBBOUS

ATTRACTION

ASTRONAUT

72

Natural Resources

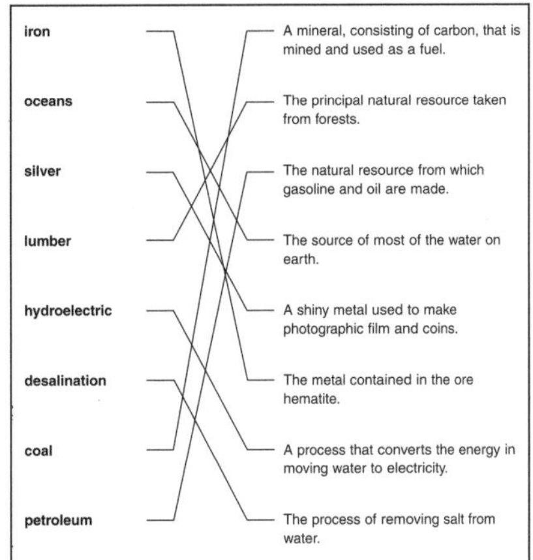

73

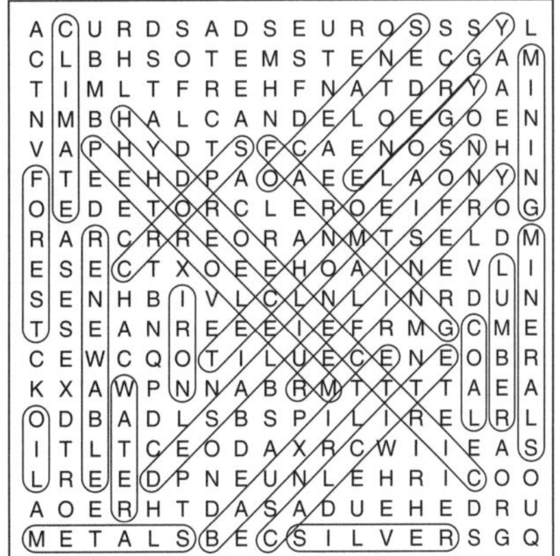

74

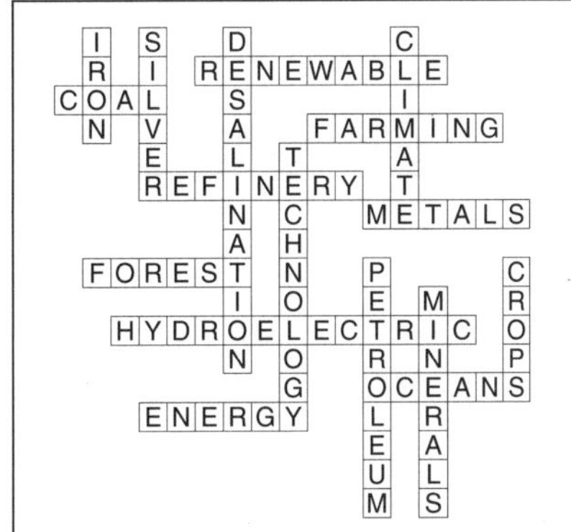

75

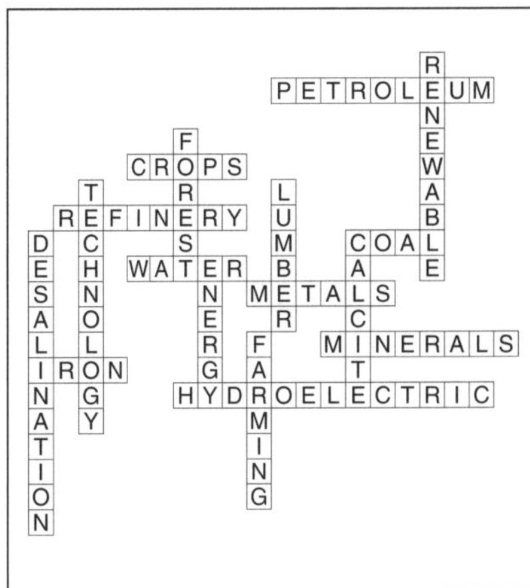

76

DESALINATION

LUMBER

CLIMATE

CROPS

TECHNOLOGY

MINERALS

77

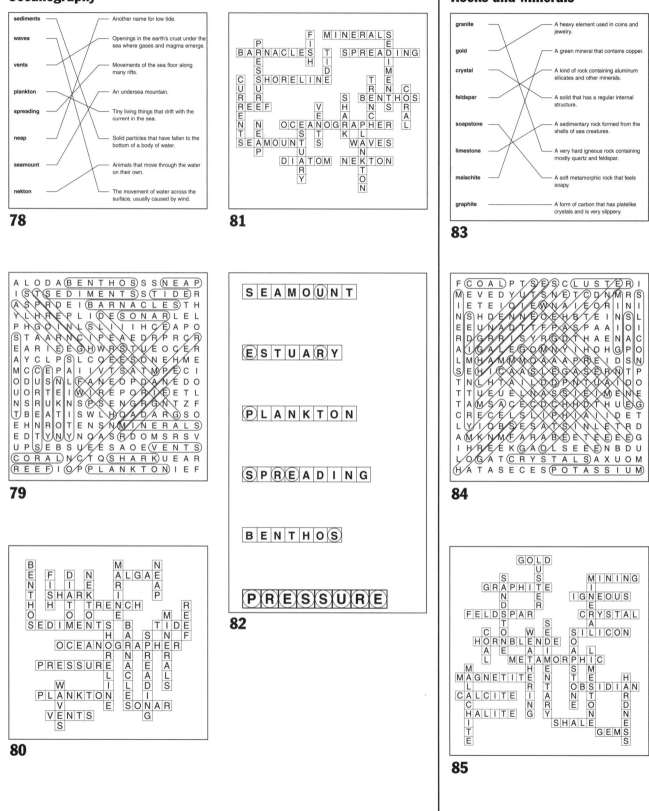

Oceanography

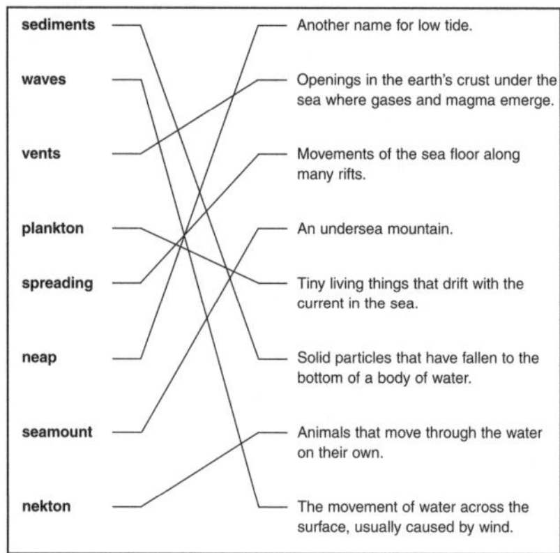

78

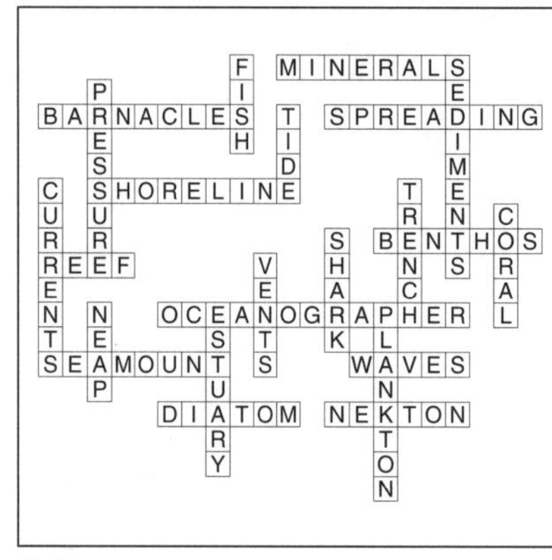

81

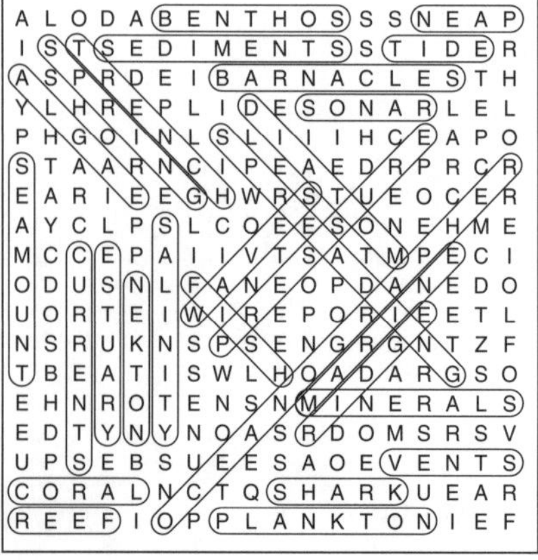

79

SEAMOUNT

ESTUARY

PLANKTON

SPREADING

BENTHOS

82

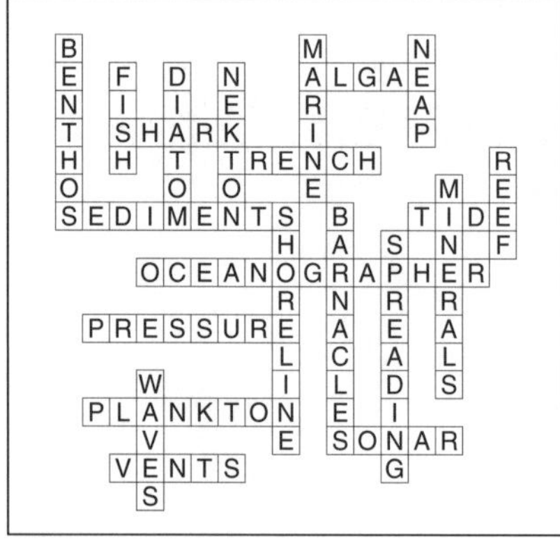

80

Rocks and Minerals

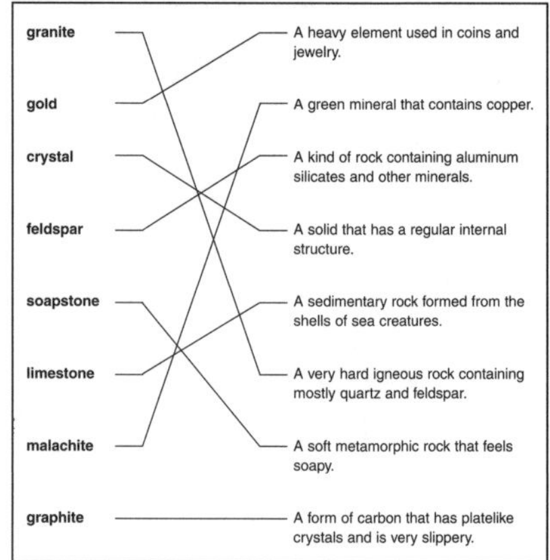

granite
gold
crystal
feldspar
soapstone
limestone
malachite
graphite
A heavy element used in coins and jewelry.
A green mineral that contains copper.
A kind of rock containing aluminum silicates and other minerals.
A solid that has a regular internal structure.
A sedimentary rock formed from the shells of sea creatures.
A very hard igneous rock containing mostly quartz and feldspar.
A soft metamorphic rock that feels soapy.
A form of carbon that has platelike crystals and is very slippery.

83

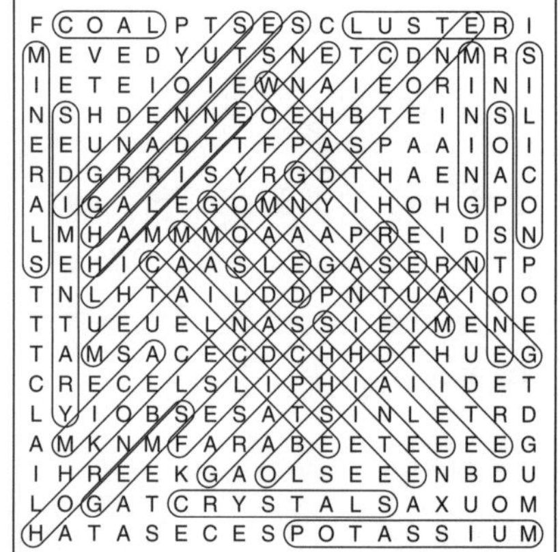

84

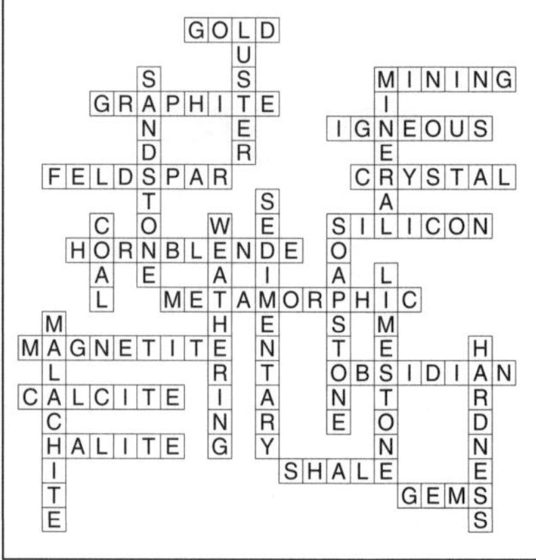

85

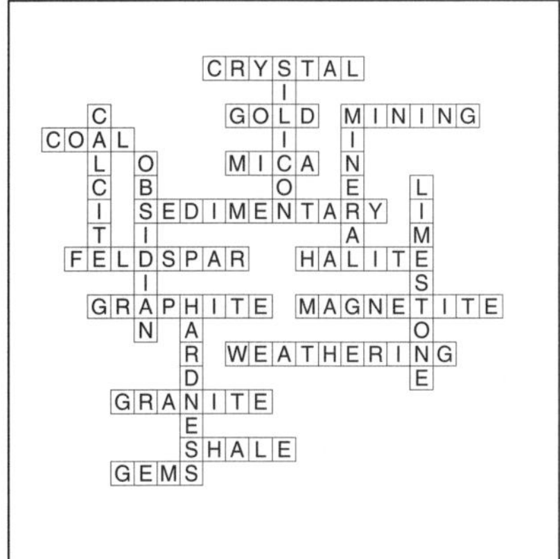

86

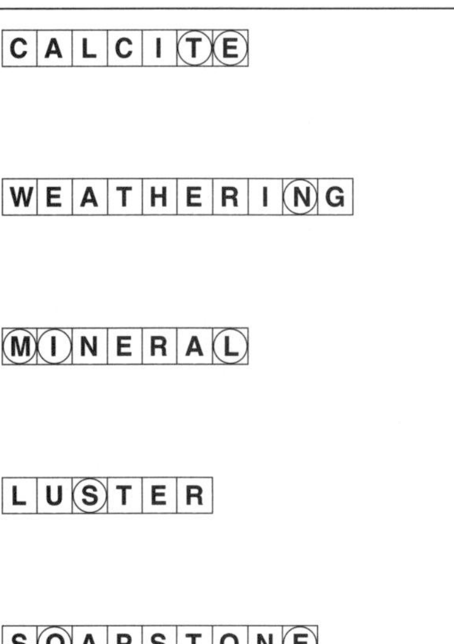

LIMESTONE

87

Solar System

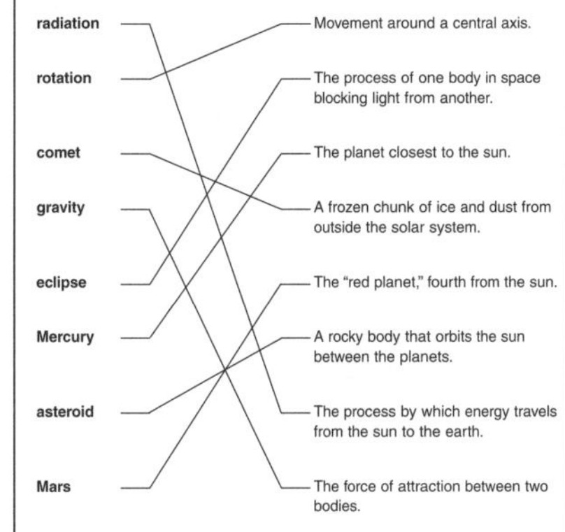

88

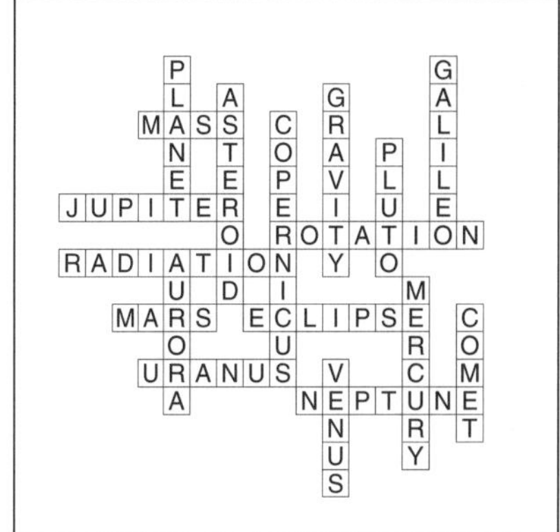

91

I S D E T U N A I T A G K I I D E U
Y E G A L I L E O A A I A T A Y T N
E P E C M A A F C M O O N R S A C E
F K M C S B U T R G R A V I T Y E N
W L A O O H C R P H E A L E E E S T
E I S P S H N K O L I P T M R E W E
X W S E T C A L U R A L B N O T N H
L A U R A N U S H W A N H O I M O R
A C S N C F E H E D A N E Y D E E D
P O X I A O P T A C O D R T A A R V
L N N C E X M S U I L U A Y S L O E
U P L U A T D E T O C I N I H N T N
T N M S U E R A T R E S P T C S A U
O I E U T E I S E D T S Y S O N T S
U C T O N D N M R S R T N E E E I H
E N E H A A E E B A E O T O U Y O S
E I S R T R L I M N E P T U N E N E
L I N O R B I T S S A J U P I T E R

89

NEPTUNE

PLUTO

PLANET

GRAVITY

RADIATION

ROTATION

92

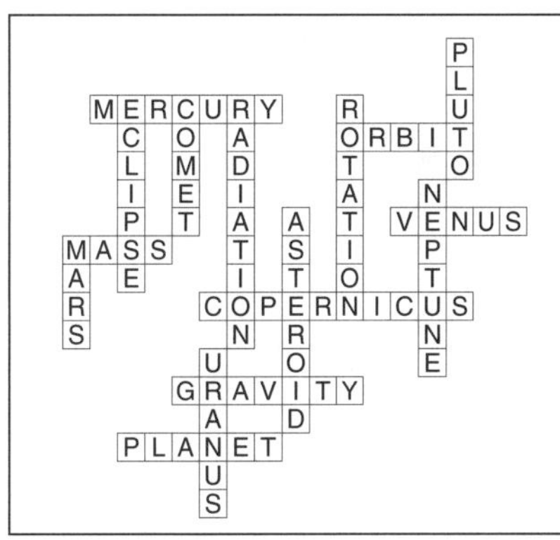

90

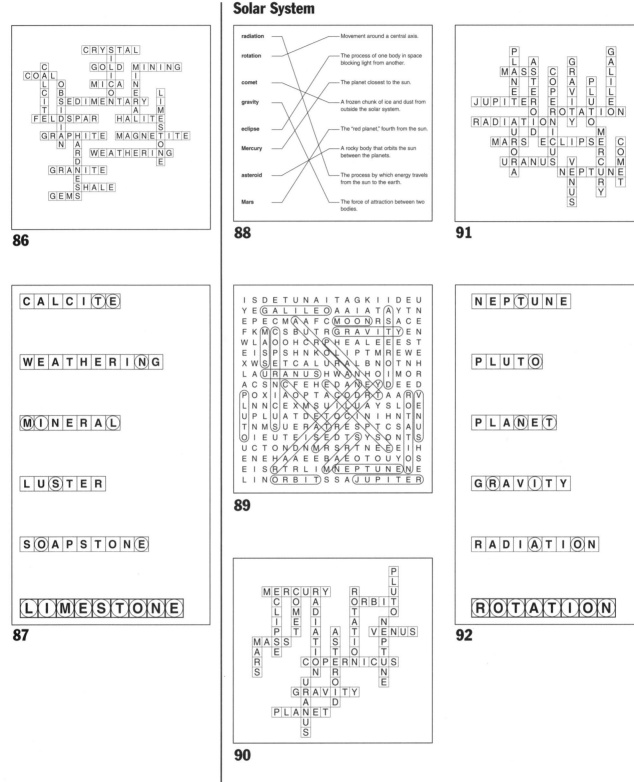

Earth SCIENCE Answer Key

Space

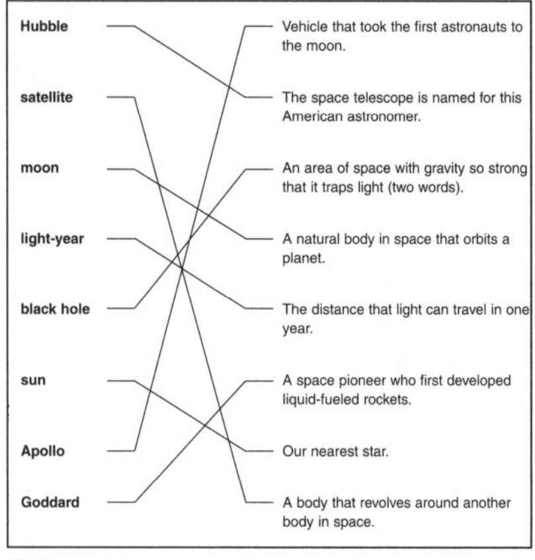

93

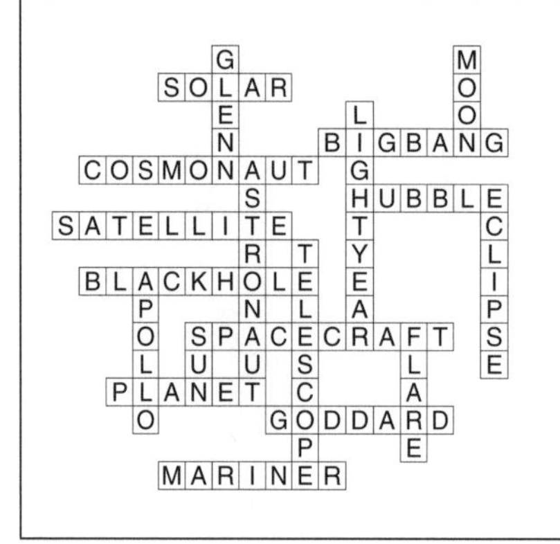

96

94

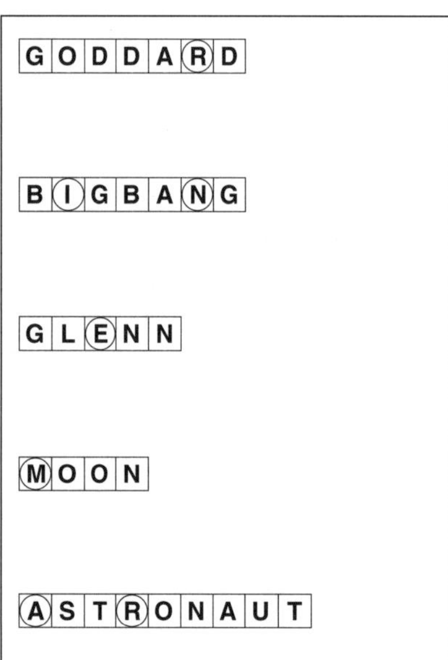

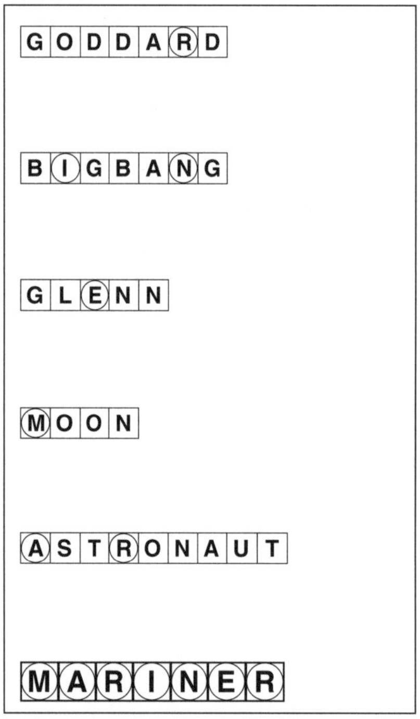

97

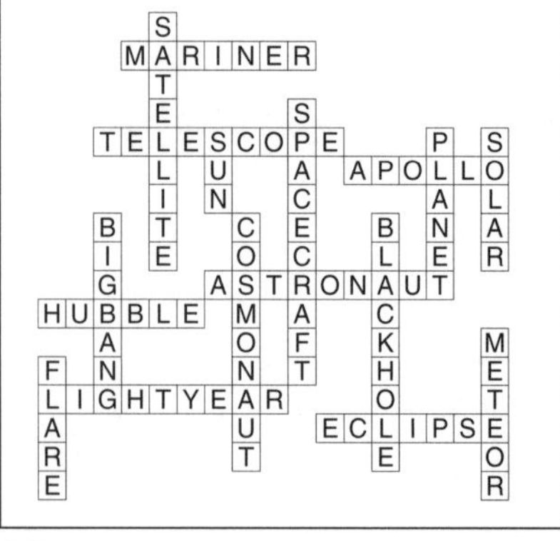

95

The Stars

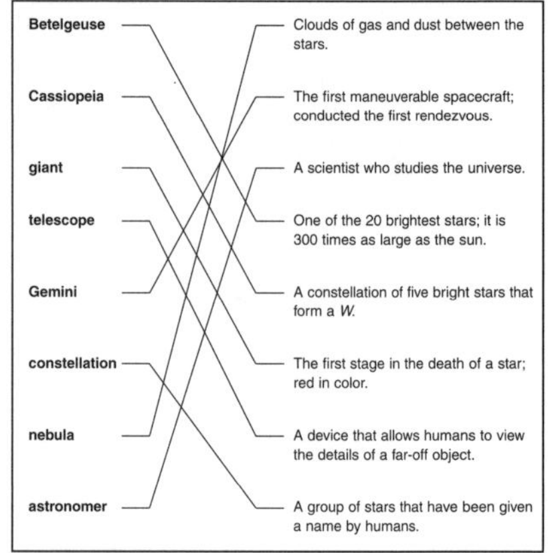

98

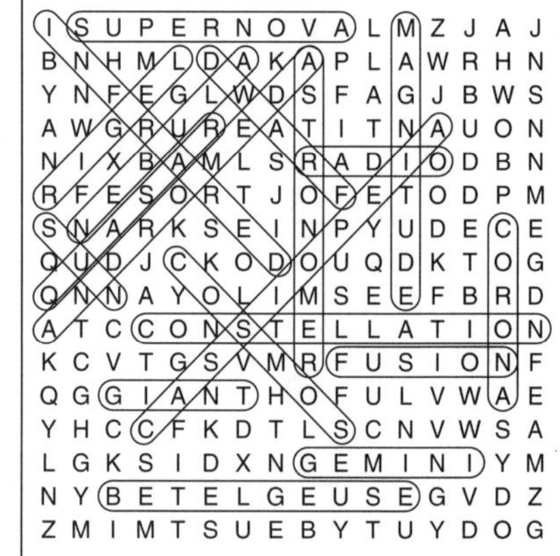

99

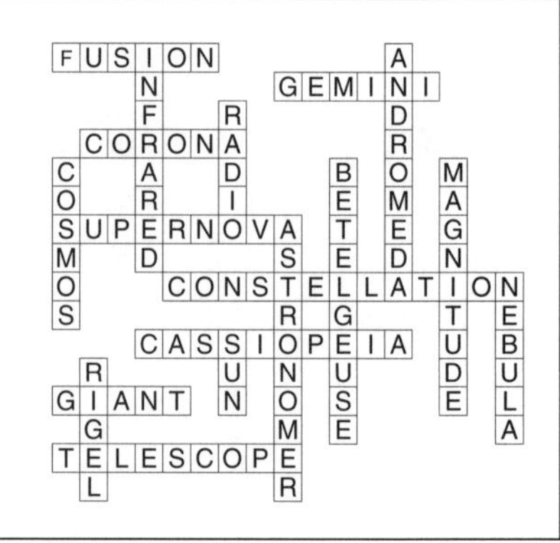

100

Volcanoes

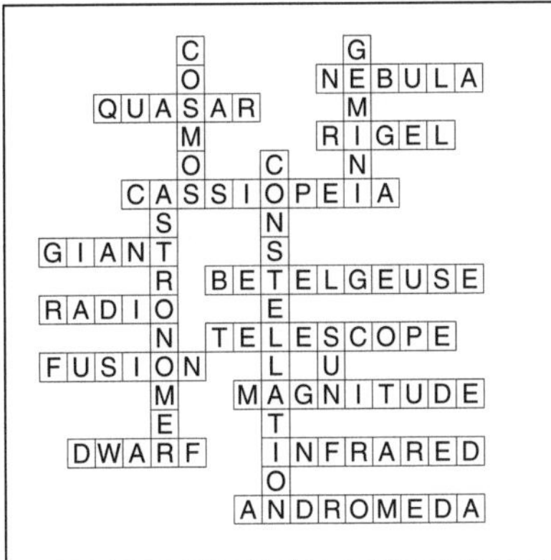

101

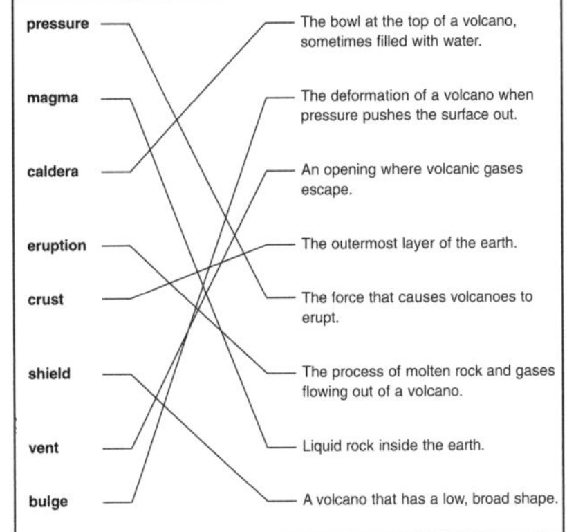
pressure
magma
caldera
eruption
crust
shield
vent
bulge
The bowl at the top of a volcano, sometimes filled with water.
The deformation of a volcano when pressure pushes the surface out.
An opening where volcanic gases escape.
The outermost layer of the earth.
The force that causes volcanoes to erupt.
The process of molten rock and gases flowing out of a volcano.
Liquid rock inside the earth.
A volcano that has a low, broad shape.

103

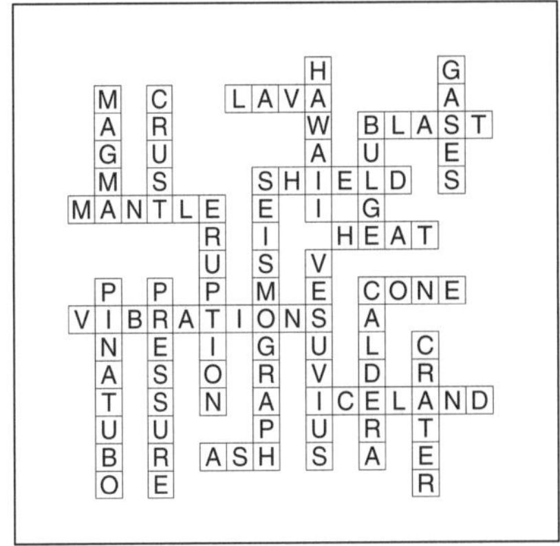

106

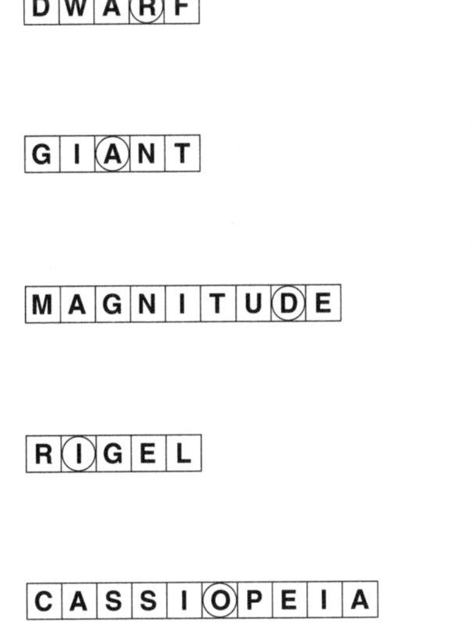
DWARF
GIANT
MAGNITUDE
RIGEL
CASSIOPEIA
RADIO

102

104

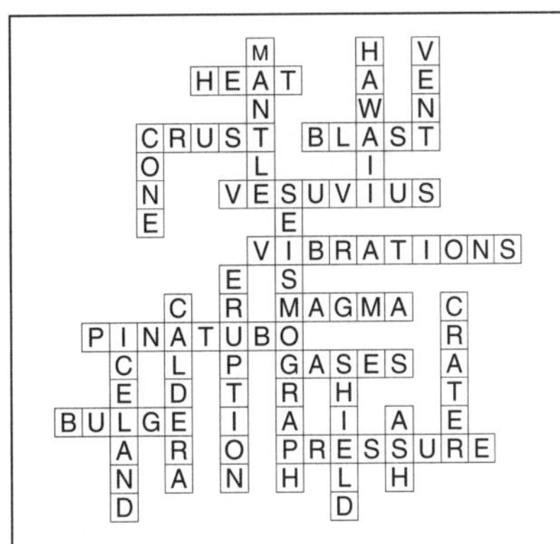

105

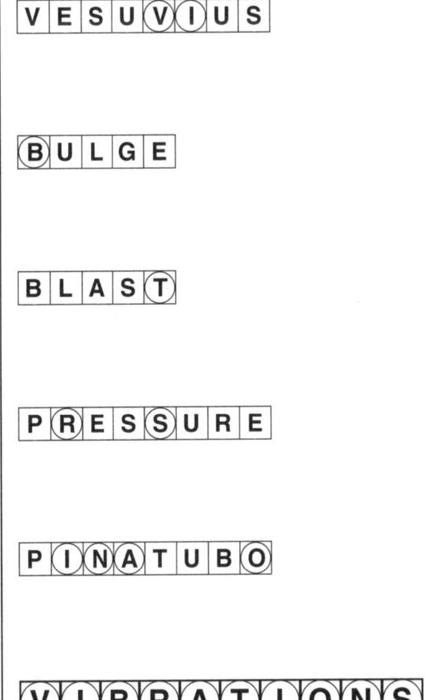
VESUVIUS
BULGE
BLAST
PRESSURE
PINATUBO
VIBRATIONS

107

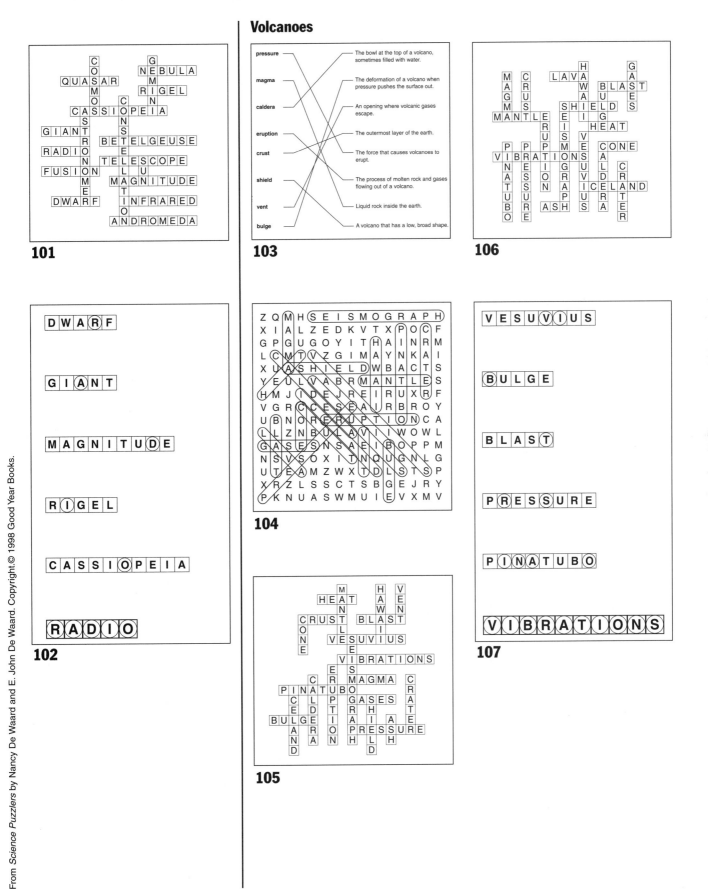

Weather

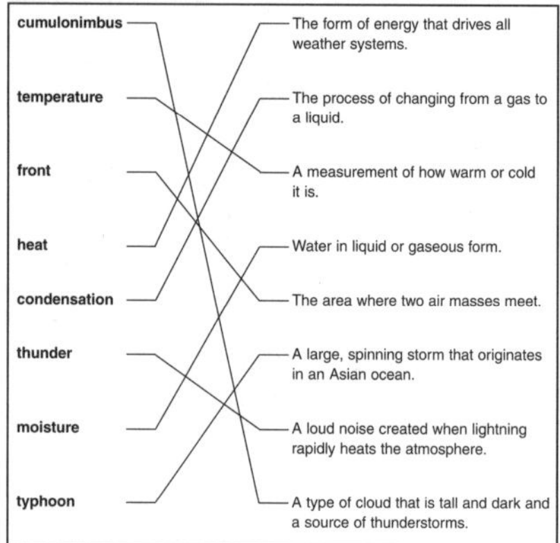

cumulonimbus
temperature
front
heat
condensation
thunder
moisture
typhoon
The form of energy that drives all weather systems.
The process of changing from a gas to a liquid.
A measurement of how warm or cold it is.
Water in liquid or gaseous form.
The area where two air masses meet.
A large, spinning storm that originates in an Asian ocean.
A loud noise created when lightning rapidly heats the atmosphere.
A type of cloud that is tall and dark and a source of thunderstorms.

108

POLAR, LOW, CLOUD, CONDENSATION, TEMPERATURE, FRONT, THUNDER, STORM, ATMOSPHERE, HURRICANE, MOISTURE, TORNADO, CUMULONIMBUS, HUMIDITY, WIND, TYPHOON, PRECIPITATION

111

C Q C A U K I Y S L U I P V Q U
S L H U R R I C A N E A I T E T
T Z O Q M H Q K R V T P N Y S Y
O M N U N U L A J M E O E J K P
R O M I D M L I W G R R A O J H
M I C F K O V O G F E Y F P S O
W S G S P E L A N H T B U W H O
C T N P R E C I P I T A T I O N
C U T N R M A S D D M N K N M Z
L R O A I C O I R A P B I D A H
I E R S Z M M O Z H N K U N C I
M Z N U T U W T R O P I C S G G
A S A A H E D V O Y J Q Z S F H
T X D N O H E A T M T F G J B Q
E C O N D E N S A T I O N U B G
K X A J S A T U R A T E D O M Q

109

TEMPERATURE

CLOUD

STORM

SATURATED

PRECIPITATION

TROPICS

112

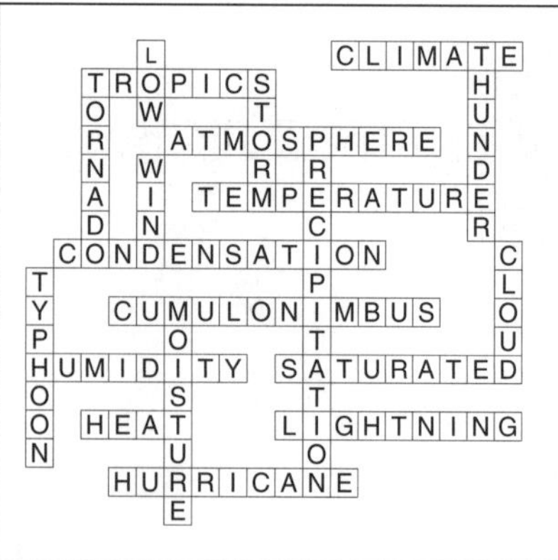

110

Weathering and Erosion

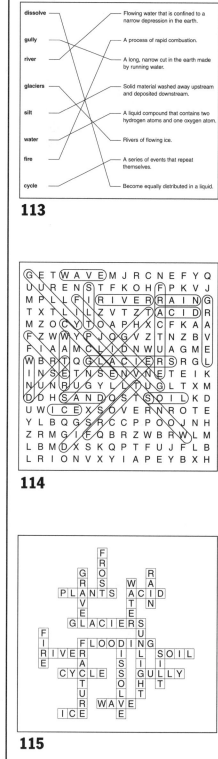

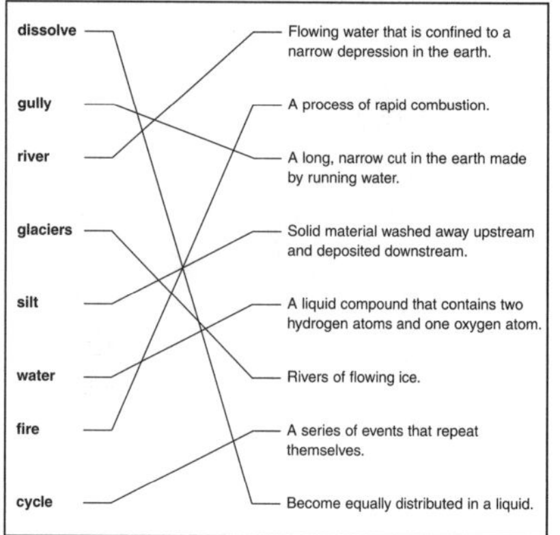

dissolve
gully
river
glaciers
silt
water
fire
cycle
Flowing water that is confined to a narrow depression in the earth.
A process of rapid combustion.
A long, narrow cut in the earth made by running water.
Solid material washed away upstream and deposited downstream.
A liquid compound that contains two hydrogen atoms and one oxygen atom.
Rivers of flowing ice.
A series of events that repeat themselves.
Become equally distributed in a liquid.

113

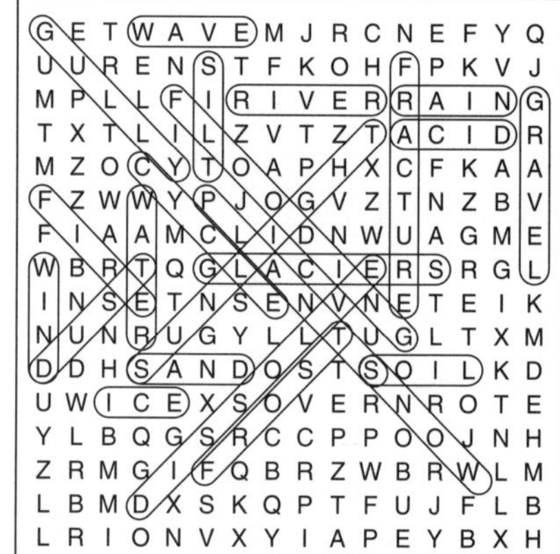

114

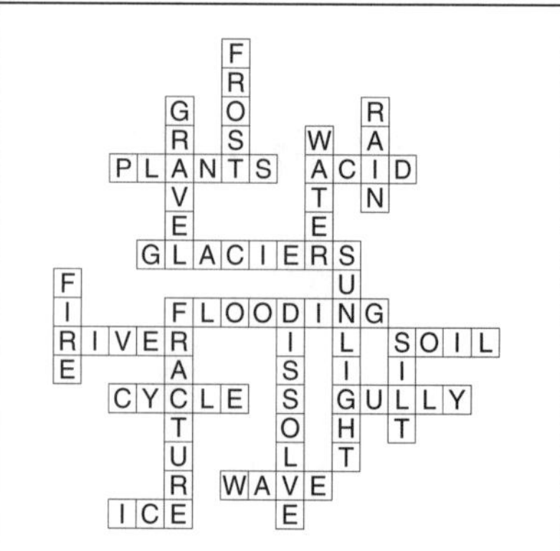

115

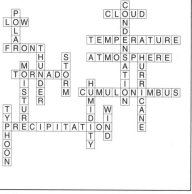

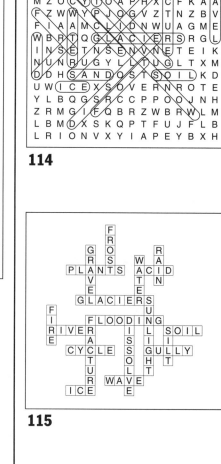

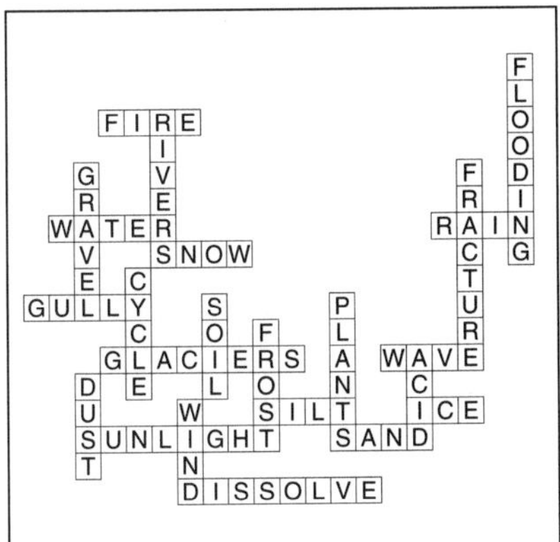

116

Atoms and Matter

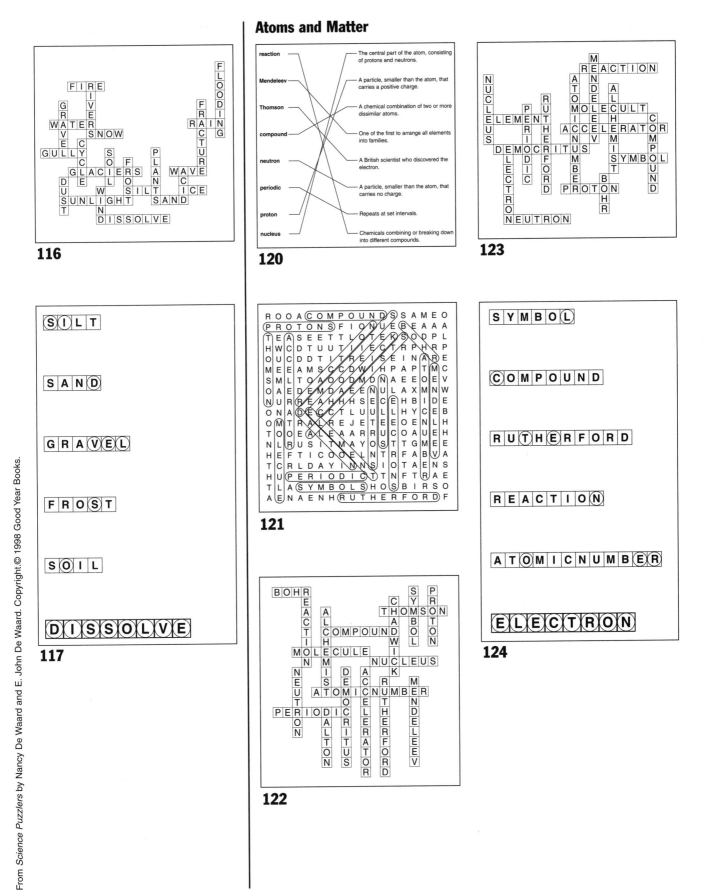

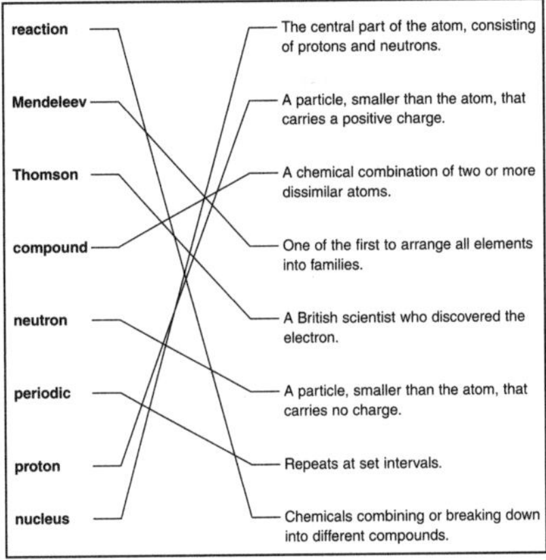

reaction
Mendeleev
Thomson
compound
neutron
periodic
proton
nucleus
The central part of the atom, consisting of protons and neutrons.
A particle, smaller than the atom, that carries a positive charge.
A chemical combination of two or more dissimilar atoms.
One of the first to arrange all elements into families.
A British scientist who discovered the electron.
A particle, smaller than the atom, that carries no charge.
Repeats at set intervals.
Chemicals combining or breaking down into different compounds.

120

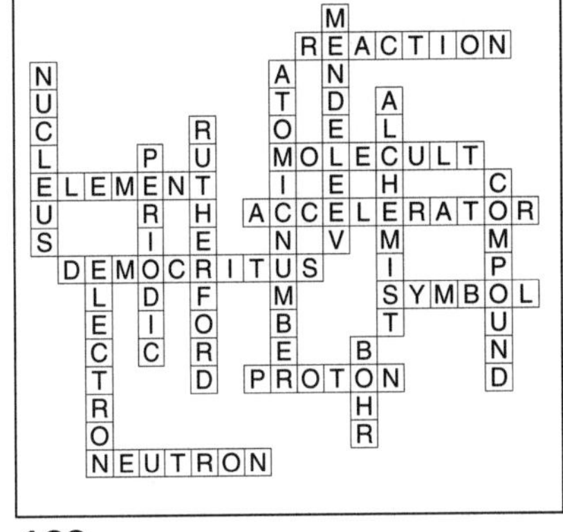

123

SILT

SAND

GRAVEL

FROST

SOIL

DISSOLVE

117

R O O A C O M P O U N D S S A M E O
P R O T O N S F I O N U E B E A A A
T E A S E E T T L O T E K S O D P L
H W C D T U U T I I E C T R P H R P
O U C D D T I T R E I S E I N A R E
M E E A M S C C D W I H P A P T M C
S M L T O A O O D M D N A E E O E V
O A E D E M D A E E N U L A X M N W
N U R R E A H H H S E C E H B I D E
O N A D E C C T L U U L L H Y C E B
O M T R A L R E J E T E E O E N L H
T O O E A L E A A R R U C O A U E H
N L R U S I T M A Y O S T T G M E E
H E F T I C O O E L N T R F A B V A
T C R L D A Y I N N S I O T A E N S
H U P E R I O D I C T T N F T R A E
T L A S Y M B O L S H O S B I R S O
A E N A E N H R U T H E R F O R D F

121

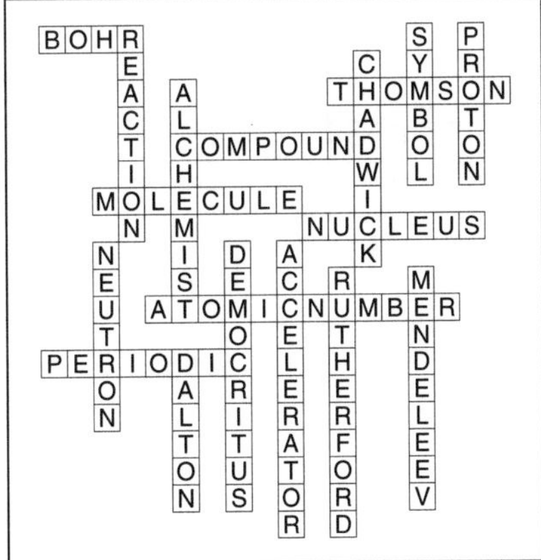

122

SYMBOL

COMPOUND

RUTHERFORD

REACTION

ATOMICNUMBER

ELECTRON

124

Physical SCIENCE Answer Key

Matter and Its Changes

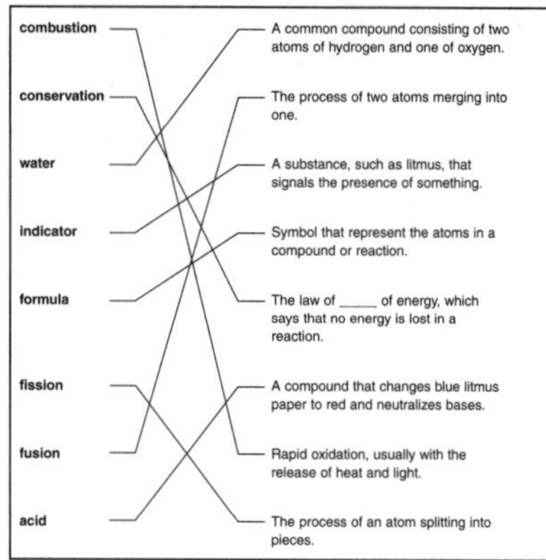

combustion
conservation
water
indicator
formula
fission
fusion
acid
A common compound consisting of two atoms of hydrogen and one of oxygen.
The process of two atoms merging into one.
A substance, such as litmus, that signals the presence of something.
Symbol that represent the atoms in a compound or reaction.
The law of _____ of energy, which says that no energy is lost in a reaction.
A compound that changes blue litmus paper to red and neutralizes bases.
Rapid oxidation, usually with the release of heat and light.
The process of an atom splitting into pieces.

125

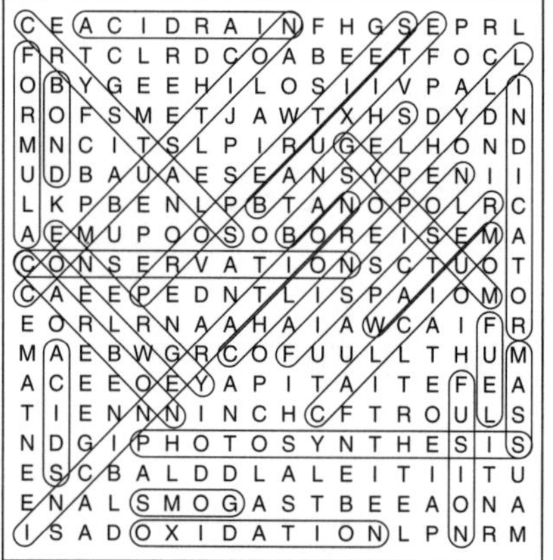

126

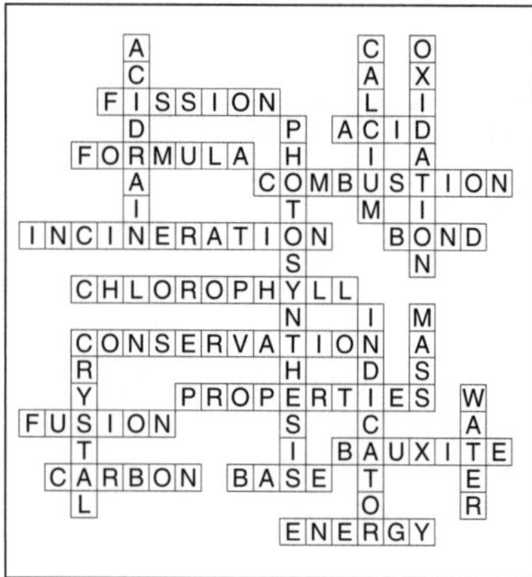

127

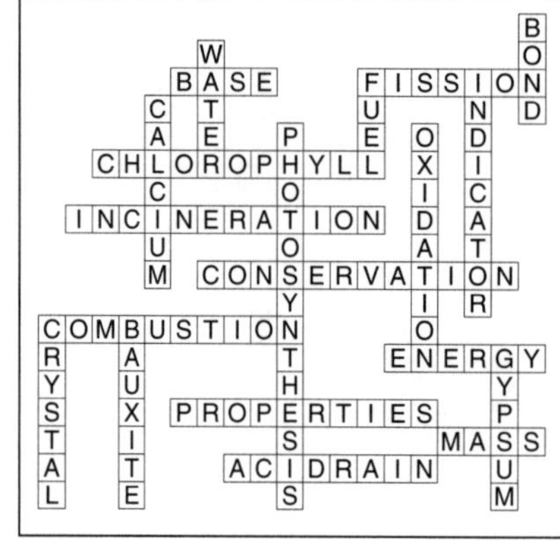

128

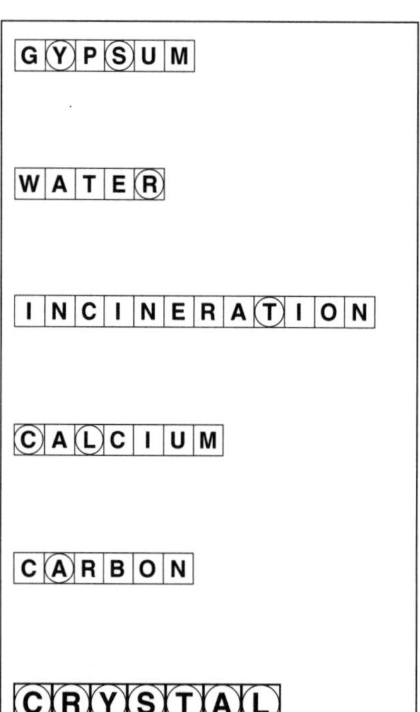

129

Electricity and Magnetism

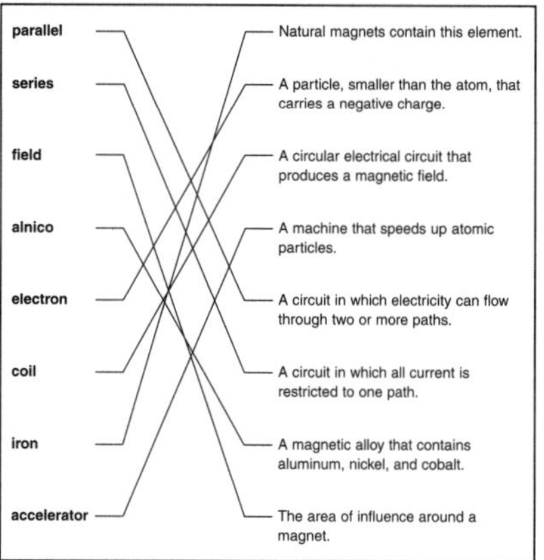

parallel
series
field
alnico
electron
coil
iron
accelerator
Natural magnets contain this element.
A particle, smaller than the atom, that carries a negative charge.
A circular electrical circuit that produces a magnetic field.
A machine that speeds up atomic particles.
A circuit in which electricity can flow through two or more paths.
A circuit in which all current is restricted to one path.
A magnetic alloy that contains aluminum, nickel, and cobalt.
The area of influence around a magnet.

130

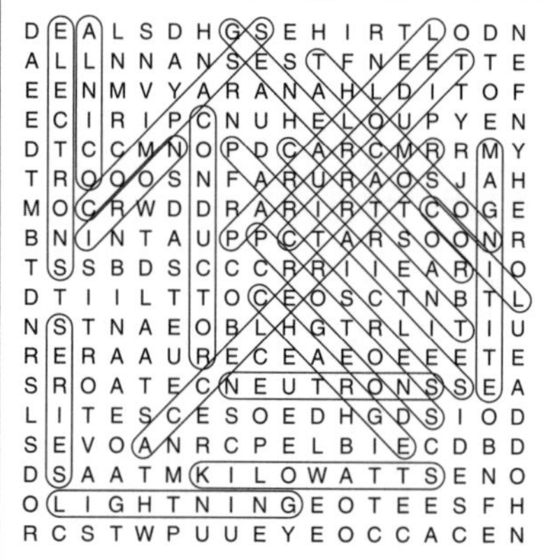

131

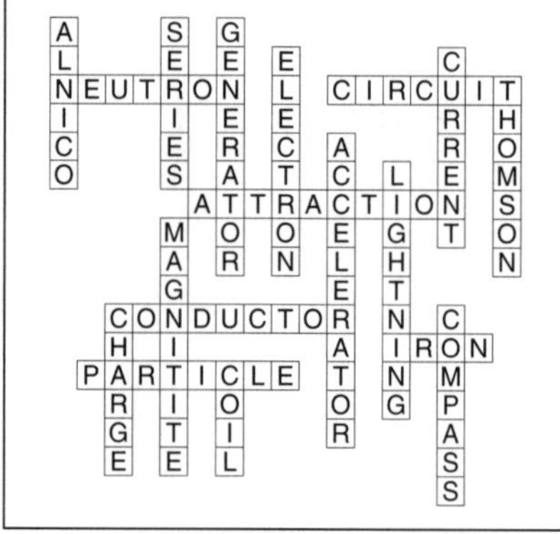

132

Elements

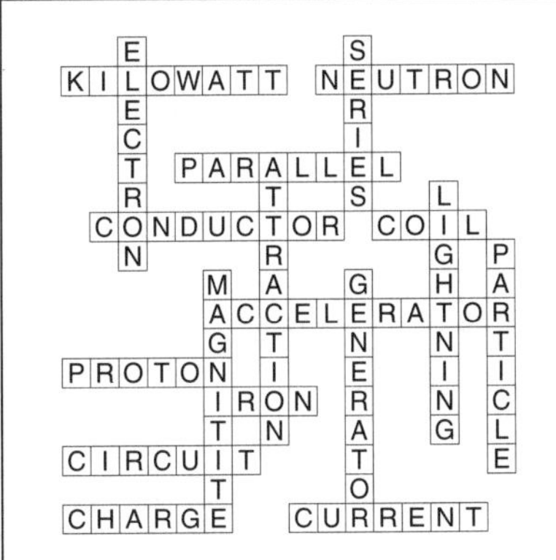

133

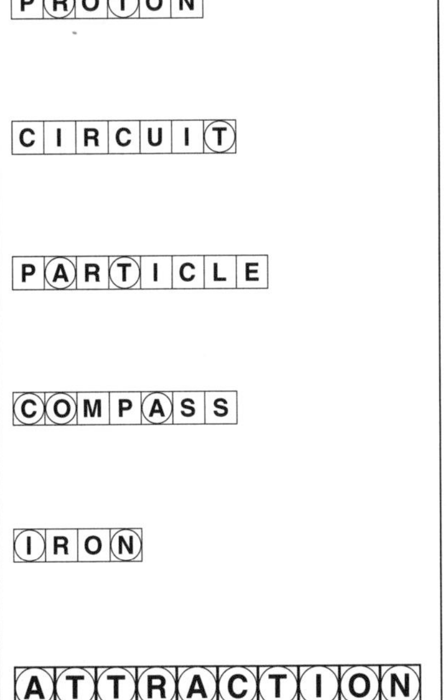

PROTON
CIRCUIT
PARTICLE
COMPASS
IRON
ATTRACTION

134

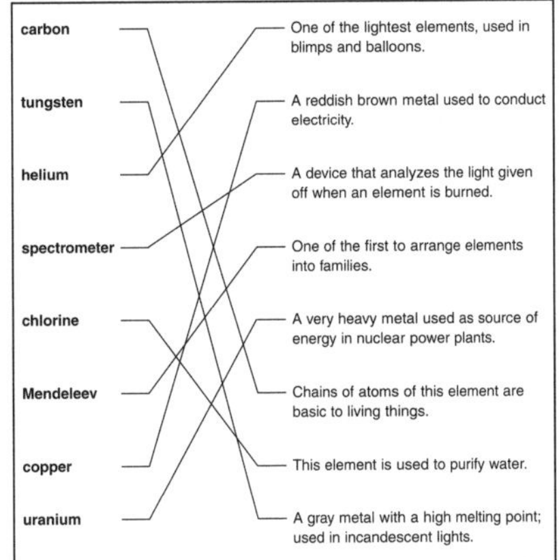

carbon
tungsten
helium
spectrometer
chlorine
Mendeleev
copper
uranium
One of the lightest elements, used in blimps and balloons.
A reddish brown metal used to conduct electricity.
A device that analyzes the light given off when an element is burned.
One of the first to arrange elements into families.
A very heavy metal used as source of energy in nuclear power plants.
Chains of atoms of this element are basic to living things.
This element is used to purify water.
A gray metal with a high melting point; used in incandescent lights.

135

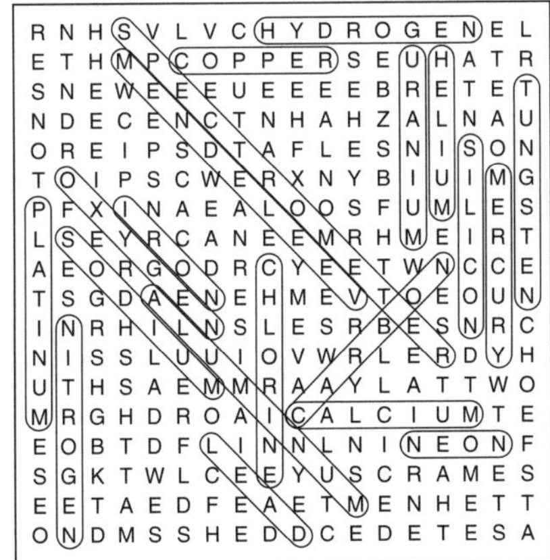

136

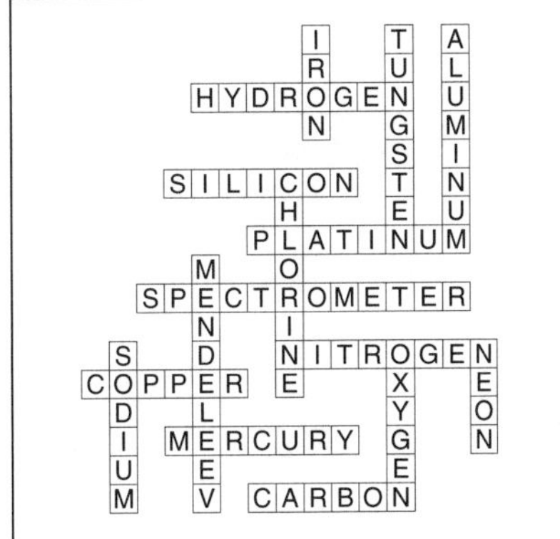

137

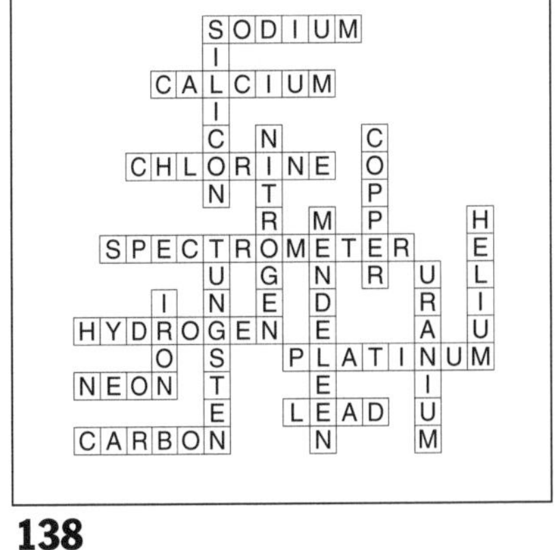

138

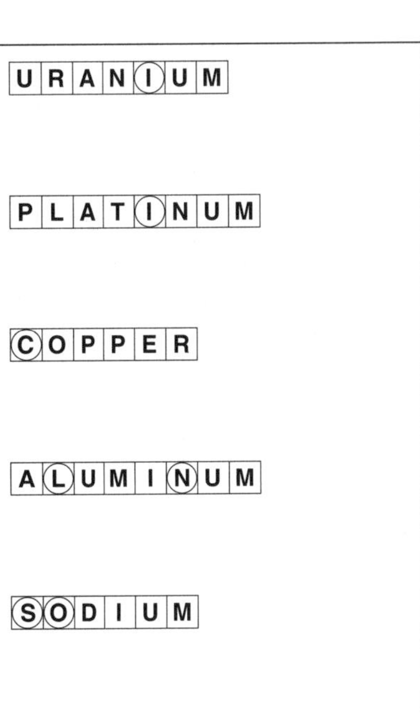

139

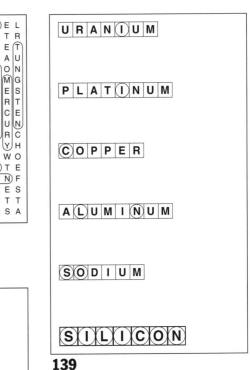

Light and Heat

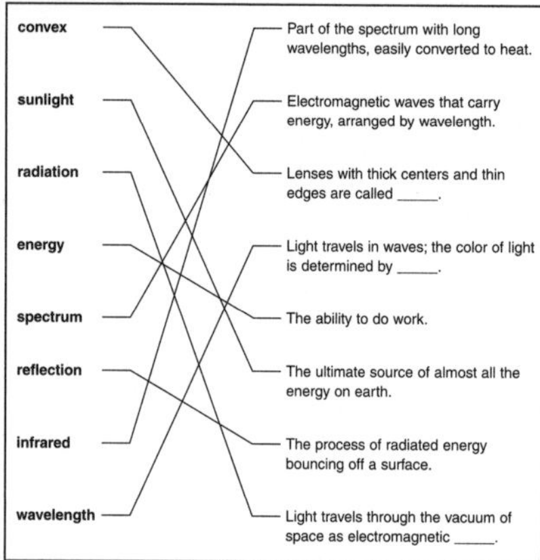

140

141

142

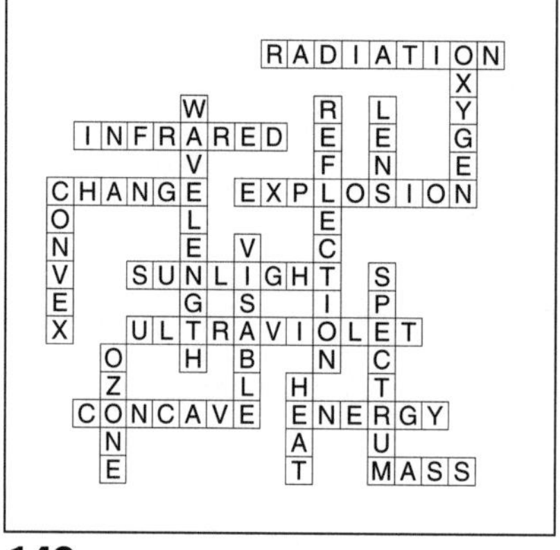

143

CONCAVE

OZONE

WAVELENGTH

OXYGEN

VISIBLE

CONVEX

144

Simple Machines

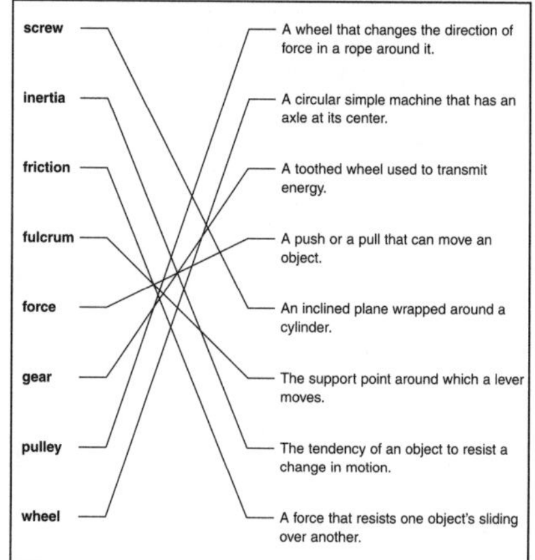

screw
inertia
friction
fulcrum
force
gear
pulley
wheel
A wheel that changes the direction of force in a rope around it.
A circular simple machine that has an axle at its center.
A toothed wheel used to transmit energy.
A push or a pull that can move an object.
An inclined plane wrapped around a cylinder.
The support point around which a lever moves.
The tendency of an object to resist a change in motion.
A force that resists one object's sliding over another.

145

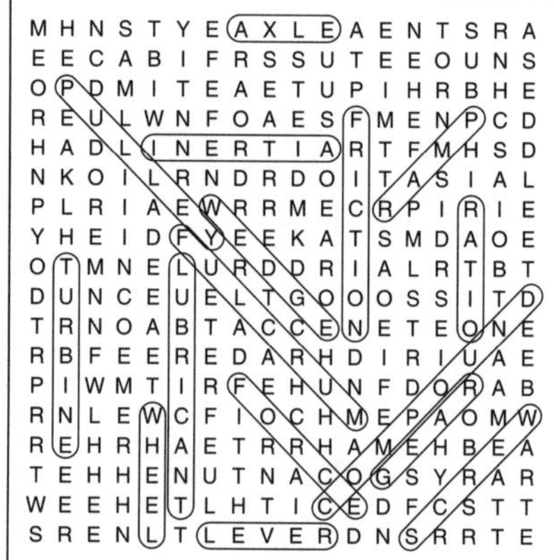

146

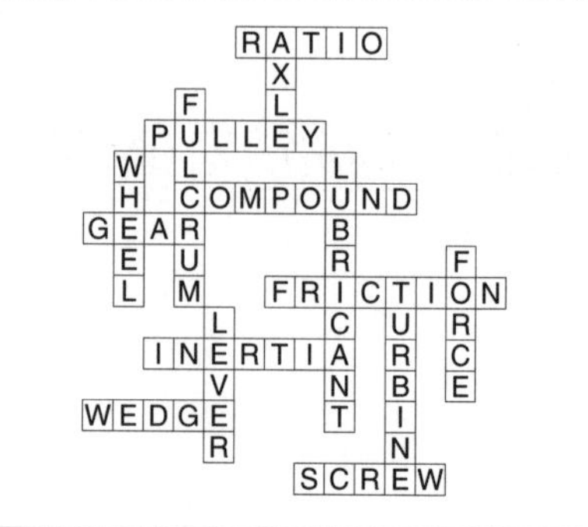

147

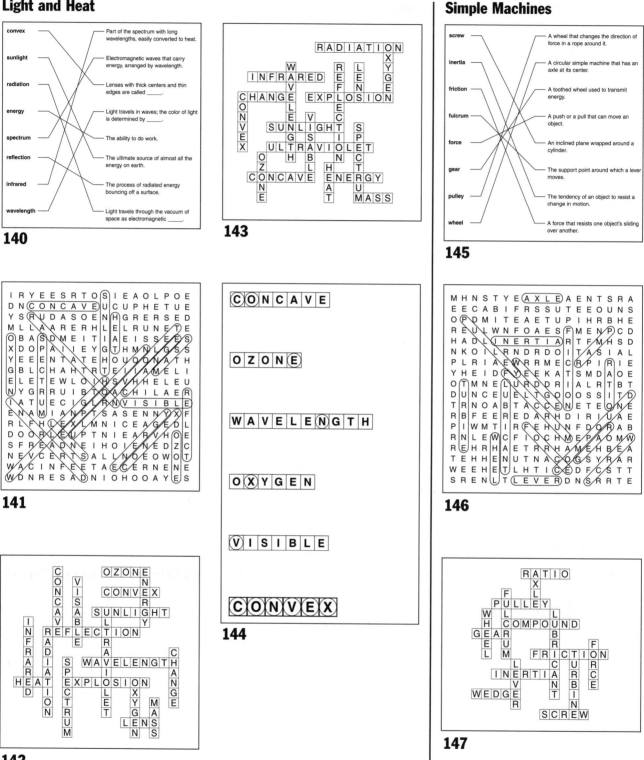

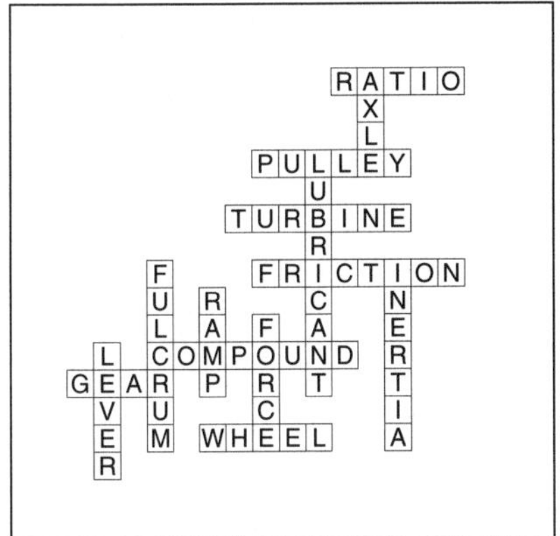

148

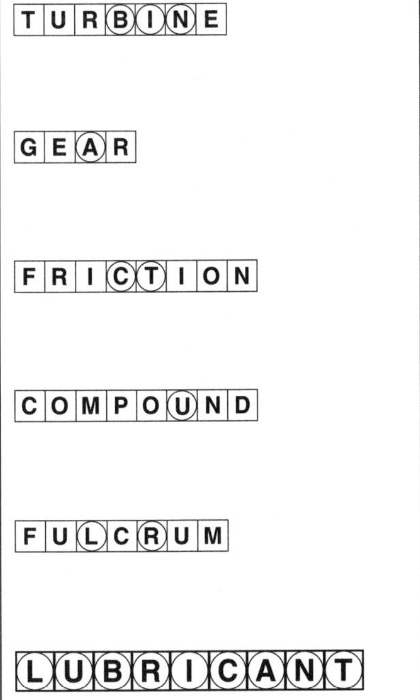

149

Motion

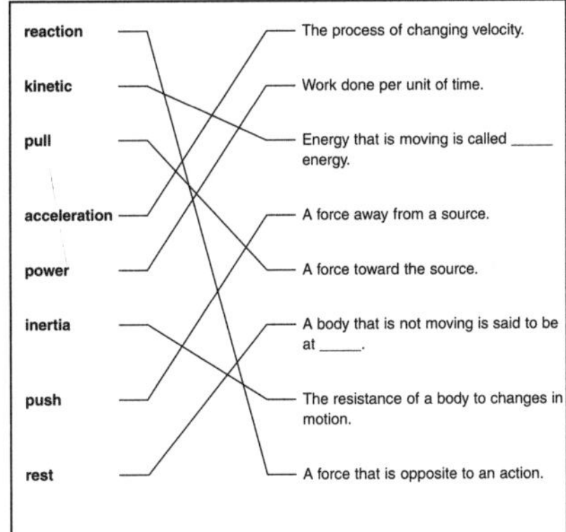

150

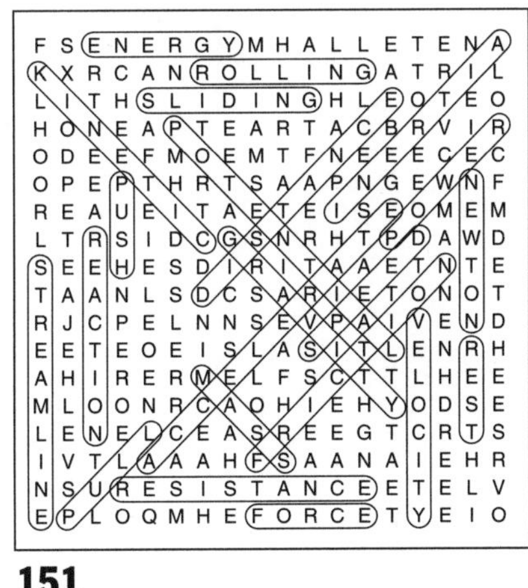

151

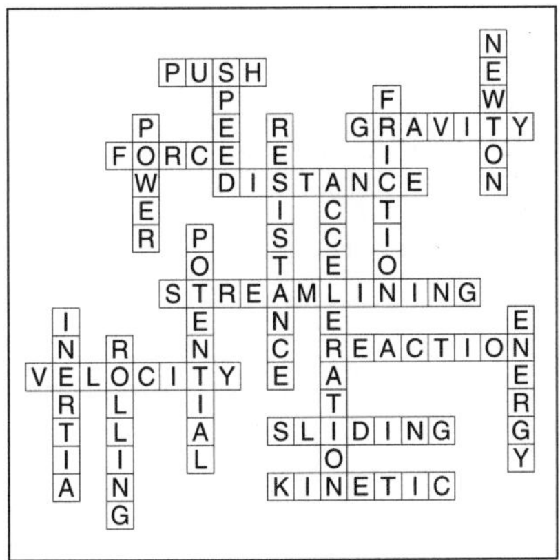

152

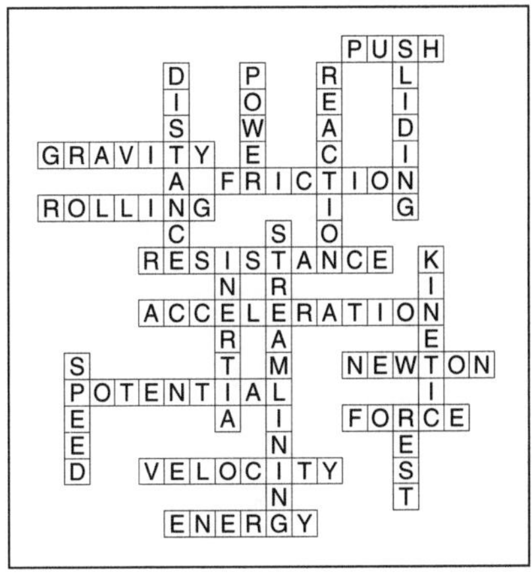

153

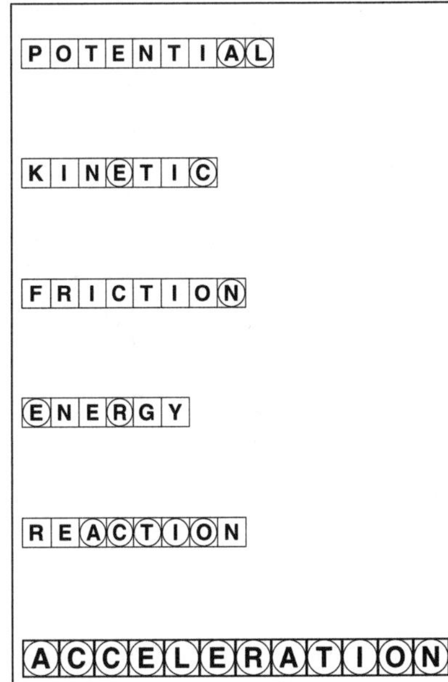

154

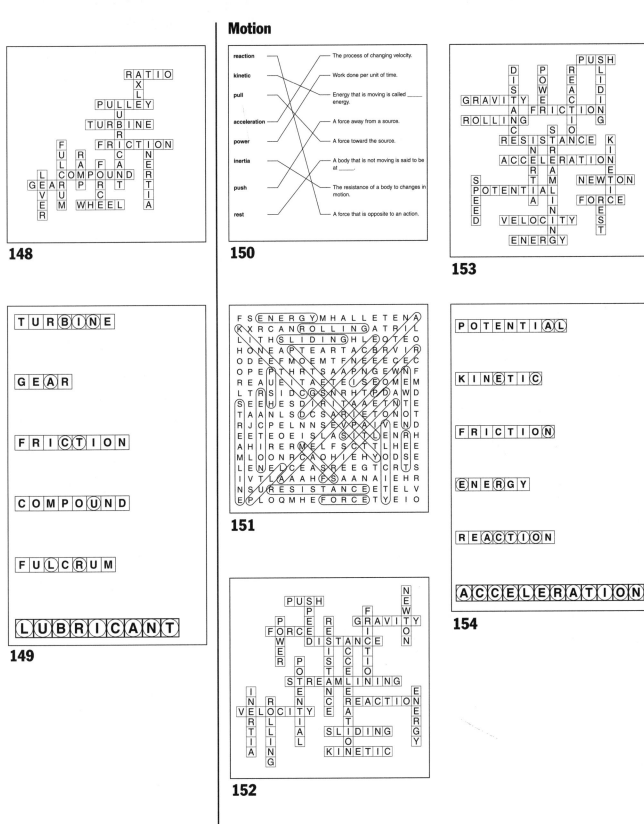

Sound

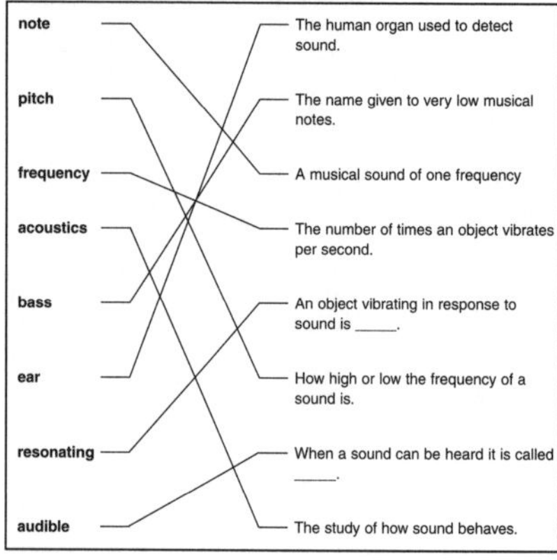

note
pitch
frequency
acoustics
bass
ear
resonating
audible
The human organ used to detect sound.
The name given to very low musical notes.
A musical sound of one frequency
The number of times an object vibrates per second.
An object vibrating in response to sound is _____.
How high or low the frequency of a sound is.
When a sound can be heard it is called _____.
The study of how sound behaves.

155

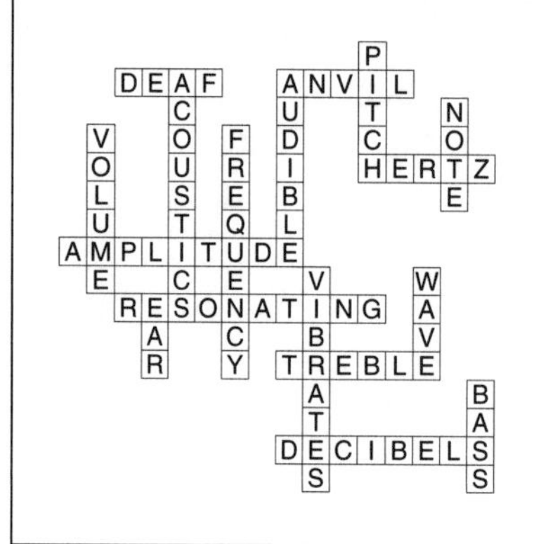

158

156

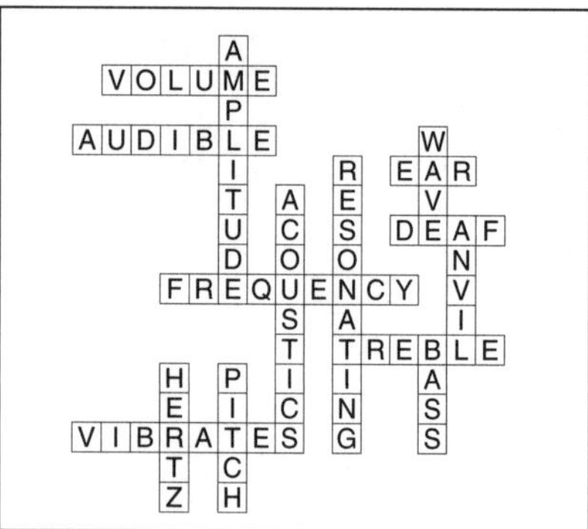

157

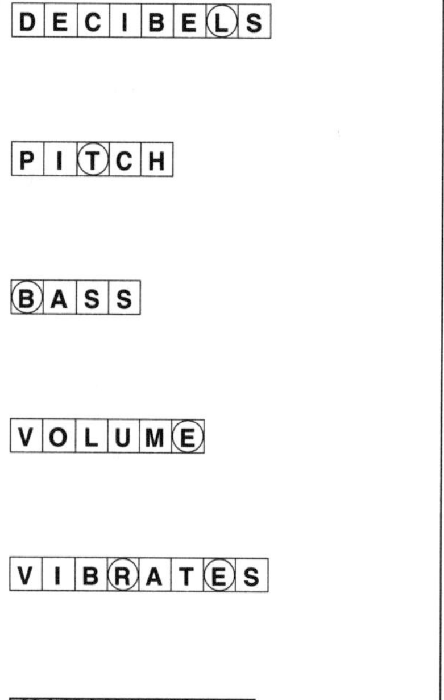

DECIBELS
PITCH
BASS
VOLUME
VIBRATES
TREBLE

159

Digestion

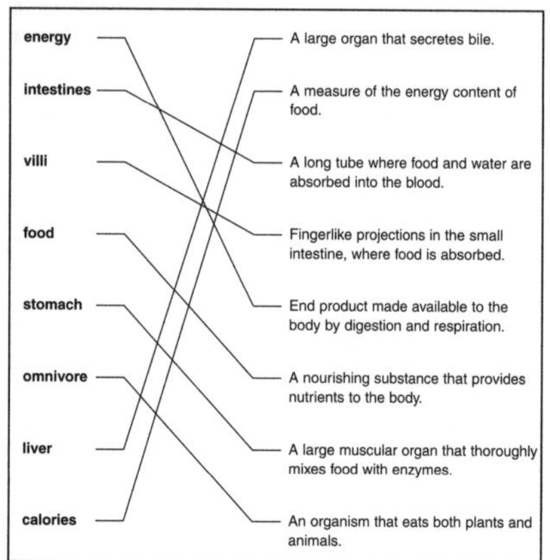

energy
intestines
villi
food
stomach
omnivore
liver
calories
A large organ that secretes bile.
A measure of the energy content of food.
A long tube where food and water are absorbed into the blood.
Fingerlike projections in the small intestine, where food is absorbed.
End product made available to the body by digestion and respiration.
A nourishing substance that provides nutrients to the body.
A large muscular organ that thoroughly mixes food with enzymes.
An organism that eats both plants and animals.

162

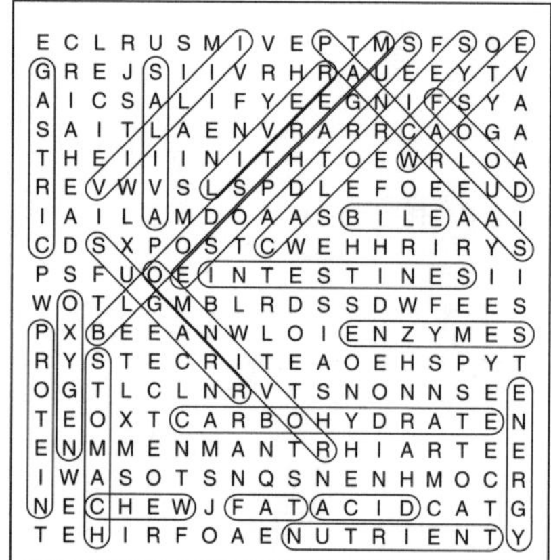

163

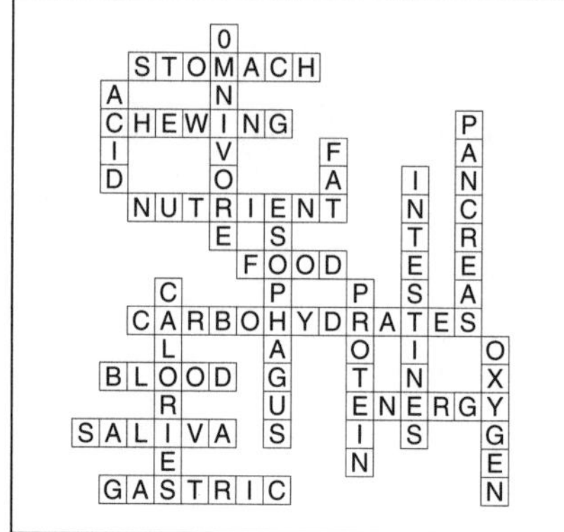

164

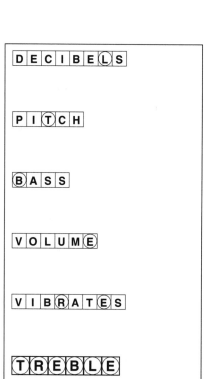

Answer Key

Circulation

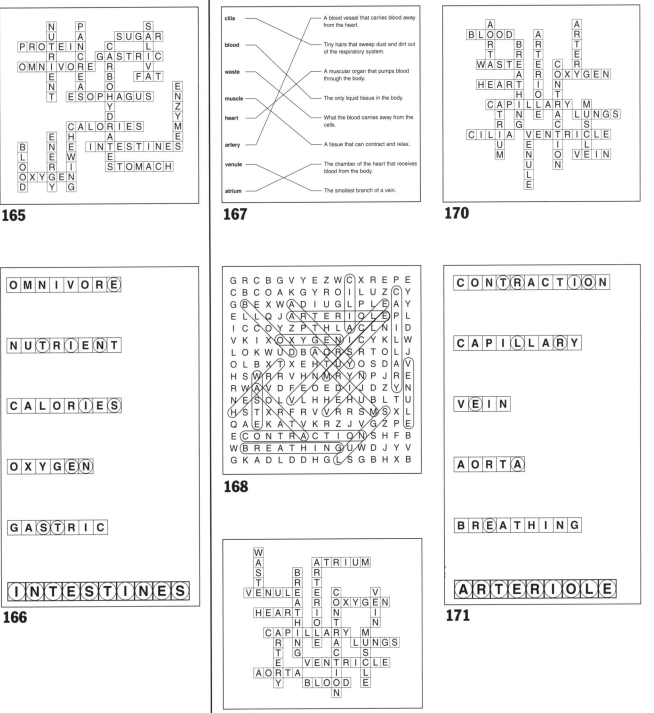

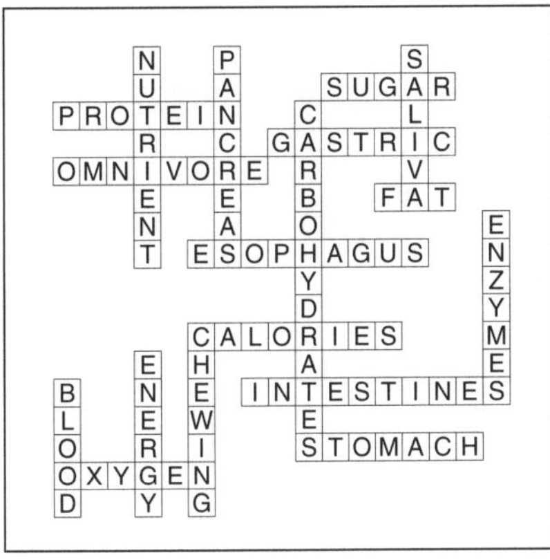

165

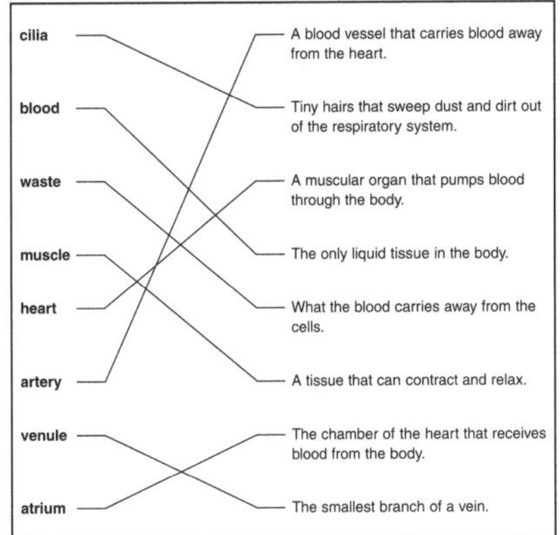

cilia
blood
waste
muscle
heart
artery
venule
atrium
A blood vessel that carries blood away from the heart.
Tiny hairs that sweep dust and dirt out of the respiratory system.
A muscular organ that pumps blood through the body.
The only liquid tissue in the body.
What the blood carries away from the cells.
A tissue that can contract and relax.
The chamber of the heart that receives blood from the body.
The smallest branch of a vein.

167

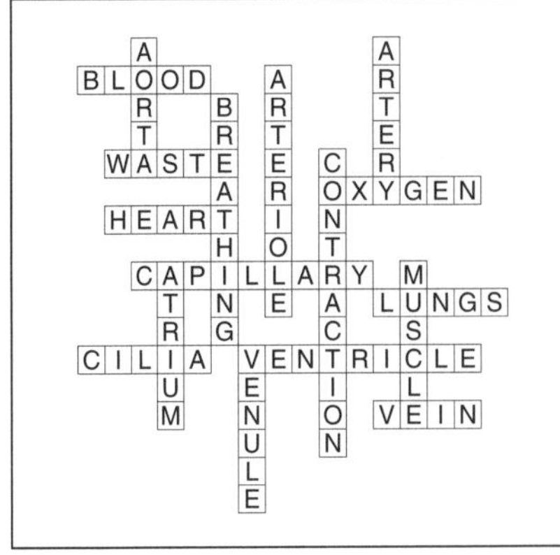

170

OMNIVORE

NUTRIENT

CALORIES

OXYGEN

GASTRIC

INTESTINES

166

168

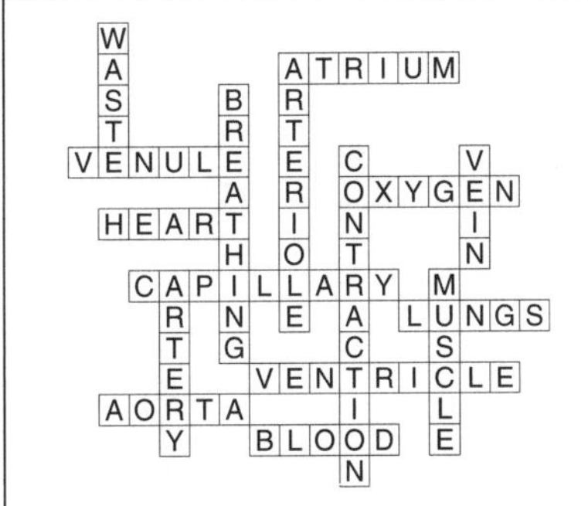

169

CONTRACTION

CAPILLARY

VEIN

AORTA

BREATHING

ARTERIOLE

171

Answer Key

Human Heredity

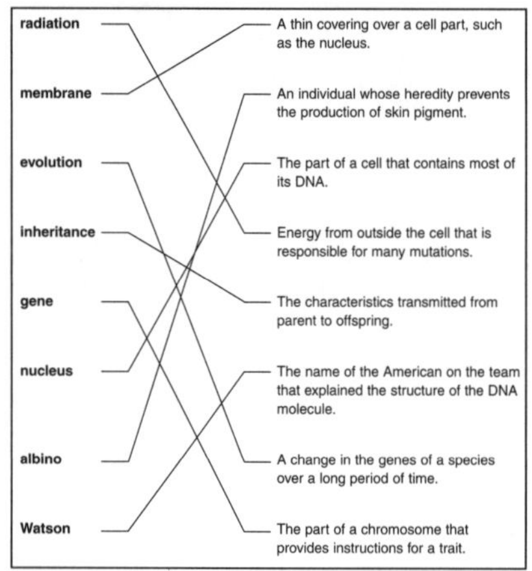
radiation
membrane
evolution
inheritance
gene
nucleus
albino
Watson
A thin covering over a cell part, such as the nucleus.
An individual whose heredity prevents the production of skin pigment.
The part of a cell that contains most of its DNA.
Energy from outside the cell that is responsible for many mutations.
The characteristics transmitted from parent to offspring.
The name of the American on the team that explained the structure of the DNA molecule.
A change in the genes of a species over a long period of time.
The part of a chromosome that provides instructions for a trait.

172

M O R A E N P Q D D D M D Y N
B N I B C U L K R B I J B C U
R U H P J E Y C A L R H U O C
F A B M E N D E L O G T R P L
E M D M O P A R Y T A X E I E
E Q E I N H E R I T A N C E U
O M U T A T I O N T D F E D S
B C X O O T G V D V E G S R E
S E L E C T I O N N X E S W I
T R E F B N S O A A S Y I K P
U J I I D A B R N A L S V E F
I M F I N Y B K E R G B E I G
I C H R O M O S O M E W I C S
T E N H E L I X U M N Z D N G
M Q Q M A D D W J M E T Z C O

173

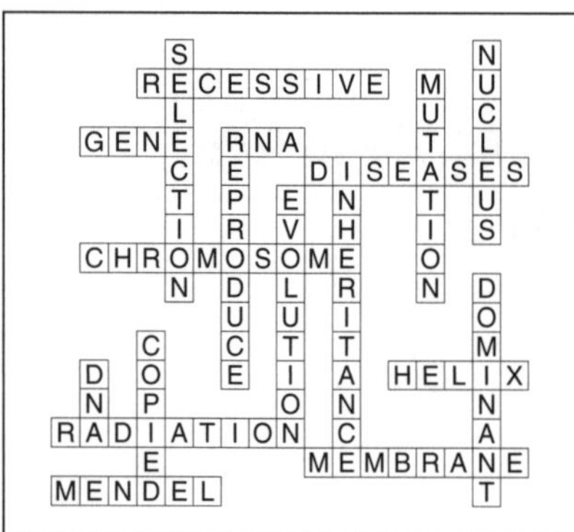
SELECTION
RECESSIVE
MUTATION
NUCLEUS
GENE
RNA
REPRODUCE
DISEASES
EVOLUTION
INHERITANCE
CHROMOSOME
DOMINANT
HELIX
DNA
RADIATION
MEMBRANE
MENDEL

174

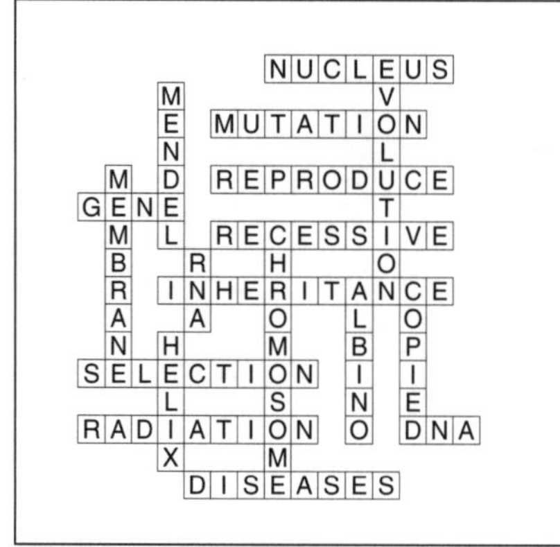
NUCLEUS
MENDEL
MUTATION
EVOLUTION
MEMBRANE
REPRODUCE
GENE
RECESSIVE
INHERITANCE
RNA
HELIX
CHROMOSOMES
ALBINO
SELECTION
RADIATION
DNA
DISEASES

175

GENE

MENDEL

CHROMOSOME

NUCLEUS

EVOLUTION

SELECTION

176

Hygiene

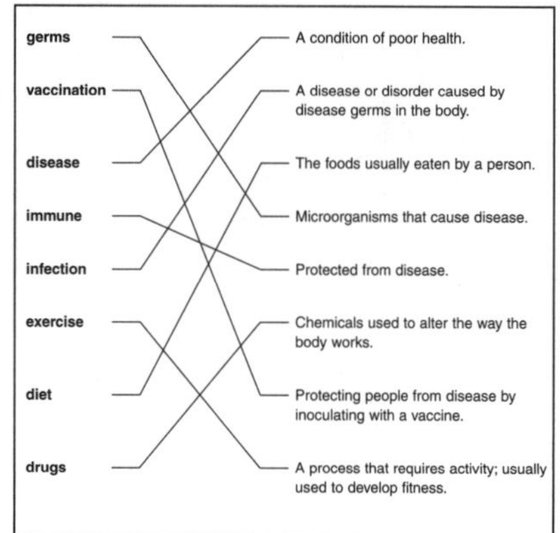
germs
vaccination
disease
immune
infection
exercise
diet
drugs
A condition of poor health.
A disease or disorder caused by disease germs in the body.
The foods usually eaten by a person.
Microorganisms that cause disease.
Protected from disease.
Chemicals used to alter the way the body works.
Protecting people from disease by inoculating with a vaccine.
A process that requires activity; usually used to develop fitness.

177

D S S E D O H U C A F H E A L T H A
V H N N N B N A D A D I D E N D A I
F T C V I A O C N P U E D C O I S R
T S A I S M S N D N H E I I I S T I
H I G R M T M I E N V X N V N E C D
E U E O A E C U O S A E D E T A T A
E T R N H E R I N D C R S R P S S T
N T M M W T T C E C C R N I E N C
I L S E E I S L I S I I E T T E B N
I W E N R O O O S E N S N E C A E A
N O A T T S M T N O A E I S W S I Y
F E U S G N O H F I T D E I A R R I
E N G U H Y E I I N I L D E E A M N
C N R R O I R N O B O O D T T T T O
T D F E O T N G A D N A C I N U S I
I R P O U W P G A N W A N O A S H R
O S R E S T T F S I B A A N A A D R
N O T S H I N H H T S E H I R W O E

178

DISEASE
IMMUNE
HEALTH
EXERCISE
VACCINATION
BACTERIA
REST
WASHING
INFECTION
ENVIRONMENT
NUTRITION
CLOTHING
GERMS
DRUGS
SOAP

179

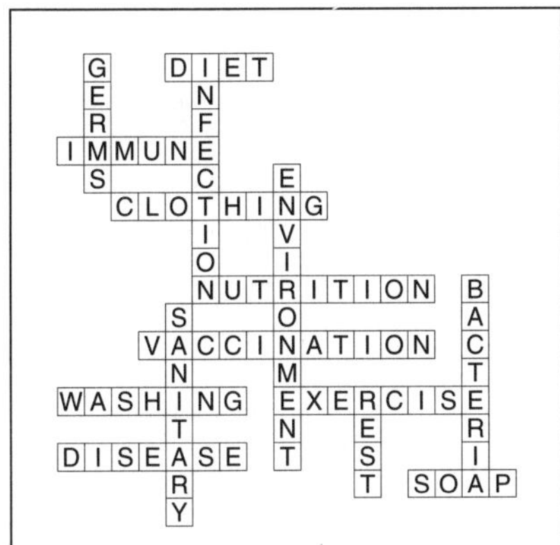

180

IMMUNE

GERMS

WASHING

DIET

DRUGS

DISEASE

181

Nutrition and Health

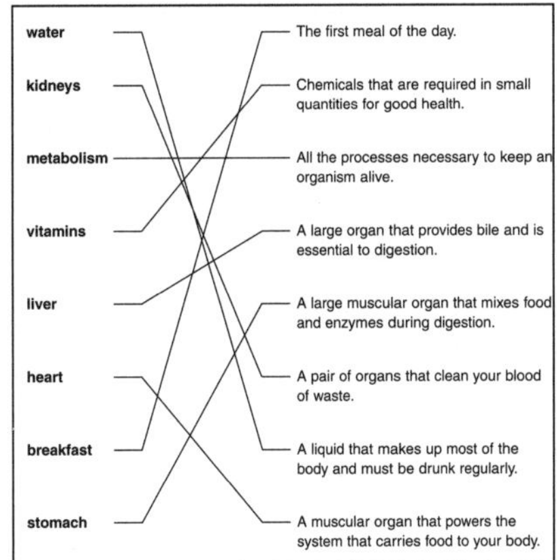

182

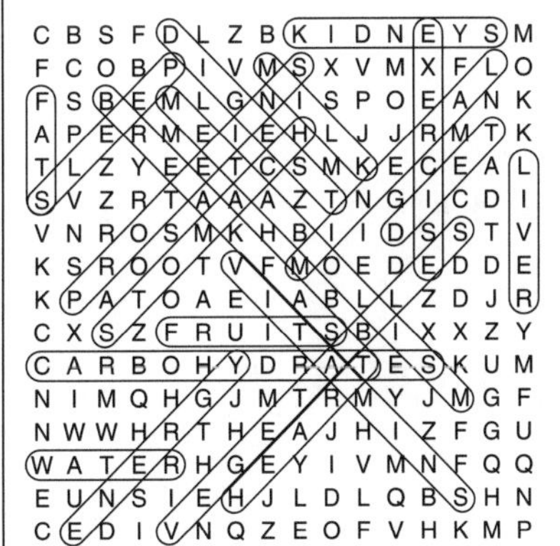

183

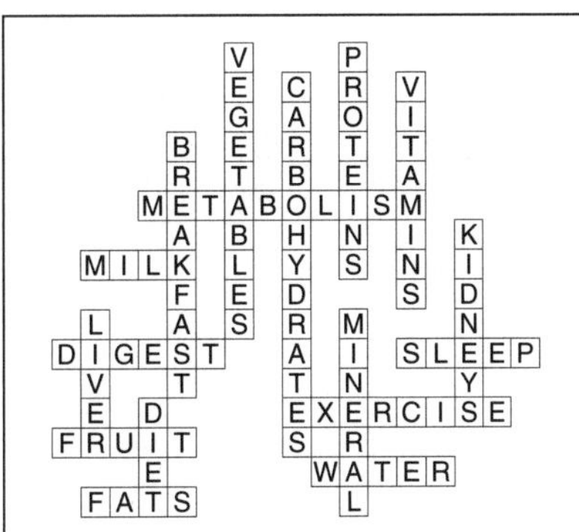

184

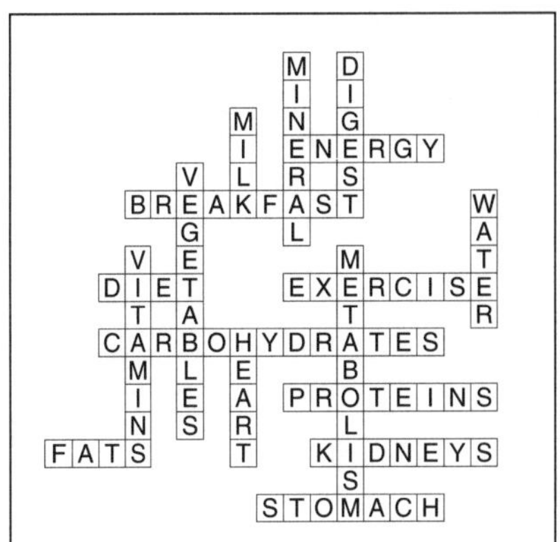

185

KIDNEYS

VEGETABLES

STOMACH

ENERGY

MILK

MINERAL

186

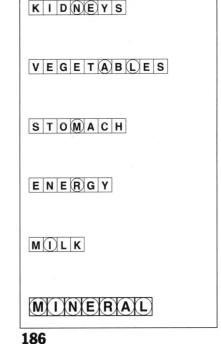

Answer Key

Safety

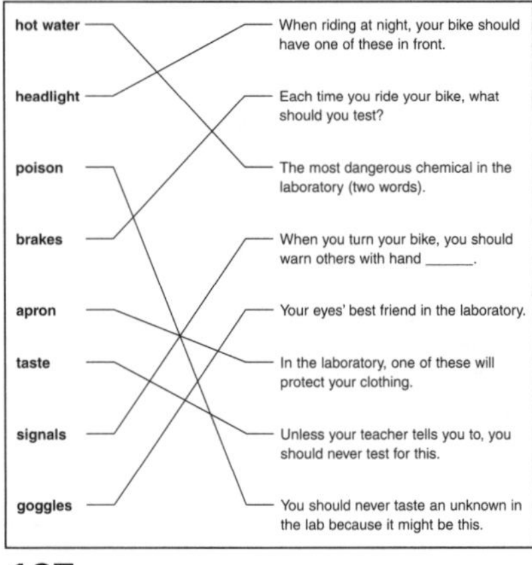

187

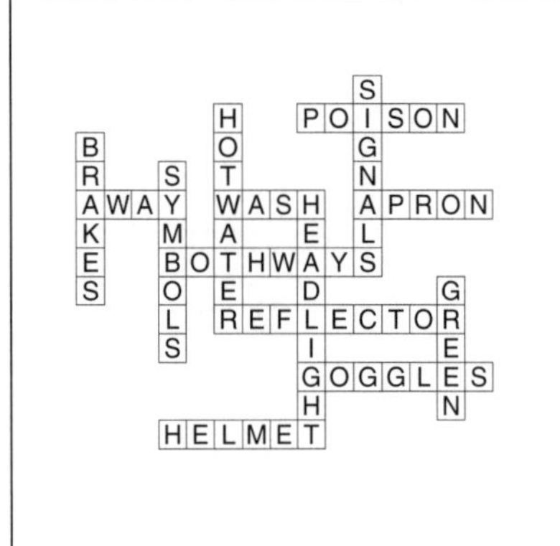

190

188

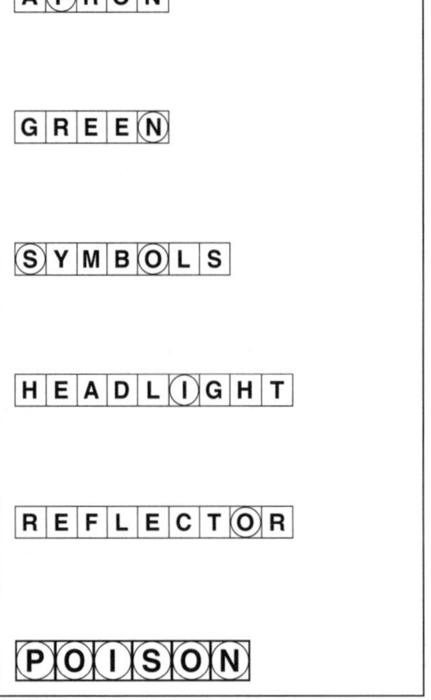

191

189

Senses

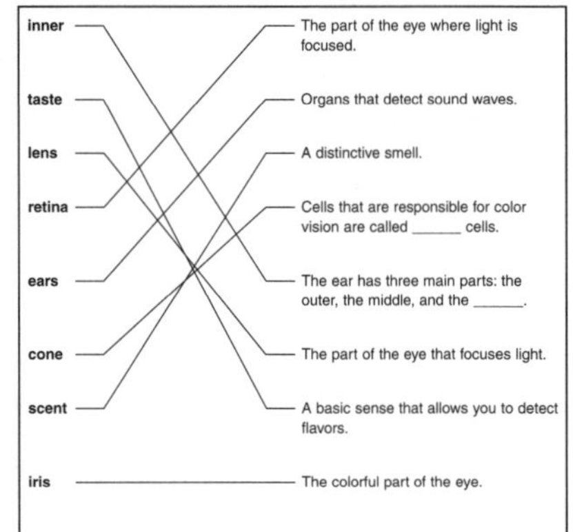

192

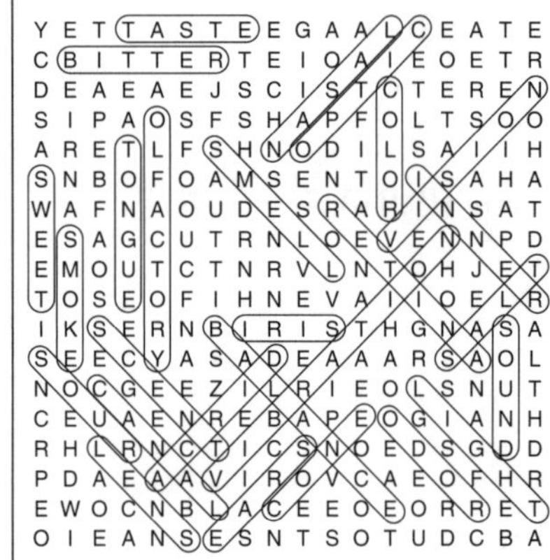

193

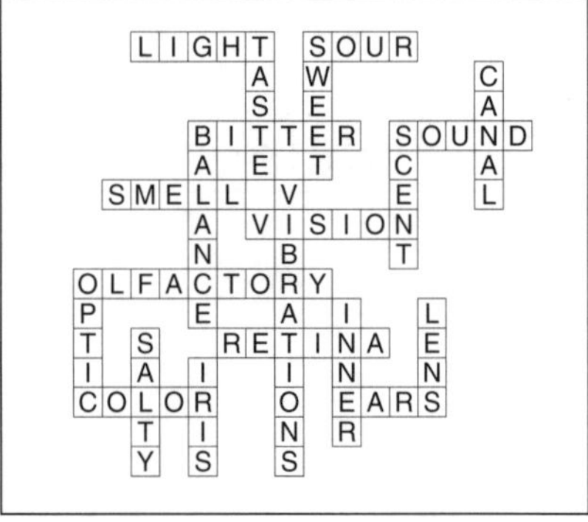

194

Skeletal-Muscular System

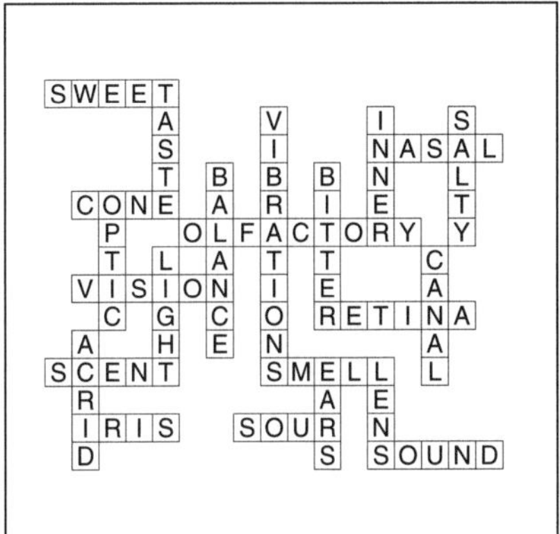

195

OPTIC

VIBRATIONS

BITTER

LIGHT

SOUND

COLOR

196

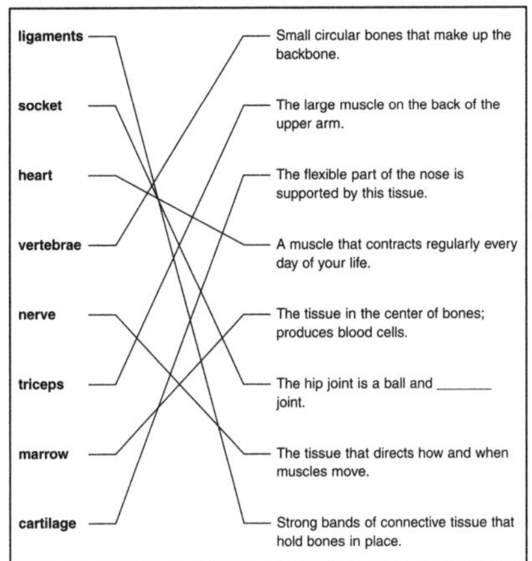

ligaments	Small circular bones that make up the backbone.
socket	The large muscle on the back of the upper arm.
heart	The flexible part of the nose is supported by this tissue.
vertebrae	A muscle that contracts regularly every day of your life.
nerve	The tissue in the center of bones; produces blood cells.
triceps	The hip joint is a ball and _______ joint.
marrow	The tissue that directs how and when muscles move.
cartilage	Strong bands of connective tissue that hold bones in place.

197

198

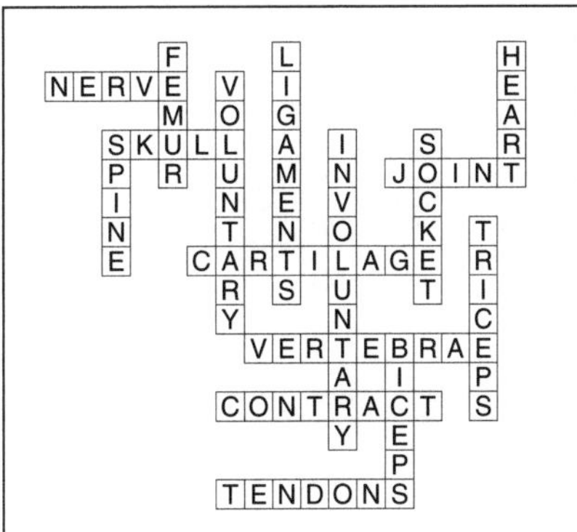

199

TENDONS
SPINE
FEMUR
BICEPS
VOLUNTARY
SKULL
INVOLUNTARY
NERVE
LIGAMENTS
CARTILAGE
VERTEBRAE
JOINT
SOCKET
CALCIUM
HEART
TRICEPS
MARROW

200

SKULL

SPINE

BICEPS

TENDONS

CONTRACT

SOCKET

201

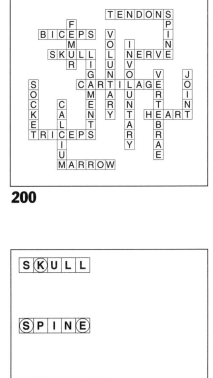

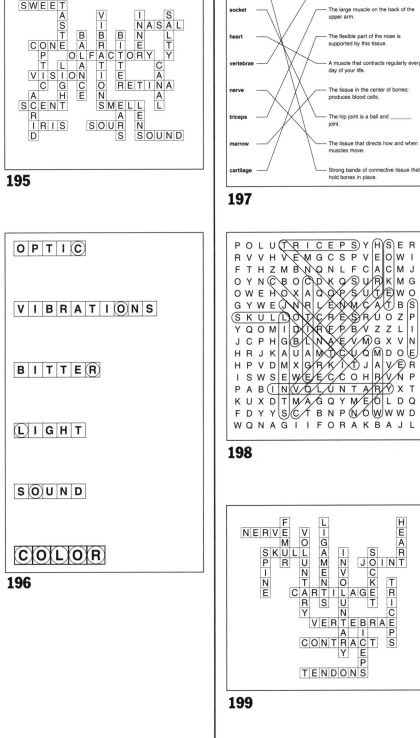

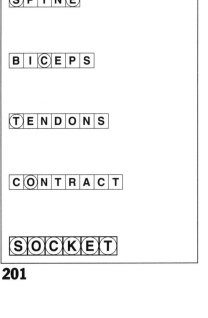